RECITING ROBERT FROST IN THE ICU

Surveying the whole field of medicine, Taylor Prewitt, a retired cardiologist, shows himself to be an entertaining guide as he brings us a commentary on a collection of some sixty books written by or about doctors, patients, and others who help in time of need—such as Florence Nightingale, whose name is almost synonymous with nursing, and Thomas Lynch, a Michigan undertaker who is also a poet.

This collection illustrates the same variety that doctors encounter at their offices, the same variety that any of us encounter in walking down a crowded street. There are several examples of the history of medicine, going back five hundred years to the time when Theodore de Mayerne was a physician to King James I of England. The world of the twenty-first century is shown in the essays of Atul Gawande and Phillip R. Reilly, ranging from present-day delivery of health care to the genetic revolution.

We see front-line primary care and research into the basic secrets of life; life in its beginning and at its end; the care of the poor and the care of the kings; health care on the plains of Kansas and the jungles of Africa; sick folks one at a time and millions at a time.

This is hardly a list of the best sixty books about medicine. However, they are good books, and they illustrate the richness and the depth of the field. Times are changing; wherever we are going, these reviews help us understand where we have been and where we are now.

RECITING ROBERT FROST IN THE ICU

Essays on the Literature of Medicine

Taylor Prewitt

foxboro press

ISBN 978-097933561-7

foxboro press
Fort Smith, Arkansas

For Mary
My Partner in Crime

CONTENTS

NONFICTION

INTRODUCTION

"Let me tell you a story," says the stranger sitting next to you on the airplane. And if he is an ancient mariner who fixes you with his glittering eye, you listen. If he begins by saying, "Let me tell you about my operation," you groan inwardly. But if you're first fixed by his glittering eye, he can tell you about his operation, or his children, or his summer vacation, and you'll listen. A good storyteller can get away with things like that. The stories in this book are told by ancient mariners with glittering eyes. They happen to be stories from the literature of medicine, which may be considered as the literature that deals with efforts to understand and improve our health. Does this bring a groan? Only if you escape the glittering eye. They are not all billed as stories. Some are biographies, some are nonfiction, some poetry, and there is even one play. And quite a few are indeed fiction; some novels, some short stories, some in between. But they are basically stories of a life, of a disease, of something having to do with medicine, but basically stories, no matter how they are packaged.

This collection of book reviews is intended to advertise some *good* books in the genre of medical literature. The field of medical literature is already well advertised if the large number of such books on booksellers' shelves and lists is any indication. I counted some two hundred titles in the "Medical" section of one of the large chain bookstores recently. If I read them all, I don't think I would recommend them all to my reading friends. But I certainly can recommend some of them and some of the titles I spied in that informal survey were already included in my table of contents for this volume.

The books reviewed here were written for the general reader and also, presumably, for those with experience in the field of medicine. Some of them have been bestsellers, and some have been honored with prizes in general literature. As with the books themselves, so these reviews are intended for general readers, including medical readers.

Why these particular books from the surprisingly rich literature of medicine? I can't say that I formulated a list in the way a professor selects a syllabus for a course. The books were selected just as everyone selects books to read: books recommended by a friend, those with interesting reviews, those on subjects of particular interest, or those with an interesting title or cover art. If there were a canon of the literature of medicine, this would not be it. If I were voting on a list of the fifty or hundred best, some of these would not be included. But quite a few would be on my list, and I daresay that quite a few would be on a consensus list if one were ever to be generated.

Some of these books are probably worth plowing through to the end for only a few with particular interests. But they all contain nuggets of worth and the reviews are intended to extract these for the general reader. Of all these books, it can be said that it's good to know that they're out there, and what the "good parts" are. In other words, if I might not issue a general recommendation for all these books, I highly recommend the reviews.

But after the fact, the list appears to be a pretty good one. It illustrates the same variety that a doctor encounters in his office, the same variety that any of us encounter in walking down a crowded street. There are several samples of the history of medicine, going back five hundred years to the time when Theodore de Mayerne was physician to King James I of England; and there are several looks at the Victorian era and the early twentieth century. The world of today is seen in several accounts of the world of the twenty-first century, such as the essays of Atul Gawande, which appeared recently in *The New Yorker*.

We see front-line primary care medicine in the fictional life of Bruno Sachs in rural France in *The Case of Dr. Sachs* and in the career of the iconic *Horse and Buggy Doctor* who braved Kansas blizzards a hundred years ago. At the other end of this spectrum is the basic research into the secrets of life as told by two Nobel Prize winners, James Watson and Arthur Kornberg. We see life from its beginning in the dramatic delivery of twins described in *Cutting for Stone*; and there are several accounts of death and dying, including the views of the funeral director in *The Undertaking*. We see the care of the poor in the story of Paul Farmer, *Mountains Beyond Mountains,* and we see the care of kings in *Europe's Physician* and *The Madness of King George*.

"Some of these books are too deep for me," friends have sometimes said. No, they're not! I confess to a personal bias that we run the risk of being scientifically illiterate for lack of effort. Much basic science material is as important as anything that appears in our daily newspapers. The object in presenting apparently complicated material is to present it so simply and clearly that it is transformed into something "any fool can plainly see," to borrow a phrase from a hero of the comics of my childhood, Li'l Abner. By and large, the authors of these texts have done a good job in this regard. My job here was to present reviews that meet the same high criterion. If I didn't always succeed, it wasn't because I wasn't trying.

Several of these books have withstood the test of time. Who knows which ones will survive even the next few decades? They comprise my list for today, but tomorrow they will be yesterday's list. That the literature of medicine is a field of dynamic growth is apparent from the new titles continuing to appear, addressing economic, ethical, and cultural issues related to medicine. Some of these are works of artistic merit warranting inclusion in the literature of medicine. We live in interesting times and a sound footing in the medical humanities affords a more stable balance as medicine continues to evolve.

Here is where the stories come in. I'm not sure I know why I became a doctor, but I learned pretty early on that health is important. Good health is near the top of the lists of what people want most in life. And then comes the pondering: "What's it all about?" ·What is this person all about?" "What is their story?" The questions are hard; but stories seem to be a way of getting at them.

Some of the stories reviewed in these pages are ones I read when I was a boy, some as I went through the practice of medicine and cardiology, and others since I retired some seven years ago. They are not my stories, but they do intersect with my own story, as books that are important to us tend to do. Bits and snatches of my own story pop up here and there, so a bit of orientation may be in order.

I grew up in a small farm and railroad town in the southeast Arkansas delta, the son of an automobile dealer/farm owner. I was editor of the high school newspaper for two years and doubted my interest or aptitude for science until my experience in biology and chemistry courses at the University of Arkansas convinced me that, like the aspiring dancer in *A Chorus Line*, "I can do that!" Looking through the course catalogs and pre-med requirements, I saw that I could take all the required science courses and still have time to major in English just for fun.

There was no department of medical humanities when I was in medical school, but about a half dozen of us found time in our senior year (1962-1963) to have our own small group seminar, meeting every three or four weeks. Several of us were married, and our spouses, who were a gifted lot, read and discussed along with us. We read *Job, J. B., Murder in the Cathedral, Becket, Death in Venice, The Brothers Karamazov, The Bear* and a few other favorites. Perhaps a cross between a journal club and a book club, I counted this as one of the more fruitful of my medical school experiences. Without realizing it, we were forerunners of courses in medical humanities, which are now featured at some medical schools.

The books in this evolving list are part of my window to the world, no less a part of my continuing medical education than the credit hours I receive for attendance at meetings and courses. "Don't let your schoolwork interfere with your education," my dad sometimes reminded me, and we must remember that education may come in surprising ways. "Try to have a little fun every day," was another paternal maxim, and these books have been fun to read.

Just one more thing: What about reciting Robert Frost in the ICU? There were probably times when Dr. Prewitt was standing at the bedside of an unresponsive patient in the Intensive Care Unit, staring at the monitors or watching the iv drip, and the nurses may have heard him mutter a little poem by Frost which concludes, "But the Secret sits in the middle and knows." Keep an open mind, consider all possibilities. We may think we know something, but there is always a reality that may not be the same as what we think we know.

The practice of medicine poses many challenges, but it does have its compensations. For one thing, it's the greatest show on earth. It's a three-ring circus. It's life itself. Who can take it all in? But we do have front row seats. Don't blink your eyes.

BIOGRAPHY

Woe to that person who no longer delighteth in hearing the story of another; for truly that person shall be weary of life itself; nor shall the physician any longer be happy in his work, when the pleasure in hearing a patient's life story shall have passed away. Though these words may not have fallen from the lips of the psalmist or even Hippocrates, they do express the appeal of biographies. Our species is coded to enjoy hearing stories, particularly life stories.

The biographies included in this section are those of health care providers: physicians (and, in one case, their offspring), some of them private practitioners, some researchers, some teachers, some all of the above; and one immortal nurse, the iconic Florence Nightingale. My claim is that these stories are worth reading because they are entertaining; and they are. But I can't deny that I'm a sucker for inspirational stories. For the most part, the subjects of these biographies are heroic figures, larger than life. But they are not all heroic to the same extent. Borrowing Henry James' comment about a great man he had visited, some of them can be measured readily enough. And we find that all of them had their "little ways." But John Hunter, William Osler, Florence Nightingale: they were made of stern stuff.

I read two of these books in my high school days: *The Horse and Buggy Doctor* by Arthur Hertzler, and *Out of My Life and Thought* by Albert Schweitzer – the latter after strong urging by my mother, as Schweitzer was her great hero. Their influence on my thinking defies my estimation, but they set a standard somewhere in my approach to life. I tracked down and read a copy of Cushing's biography of Osler during my leisurely days in the U. S. Public Health Service, back when finding a copy of an out-of-print book was not just a matter of touching a few keys on a computer. My obligatory two-year military service turned out to be a hiatus between training and practice, giving me an opportunity to charge my batteries for the challenges of private practice. Sir William served me well in this capacity.

The biography of James Mackenzie provided reading material while riding the train to and from the Brompton Hospital during my year in London in 1974. (The opportunity to read widely during the three hours of commuting each day was one of the many benefits of this year of "sabbatical" research.) I read the Cushing and Kornberg books while in practice, as well as a biography of Schweitzer in addition to his memoirs. I have read or re-read all of these books since retirement, the time in my life when I somewhat facetiously remarked that I would pursue "scholarship, exploration, and pleasant conversation." One of my friends caught on to this. "I know, Taylor. You'll read some books, take some trips, and go to a lot of parties."

I did a little extra reading on some of the biographies. More recent biographies had appeared for Schweitzer, Osler, and Cushing; and in the case of Cushing, I couldn't resist the opportunity to review the account of his three daughters, which I had first read when it came out in 1992.

And how were these particular life stories selected? Not, I must confess, in any systematic fashion. The books were read for enjoyment; there was no effort to include only the greatest in any field, though some rank as giants by any measure. They all led fascinating lives and though I read their stories for fun, I must admit that I understand the field of medicine better after having done so.

A MAN FOR MANY SEASONS

EUROPE'S PHYSICIAN
The Various Life of Sir Theodore de Mayerne
By Hugh Trevor-Roper

A word of advice to the young boy or girl who would be President of the United States: don't go to medical school. An MD degree will open many doors, perhaps even to the White House, but nobody has done it yet. Fifty-one doctors have become U.S. Senators, but none of them are household names. A physician can be a governor; for example, the Jamestown colony elected Dr. John Pott as the first physician to be an American governor in 1628. But none of the illustrious names in the history of the government of the United States are followed by the letters MD.

Of the physicians who have played a role in the government of the English-speaking world, the most eminent in his own time was Sir Theodore de Mayerne, a Renaissance man of many talents who moved to England toward the end of the English Renaissance and served as first physician to King James I. Not known to many today, his role in the complex political, religious, and scientific world of the early seventeenth century was brought to light in a biography discovered among the posthumous papers of Hugh Trevor-Roper, Regius Professor of History at Oxford. It was edited by Blair Worden and published in 2006 by the Yale University Press under the title, *Europe's Physician: The Various Life of Sir Theodore de Mayerne.*

Sir Theodore was a man of many parts. A French Huguenot at a time when France was busy ridding itself of Huguenots and establishing itself as a Catholic nation, he became a citizen of the world – almost a man without a country. He was born in

Switzerland and took his medical degree in Montpellier, one of the centers that dared to doubt the authority of Galen and insist on observation and verification of medical teachings. He rapidly became a successful private practitioner in Paris, even though he hadn't attended the medical school there, and he became the trusted physician of Henri IV, though not recognized as the first physician because of the Queen's objection to his failure to convert to Catholicism.

James I of England had no such scruples about Mayerne's Protestantism. After Mayerne made his way to England, King James invited him to court, where he subsequently became first physician to the king in 1611. By 1615, Mayerne was undertaking a secret mission to France for King James. His "cover" was that he was going to Paris to see his French patients, but he also had some secret royal errands; one of these was probably to promote a revolt against the French king's plans for an alliance with Spain through royal marriages. If so, the attempt was unsuccessful. The weddings took place.

Of course, one can never be sure about all the details of secret missions, designed to prevent discovery, and the task of sorting them out is no easier after the passage of four or five centuries. But Trevor-Roper does quote a letter thought to have been carried on Mayerne's person, from one of the Huguenot leaders to King James: "M. de Mayerne... is a man whom you and I both trust, and being full of judgment, he will tell you our affairs better than I can write them."

Besides such international intrigues, Mayerne maintained a private practice where few celebrities of the day failed to seek consultation, including the kings of England and France, the future Cardinal Richelieu, John Donne, Oliver Cromwell (in later years), and most members of the royal court. He was active in many phases of public life, as when he intervened in the apothecaries' request to be separated from their joint guild with the grocers. He encouraged the king, who granted the request; the apothecaries were given a charter as a separate City guild with a monopoly on compounding and selling medicines. The king's preamble stated he was moved by concern for the public good and also by certain petitions, including one from Theodore de Mayerne.

Mayerne also promoted the publication of a list of physicians' remedies, the first such document in English medical history. Mayerne's reputation in the medical community was enhanced by his scrupulous clinical methods, his charm and courtesy, and his consideration for both his colleagues and his patients, being careful not to embarrass or humiliate either.

Along with two other physicians, he submitted a thirty-eight-page report to the Privy Council in 1630 with detailed recommendations for dealing with "the Great Plague," as it was known until the even more devastating epidemic of 1665. Several of these recommendations were new to England: a central Office of Health with power and authority, new hospitals with central management, and a group of specialized officials. As it happened, the plague receded and since Parliament had been disbanded by Charles I, there was no source of funding for building the new hospitals. These ideas were dropped.

The historian had abundant material for reconstructing the life of Mayerne: there are twenty-five volumes of his papers in the British Library, including most of the *Ephemerides Morborum* (Diaries of Disease), his case notes. In other words, his medical records[1] are available for review. One of these records is his summary of the case of his royal patient, King James I, giving a snapshot of the function of the king's private physician. Mayerne was preparing to go to Switzerland in 1624 to visit his estate, the barony of Aubonne, and he wrote lengthy instructions for those who would be caring for the king – in the slang of today's hospital residents, an "off-service note."

The first section of this document was a physical account of the king's health and habits; the second was his medical history from birth; then a list of the medicines that had been helpful;

---

[1] A more thorough analysis of the case records was published in 2001 by Brian Nance: *Turquet de Mayerne as Baroque Physician: The Art of Medical Portraiture.*

and, finally, a summation of problems the physicians might face in the near future, and decisions that would have to be taken. The royal physicians were told that the king had had unfortunate care in his first year, having been entrusted to a Scottish nurse whose drinking habits resulted in alcoholic milk, leaving him barely strong enough to walk for his first six years. A survey of his current habits listed a few challenges:

> "In drink he errs in quality, quantity, frequency, time and order. He drinks promiscuously beer, ale, Spanish wine, French sweet wine, and especially, his ordinary drink, thick white muscatel; whence diarrhea. Sometimes, when his stomach is loose, he takes red Alicante wine, but he does not care whether the wine is good so long as it is sweet. He hates water and anything watery."

He required careful handling, especially since he had little use for physicians, laughing at their medicines and having scant respect for their opinions.

Mayerne's departure was delayed for eight months and he wrote a postscript on the king's care just before leaving, setting out some principles of the king's care. No amateurs, only the heads of the profession were to be admitted. There must be free and open deliberation. Only the doctors must decide and all differences must be resolved so no doubts could be exploited later. Decisions were to be recorded in writing on the spot; prescriptions were to be signed by all; and nothing must be said in public about their discussions.

A list of the king's ailments included a weak stomach, an obstructed liver resulting in occasional jaundice, catarrh, arthritis, and piles. Mayerne feared dropsy, scurvy, kidney ulcers, apoplexy, and "corruption" of the lungs. Of course, prescription would be difficult because this wasn't a prince who could be managed by the rules of the art. It was hoped that something could be done about his drinking habits. A list of remedies he would take that had proven useful was appended, including "vomitories of metallic mould in wine followed by restorative possets[2]; laxative infusions; mineral diuretics in sweet broth, 'cream of tartar,' 'vitriol of tartar,' diuretic powder compounded of crab's eyes, fish heads, crickets, grasshoppers, millipedes, etc."

Unfortunately, the worst fears of both patient and physician were realized: the king died while his chief physician was away. The wisdom of Mayerne's instructions was validated by the consequences of their being ignored. An amateur remedy was advised by the king's favorite, the Duke of Buckingham, in the form of a posset drink and certain plasters applied to his wrists and stomach, after the king had appeared to recover from an epidemic fever. A charge was made that the king had been poisoned by Buckingham with the knowledge of his son, the future King Charles. This charge was later revived in the Puritan Revolution and used by John Milton, the king's "most eloquent hack-writer," to justify executing the king. King Charles was crowned on February 2, 1626, and anointed with coronation oil prepared according to a recipe devised by Theodore de Mayerne. The same recipe was later used in the coronation of Queen Elizabeth II in 1953.

When I was a small boy seeing an ophthalmologist in the Donaghey Building in Little Rock, my parents stopped in the hall to speak with an elderly physician who alluded to his success in surviving the hard times of the Great Depression. "If you take care of your office," he told us, "your office will take care of you." I've subsequently taken this oracular wisdom to mean that a doctor's greatest asset is the loyalty of his patients, a simplistic axiom which may or may not survive the turbulent changes in the delivery of health care in present times. In any event, Theodore de Mayerne survived the wars of religion in Europe as a member of the losing side, the Huguenots; and he maintained his position as first physician to the king after the succession of Charles I, but he never had the close relationship with Charles that he had had with James. He even maintained his position

---

[2] A British hot drink of milk curdled with wine or ale, often spiced.

after the Puritan Revolution and was formally placed on the parliamentary establishment with a salary of £200 a year. It is certainly quite reasonable to conclude his office took care of him. He survived the revolutions of his time with the help of his friends – his friends in court, many of whom were his patients, whose loyalty to him trumped the doctrinal divisions of the day.

He earned this loyalty with careful attention to every symptom, never despairing of recovery, showing his pride when recovery occurred, and counting the years of survival as he followed the patient's progress.

Sir Henry Slingsby described him as "corpulent and unwieldy," not unexpected in one who was a wealthy knight and physician to the king. But before venturing a new prescription, he always consulted his book, reviewing previous visits from the same patient – one of his compulsive practices that helped justify the high cost of his care.

Physicians are obliged to use the knowledge and tools of their times. Theodore de Mayerne lived during the time of bitter conflict between the disciples of Galen's school of reliance on authority and a revolutionary school of thought claiming Paracelsus as an advocate of observation and empiricism – something a bit closer to the scientific method of later centuries. Mayerne was schooled in this latter thought, believing in "chemical" medicine – the compounding and use of chemical remedies as opposed to the use of only animal and plant material in Galen's system. And indeed some of Mayerne's success is to be attributed to the simplicity and, sometimes, the effectiveness of the new chemical remedies – denounced by his opponents as poisonous and expensive, but generally preferred by the patients.

Herein lay the value of Mayerne's contribution in promoting the London *pharmacopoeia*, defining and giving legitimacy to the chemical medicines. To the modern mind, the field of chemical medicine of that day is indeed a murky one. Mayerne considered himself an alchemist and it must be remembered that alchemy wasn't solely the attempt to transmute lead into gold; it included the audacious attempts to alter and even synthesize chemical substances. The crucible and the distilling flask were essential tools of the trade – or the secret art. This was not an age of open publication of scientific discoveries, though it was urged by Francis Bacon. Even Mayerne had his own secret remedies that he withheld from the *pharmacopoeia*.

Trevor-Roper was trained in history, not in medicine. With the caveat that his book considers Mayerne not so much in his medical as in his social and intellectual context, Trevor-Roper explores the thought world of that time in detail. He shows Mayerne as a member of the Protestant International, the group of Calvinists who may or may not have paid much attention to Calvin's theology, but were certainly not prepared to accede to the tyranny of Rome. These Protestants were driven away from their homelands by conflict with the Catholics in a migration of talent that he likens to the dispersal of Jews across Europe and America by Nazi Germany.

Mayerne himself was characteristic of these displaced persons. Energetic and acquisitive, he migrated from Switzerland to France to England, where he made his fortune, purchased an estate in Switzerland, and styled himself the "Baron d'Aubonne." He intended to establish a dynasty upon retirement from his duties in England. Here we see feudalism red in tooth and claw as Mayerne surveys his estate, inspecting its fields that would produce tithes and rents, taxes and tolls – various seigneurial perquisites complete with respectful peasants and obedient Calvinist ministers of the gospel.

As it happened, the dream didn't work out all that well. There was no dynasty; Mayerne's two older sons died in their twenties of drink and dissipation, and his two younger sons by his second wife died in childhood. Mayerne never saw Aubonne again after returning to England in June, 1625. King Charles wouldn't let him go, probably for political reasons – thus validating his father's warning that if he served princes, he would be a life-long slave, as Mayerne wrote in a letter to his sister.

A slave, perhaps, but a wealthy one. Court doctors received a nominal salary, but their real income came from private practice and from the advantages of being in the royal court. Doctors applied for forfeited lands, confiscated goods of outlaws, and offices of profit. The Regius Professor of Medicine at Oxford had a concession to garble (sift for impurities) tobacco. Mayerne himself was Garbler of Spices and Seeds under Charles I; some of his other entrepreneurial ventures were in Scottish coal mines, English lead mines, and English oyster beds.

He had a lifelong preoccupation with chemistry and maintained his own laboratory, primarily to concoct his medications, but he also used his interest in distilling to found a new company: the Distillers of London. He compiled a cookery book, invented a cordial, kept deer, and grew medicinal herbs.

He may be better known in the field of art than in medicine, on the strength of the "Mayerne manuscript," discovered in the 1840s and now in the British Museum. In it, he described the many technical details of preparing pigments, varnishes, enamels, and other art materials. The manuscript is considered by an English scholar to be nothing less than the most important original source on the techniques of North European art in the Baroque era. Mayerne had his portrait painted by Rubens, counting him and Van Dyck among his personal friends.

It is apparent that physicians were less specialized at that time. Mayerne's royal duties included the care of the king's horses and dogs; veterinary medicine was not yet a field in itself. He often performed autopsies on his patients. "Physician, chemist, courtier, diplomatist and entrepreneur" – surely there were few who could match his energy and versatility.

Blair Worden explains in an editor's foreword that Hugh Trevor-Roper, who died in 2003, had a lifelong interest in the relationship of medicine and society. His research in preparation for writing *The Last Days of Hitler* led him to the power struggle among Hitler's doctors during the Führer's last few days. Trevor-Roper described this research in a lecture on "Medicine and Politics" at the annual meeting of the American College of Cardiology in 1980 – one of the few annual meetings I missed in those years. Most of his book was written in 1979, the year before the ACC lecture. It was left as an unfinished project and was found among his papers after his death. Worden states that he polished some of the unfinished passages, made only a few small additions, and checked the references. The result is a challenging work, full of the thought world of the seventeenth century, but one that includes a well-rounded portrait of the man who gazes at us from the cover with the eyes of one who has seen it all. The reader can hardly doubt it.

"IN THE HANDS OF ANY RASCAL"

THE KNIFE MAN
The Extraordinary Life and Times of John Hunter,
Father of Modern Surgery
By Wendy Moore

What physician hasn't assembled his own little list of stories about John Hunter, the eighteenth century English surgeon often referred to as the Father of Surgery? He was a man of great energy and stamina, seemingly unlimited curiosity, courage and audacity, skill and ingenuity. Here are a few of my own favorites from the Hunter lore:

Sir William Osler, in his "Lectures on Angina Pectoris and Allied States", described Hunter's terminal illness, in which his episodes of chest pain became more frequent and were brought on not only by exercise, but also by "worry and anger," so that he sometimes said that "his life was in the hands of any rascal who chose to annoy and tease him." And indeed this was the case. He died after becoming angered at a meeting of the St. George's Hospital governors on October 16, 1793. "When contradicted flatly, he left the board room in silent rage, and in the next room gave a deep groan and fell down dead. The coronary arteries were found to be converted into open bony tubes, and the aorta was dilated."

And so, to the cardiologist, this is surely one of the most famous case reports of sudden cardiac death. But my brief career as a specialist in venereal diseases in the United States Public Health Service provided another encounter with Hunter, who described his own legendary inoculation of himself with venereal disease in *A Treatise on Venereal Disease*. The story is one that will never die, and it has recently been recounted by Jon Franklin and John Sutherland in *Guinea Pig Doctors: The Drama of Medical Research through Self-Experimentation* (William Morrow and Company, Inc., 1984), and by Sherwin Nuland in *Doctors* (Alfred A. Knopf, 1988). Convinced that syphilis and gonorrhea were separate manifestations of the same disease, he inoculated some gonorrheal pus into his own foreskin, and he subsequently developed both gonorrhea and syphilis. Little did he know that the man from whom he had obtained the pus had both diseases; Hunter concluded that the results strengthened his contention that they were both the same disease.

An original copy of the 1817 edition of *A Treatise on the Blood, Inflammation, and Gunshot Wounds* by John Hunter, leather-bound, is probably the oldest volume I own. It was included in a box of old medical books belonging to the grandfather of a family practitioner in Mena, who gave them to me in 1976. Not much browsing is required to show that Hunter's interests extended beyond the title. On page 147 he writes,

> The carotid artery of the camel, among quadrupeds, and of the swan, among birds, are very proper arteries for such experiments. To be as accurate as possible, I injected the arteries of two camels, and of the swan; and that one end might not be more distended than the other, the artery was well warmed, and placed in a perfectly horizontal position;

This experiment was done to address the question of whether the vascular bed increases in capacity as it is farther from the heart. He concludes that this is the case and, "as arteries divide, they increase in size much faster than if they did not."

The Transactions of the Hunterian Society 1961-1962 are recorded in a slim volume I found in England in 1974. Here, the memory of John Hunter was kept alive in reports such as one from the Hunterian Oration of 1962, "John Hunter's Patients,"[3]

---

[3] Delivered by A. Lawrence Abel, Esq., M. S., F. R. C. S., at the Livery Hall, Guildhall, on Monday, 26th February, 1962.

which described his account of the "tumour removed from the neck of the horse of Mrs. General Pitt." In the course of his operation, he thought it was necessary to ligate the carotid artery, "but immediately the horse appeared vastly oppressed, breathed with great difficulty, so much so that I suspected that I had tied up with the artery the par-vagum." Even though the ligature was released, the horse died the next day.

Wendy Moore is described in the dust jacket of her biography, *The Knife Man: The Extraordinary Life and Times of John Hunter, Father of Modern Surgery* (Broadway Books, 2005), as a "writer and a journalist" who "has specialized in health and medical topics for more than twenty years". She lives in London and this is her first book.

Her journalistic experience has taught her to use snappy chapter titles and dramatic opening paragraphs, as in Chapter 4, "The Pregnant Woman's Womb":

> *Striding up the sweeping driveway from the Thames to the grand façade of the Royal Hospital in its pastoral setting at Chelsea, John Hunter could have been forgiven for lapsing into a relaxed frame of mind. The spring sunshine, which was bringing out the blooms in the hospital's glorious gardens, had brought an end to the first long winter in his brother's anatomy school...*

One is reminded of the young reporter who began his report of a flood, "This morning God sits on a lonely mountaintop overlooking the flood waters..."

His editor wired in reply, "Forget the flood. Interview God."

That said, however, the book assembles many fascinating episodes in Hunter's life, and the stories, many of them well known, can speak for themselves. Chapter 1, "The Coach Driver's Knee," describes Hunter's introduction of his concept of collateral circulation, demonstrated in an experiment where he tied off the carotid artery of a deer and observed the blanching (and subsequent pinking up several days later) of the antler supplied by the artery as collateral circulation began to replace the ligated artery. The coach driver had a popliteal aneurysm and Hunter tied off the femoral artery high enough in the thigh to allow collateral circulation to supply the leg. This is now known as "Hunter's operation" and the operative site is known as "Hunter's canal".

She gives many details of the grave-robbing industry in England in the eighteenth century, which provided cadavers for the anatomy classes Hunter taught. The story most likely to be retold is in Chapter 13, "The Giant's Bones," in which she recounts the story of the eight-foot- two-inch tall "Irish Giant," Charles Byrne. This young man, a victim of a pituitary tumor long before this disease was identified, died at an early age, but not until after he had taken every precaution he could to avoid having his body taken by John Hunter for display purposes. Hunter had tried unsuccessfully to obtain Byrne's permission to use his body and had then hired a private investigator to follow Byrne to keep track of his body before and after death.

After death, the mourners, who had been retained by Byrne, put the body in a concrete casket and took it to the middle of the English Channel, where they dumped it. However, Hunter had bribed the undertaker to allow some skilled workers to slip the body out of the casket while the mourners were drinking at the last tavern before they arrived at the Channel. Upon receiving the body, Hunter boiled it down to the skeleton, but it was such "hot property" that he dared not display it for several years.

In his chapter on Hunter in *Doctors,* Nuland wrote that although an abundance of information is available about John Hunter, a biographer who does justice to the life and contributions must be a person of many parts, blessed with intuition and energy. Wendy Moore has performed a useful service for the reading public. Nuland's wished-for biographer has yet to appear.

THE LADY WHO HAD SEEN HELL

Florence Nightingale 1820-1910
By Cecil Woodham-Smith

"Florence Nightingale" in Eminent Victorians
By Lytton Strachey

The Florence Nightingale window in the National Cathedral in Washington, D.C. includes an image of the nurse with her lamp at the bedside of a wounded British soldier in the Crimean War – an icon that has come to stand for the highest ideals of the healing profession. Of course, no stained window or any other visual representation of the Barrack Hospital at Scutari can convey the horror and stench of the circumstances; perhaps their reality is reflected in the devotion of the soldiers, conveyed by the survivors who returned to England to spread her legend. This legend, which afforded her the leverage to revolutionize the role of nursing, was based on twenty months of service in the Crimea. "She said she had seen Hell, and because she had seen Hell, she was set apart," Cecil Woodham-Smith writes in *Florence Nightingale* (McGraw-Hill, 1951).

Indeed, she was "set apart" all her life. A sketch by her aunt shows two little girls walking with their father; one sister holding to her father's coat-tail while Flo held no hand and walked alone. Later, at age sixteen, she had an experience of being called by God, writing in her diary that God had spoken to her and called her to his service. (Forty years later, she wrote that her "voices" had spoken to her four times – at the time of her original call, before taking her first hospital post, before going to the Crimea, and after the death of her dear friend, Sidney Hebert.)

Her background was a privileged one. When Florence was seventeen to nineteen years old, the Nightingales spent almost two years in Europe while six new bedrooms were being added to the family's country home, Lea Hurst. At age twenty-five, she wanted to set up a Protestant sisterhood, without vows, but the family squashed this plan.

Hospitals at that time were for the poor who couldn't afford private medical care; the smell was such that those entering the hospital for the first time often became acutely nauseated. There was no such thing as training for nurses; the only qualification was to be a woman. Miss Nightingale wrote in 1845, aged twenty-five, "I saw a poor woman die before my eyes this summer because there was nothing but fools to sit up with her, who poisoned her as much as if they had given her arsenic."

She didn't attain the critical velocity to escape the orbit of her home and family until she was thirty-three years old. Until this time, her "day job" was to be in charge of the still-room, pantry, and linen-room. At a friend's suggestion, however, she began to obtain and study Blue Books and hospital reports – the sort of information Members of Parliament are supposed to review and master. She really did master this information, filling her own notebooks with facts she analyzed, indexed, and tabulated. She also obtained similar information from contacts she had met on family trips in Berlin and Paris. All this studying was done in secret because her family would hardly have approved.

In addition to the knowledge she was surreptitiously acquiring, she gained friends important to her subsequent career, none more so than Sidney Herbert, future Secretary of State for War, whom she met on a family trip to Rome. Herbert was converted to her cause, and he was willing to carry out many of the projects that, as a woman, she could only suggest. Through the Herberts, she met Doctor Manning, Archbishop of Chichester and later Cardinal, who was also one of the four *Eminent Victorians* of Lytton Strachey.

Among the other critical life choices of her young adulthood, she decided not to marry the man she almost surely loved, Richard Monckton Milnes.

Her mother and sister were disappointed, to say the least; Florence responded to this crisis by becoming so ill that she often fainted. Friends offered to take her with them on a trip to Egypt, and on her way back home, she spent two weeks as a visitor at the Institute of Deaconesses at Kaiserswerth, a place she had been longing to visit for years because of its reputation for religious emphasis and ascetic discipline. She also acquired a pet owl, which she used to surprise her friends, carrying it in her pocket.

An indicator of the absence of tranquility in her relationship with her family was their reaction to her visit to Kaiserswerth. Her sister, Parthe, became hysterical and her mother was in tears, as they insisted that Florence must return home to her duties and station. Two years later, Florence managed to escape the toils of her family and spend a few months at Kaiserswerth, where she appreciated its atmosphere of devotion and concern for the sick. The nursing, however, she found to be nil and the hygiene horrible.

She rejoined her mother and sister at Cologne, where she claimed she was treated as a criminal. Her father required her to nurse him for his inflamed eyes and back she went to her domestic cage. What was her cage? She described her situation with a damning indictment: "O weary days – oh evenings that seem never to end – for how many years have I watched that drawing-room clock and thought it never would reach the ten! And for twenty, thirty years more to do this!"

She later wrote that women accumulate so much nervous energy during a day of doing nothing that by night, they are at risk of going mad.

It often happens that the interests and activities of the high-energy years of the twenties are the mainspring for subsequent achievement; Miss Nightingale's use of this period of her life is of interest in that she attended no university, didn't work, and had no apparent mentor. She stayed at home, unable to break away. Her mother and sister found her difficult to get along with and she experienced such frustration that she would sometimes fall into trances, losing all track of time. But as if the spring were being wound tighter and tighter, she prepared herself for her moment of release, when she would pour herself into her life's work with strength and determination.

Her liberation finally came in April, 1853, when her friend Liz Herbert wrote to her about a possible opening as superintendent of The Institution for the Care of Sick Gentlewomen in Distressed Circumstances. Amid the family disturbance resulting from her acceptance of this position, her father retired to the Athenaeum Club and decided to grant his daughter an allowance of £500 per year (perhaps $50,000 today). This was convenient, since the Institution's committee couldn't bring itself to offer her any remuneration for her services, although it could overcome its reservations about having a "young lady in society" in a position where she would be taking orders from a committee of other young ladies.

Undeterred by the attacks from her opposition, Miss Nightingale entered into her duties with revolutionary innovations, such as having pipes for hot water on every floor. "From Committees, Charity and Schism, from the Church of England, from philanthropy and all deceits of the devil, Good Lord deliver us."

When the Institution began running smoothly, she enlarged her scope and began visiting hospitals and collecting facts that would help in reforming conditions for hospital nurses. But there were no institutions to produce trained nurses. Then an epidemic of cholera broke out in 1854. She volunteered to supervise the nurses caring for cholera patients at the Middlesex Hospital. She was in her element here, on her feet constantly for days, caring for patients shrieking in agony.

Then the Crimean War broke out. The people of England suddenly knew more than they had ever known about any military campaign because *The Times* was publishing reports from the first war correspondent, William Howard Russell, who sent back furious reports of the suffering he found among the sick and wounded. Miss Nightingale saw her chance. Her old friend Sidney Herbert was now Secretary of State for War and he invited her to go to Scutari in command of a group of nurses, at the Government's expense. Even before receiving his letter, she had already booked passage to Constantinople with a party of nurses.

With this backing from the Cabinet, she assembled thirty-eight nurses and sailed a week later. This would be the first time that female nurses had been allowed to nurse men. The hospital at Scutari had just been built, but it was suffering from administrative collapse. Herbert had sent her as an administrator to advance the cause of nursing; direct patient care wasn't really mentioned. Her thirty-eight nurses were experienced by the standards of the day; none were young; none were "ladies." Twenty-four of them were from religious institutions. "Excellent self devoted women," wrote Miss Nightingale, they were "fit more for heaven than a hospital, they flit about like angels without hands among the patients and soothe their souls while they leave their bodies dirty and neglected."

She took money with her. *The Times* had collected contributions from the public and she had over £30,000 at her disposal, £7,000 of which she had raised personally. She did some shopping for supplies in Marseilles on the way, so she didn't arrive empty-handed. She found, however, that the Army was reluctant to accept her assistance and unwilling to accept her money or supplies. When she asked the Ambassador in Constantinople how the funds from *The Times* might best be used, he suggested they might be used for building a Protestant church.

She and her nurses were ignored by the doctors, and they were placed in cramped unpleasant living quarters, complete with fleas and rats. A surgeon reported that the nurses Miss Nightingale offered were not accepted. For her part, she was determined to follow hospital and military protocol, refusing to allow any of her nurses to enter a ward without the invitation of a doctor. They were only allowed to cook. However, a great influx of sick and wounded soldiers on November 9 overwhelmed military scruples. Crowding was intense, there was icy rain, and the filth was indescribable, with vermin-infested men lying on dirty rotten floors.

The purveyor system was so unworkable that supplies were wasted and unavailable when needed. She alone could dispense her stores with readiness; towels and soap, knives and forks, combs and toothbrushes began to appear. She reported to Sidney Herbert that she was now clothing the British army.

The bedside vigils weren't the greatest drain on her resources, however. In the face of a failed bureaucratic system, she attended to countless details without the benefit of a secretary. Her direct contact with the soldiers convinced her that they were not the "brutes" the officers had described to her. They spent all their money on drink because they had nothing else to do so she made arrangements for reading rooms and recreation rooms. The army establishment provided no means for the men to send any of their money home because they were convinced they would never do so. "The British soldier is not a remitting animal." So Miss Nightingale became the banker for the men and funds began to flow back to England.

She had ample opportunity to observe that no good deed goes unpunished. She was opposed by the army establishment and also by the nurses serving under her, among them Mrs. Bridgeman, Reverend Mother of the Crimea, known by Miss Nightingale as "Reverend Brickbat." Sir John Hall, Chief of the Medical Staff, tried to starve her out by reducing her allotted provisions, but she was a woman of means, with her own resources. Dr. Hall was recognized as "K.C.B.," (Knight Commander of the Bath), which she recognized privately as "Knight of the Crimean Burial Grounds."

She wrote lengthy reports of her efforts to her friend Liz Herbert, who forwarded them to her husband, the Secretary for

War, who in turn forwarded them to Queen Victoria. The queen replied with a request that Mrs. Herbert send all Miss Nightingale's reports directly to her, The queen complained that otherwise she, who had more interest than anyone in the details of the wounded, received no such reports at all. Such royal favor was something Miss Nightingale could later use to her advantage, but it had little power to penetrate the shield of the military establishment.

Significant improvements did indeed appear in the Barrack Hospital as a result of her efforts, but the mortality rate continued to climb with an unabated epidemic of "gaol fever." This led the government to send out a Sanitary Commission from London and the commission's findings were appalling. The whole vast building was described as standing in a sea of decaying filth. Some beds near the privy doors were fatal and every man put in them died quickly. Much of the hospital's water supply reached the men only after it had passed through a horse's carcass.

During the first two weeks, 556 handcarts and large baskets full of rubbish were removed; twenty-four dead animals, including two dead horses, were buried, with immediate effects. Finally, the death rate fell.[4]

Peace was proclaimed in April, 1856; the last patient left the Barrack Hospital on July 16, and twelve days later, Miss Nightingale sailed from Constantinople for Marseilles, traveling incognito as "Miss Smith." England desired passionately to honor her, but she was obsessed by a sense of failure, writing in a private note, "Oh my poor men; I am a bad mother to come home and leave you in your Crimean graves – 73 percent in 8 regiments in 6 months from disease alone – who thinks of that

---

[4] By February 1855 the mortality rate had dropped from 60% to 42.7%. Through the establishment of a fresh water supply as well as using her own funds to buy fruit, vegetables and standard hospital equipment, the mortality rate in the spring had dropped further to 2.2%. J J O'Connor and E F Robertson, in (see next page) http://wwwhistory.mcs.standrews.ac.uk/Biographies/Nightingale.html

now?"

Her postwar life was one of paradox: acclaimed by the people, she retreated to the seclusion of her room. So successful was her seclusion that after a few years, most of the public probably thought she had died and yet she was just now beginning to effect major reforms. Though most famous for her reforms in nursing, her primary efforts for years were directed toward reforming the War Department in an effort to improve the lot of the enlisted soldier. Thought to be on her deathbed, she lived to the age of ninety and survived almost all her peers.

While at Scutari, she had "Crimean fever," a mysterious incapacitating illness that has been variously attributed to such causes as brucellosis and, in view of her history of bouts of severe depression in her teens and twenties, bipolar disorder. After her return to England, she took to her bed and stayed there for the rest of her long life, though a few paces in the garden were documented in later years.

Her post-mortem analysis of the disasters of the Crimea combined her passion for statistics with a gift for vivid expression. She used bar graphs and she is given credit for introducing the polar area diagram, a form of pie chart. Dr. William Farr, Superintendent of the Statistical Department in the Registrar-General's Office, had provided her with information showing that the mortality rate at her hospital in Scutari had been more than twice that at the battle front.[5] It was this information that prompted her to call for the Royal Commission to review the situation. Even in peacetime, the mortality in the barracks was nearly double that in civilian life. "You might as well take 1,100 men every year out upon Salisbury Plain and

---

[5] Deaths in the British field hospitals reached a peak during January 1855, when 2,761 soldiers died of contagious diseases, 83 from wounds and 324 from other causes making a total of 3,168. The army's average manpower for that month was 32,393. Using this information, Nightingale computed a mortality rate of 1,174 per 10,000 with 1,023 per 10,000 being from zymotic (infectious) diseases. If this rate had continued, and troops had not been replaced frequently, then disease alone would have killed the entire British army in the Crimea. *Ibid.*

shoot them." She attributed 16,000 deaths in the Crimea to the many counterproductive features of the system.

Her ace in the hole, of course, was her relationship with Queen Victoria, who presented her with a brooch with the words "Crimea," and "Blessed are the merciful." Two months after her return from the Crimea, she was invited to Balmoral to meet the queen. Prince Albert and Queen Victoria were convinced of the defects she described and the reforms she proposed. There were repeated visits to Balmoral, but Miss Nightingale's agenda required concrete action, which was forbidden to the queen under the British Constitution.

Miss Nightingale's commitment to nursing reform wasn't forgotten. Backed by the £45,000 Nightingale Fund, the Nightingale Training School opened in 1860, despite opposition from the medical world, which feared that trained nurses would trespass on the province of the doctors. The directors of St. Thomas' Hospital, site of the school, held that nurses were subordinates "in the position of house-maids" and needed only the simplest instruction.

While waiting for the school to open, she wrote *Notes on Nursing*, the most popular of her works. Among other instructions, she cautioned against false assurances in an effort to cheer the sick and to remember that patients are reluctant to ask.

Though she didn't leave her room, she maintained an active interest in each nursing student, having personal interviews with each and keeping up correspondence with many of them for years afterward. She met visitors in her room one at a time and only by appointment, and such was the force of her personality that she maintained a close connection with many of them. She was apparently so charming in her relationships with men that she retained their loyalty and affection in spite of her bullying them.

Sir Harry Verney, "the handsomest man in England," Member of Parliament, baronet, and head of the house of Verney, fell in love with her and proposed marriage in 1857, which she declined. A few months later, he married her sister Parthe, and Florence and Sir Harry remained close friends. Benjamin Jowett, noted theologian and Regius Professor of Greek at Oxford, maintained a long and intimate friendship with her, mostly by correspondence, after she also declined his proposal of marriage. Her letters to him were destroyed, but his to her were published by Oxford University Press in 1987.

In the course of her efforts, in the late 1850s and early 1860s, it became increasingly apparent that to reform the army, its problems with sanitation and food supply in India couldn't be ignored. She became an expert on India, despite never having been there, by reading the government reports and acquiring through questions and correspondence the type of information she had learned firsthand in the Crimea. She continued to be a thorn in the side of the army establishment with recommendations for reform, some of which were adopted with much foot-dragging. Never in doubt, she was sometimes in error, as in her insistence on open windows for ventilation, a firm policy she carried with her from the Crimea. In vain, the old India hands attempted to tell her that opening the windows in India only let in the heat, which was miserable.

Jowett's letters sometimes scolded, sometimes praised. In his New Year's Eve letter of 1879, he recalled his romantic feelings of more than twenty years earlier, but he went on to estimate that thousands of soldiers survived their tours of duty because of the improvements she had brought about in drainage and in ventilation of hospitals. The Indian natives who were saved by her efforts, he reckoned, might number in the hundreds of thousands. Thousands of young girls, he declared, had been named after her.

She outlived her family, friends, and enemies, having become so confused in her eighties that it is doubtful she understood when she received the Order of Merit from the nation. Her last years were marked by obesity as well as senility; she died at age ninety.

The Victorian era in general, and Florence Nightingale in

particular, required a Lytton Strachey to lend a bit of perspective to its story of energy, discipline, and good works. Strachey wrote biographies in a new and different way in the early twentieth century, with the announced intention of showing the character flaws beneath the public record of accomplishment; and this he did in *Eminent Victorians,* in which he depicted four icons: Henry Edward Cardinal Manning, Dr. Thomas Arnold, Florence Nightingale, and General George Charles Gordon. They were great people, surely, but they also had their little quirks and eccentricities, which some might think of as blemishes that mark the other side of the coin of heroism.

How could an ardent iconoclast have resisted an attempt at Florence Nightingale, the saintly lady with the lamp? Strachey certainly intended his biographical sketch to be an entertaining put-down. Curiously, however, it does little to diminish her standing. Perhaps in these latter days, we have become accustomed to learning about the private lives of public figures, or perhaps Strachey became distracted from Miss Nightingale's flaws by some of the glaring flaws of the establishment she fought so furiously. In any event, The British Army turned out to be a more tempting target than the nurse.

Published in 1918, a generation before Woodham-Smith's biography, the Nightingale chapter in *Eminent Victorians* can be read as an introduction to a more lengthy account, or as a follow-up. Strachey's wit produces quotable passages that can provide the spice for any other version of her life. He declares in his opening paragraph that he will show more than the "saintly, self-sacrificing woman," and that he will show the "Demon" that possessed her. So he says. But some readers may find that the disagreeable parts he advertises are not such a high price to pay for getting things done. Such were the mores of the time that anything less than a Demon would not have done.

First, she had to deal with her family. Her mother expected her to show appreciation for her privileged upbringing "by doing her duty in that state of life unto which it had pleased God to call her – in other words, by marrying, after a fitting number of dances and dinner parties, an eligible gentleman and living happily ever afterwards." But Florence had another call, and the family couldn't understand why she felt driven to minister to the poor sick cottagers. "As if there was not plenty to do in any case, in the ordinary way, at home. There was the china to look after, and there was her father to be read to after dinner."

And when she did receive a proposal of marriage from a man she probably loved, she mustered the strength to subdue her instincts. In her own words,

> "I have an intellectual nature which requires satisfaction; and that would find it in him. I have a passional nature which requires satisfaction, and that would find it in him. I have a moral, an active nature which requires satisfaction, and that would not find it in his life. Sometimes I think that I will satisfy my passional nature at all events."

It appears, however, that the moral and active nature won out over the passional and the intellectual. Having determined to do her bit for the world in nursing, she had to contend with nursing as she found it. The typical nurse she found was some variant of Dickens' Mrs. Gamp, addicted to brandy and often a prey to worse habits. This state of affairs had changed, Strachey said, and it had done so because of Miss Nightingale.

When circumstances finally afforded her the opportunity to provide nursing care, she showed the world a revolutionary approach. This one-on-one care was the basis of her legend. Strachey described it in a memorable passage in which he abandoned iconoclasm: "Wherever, in those vast wards, suffering was at its worst and the need for help was greatest, there, as if by magic, was Miss Nightingale. Her superhuman equanimity would, at the moment of some ghastly operation, nerve the victim to endure and almost to hope."

Her mother spoke of her with amazement. "We are ducks who have hatched a wild swan." Strachey said it was no swan; it was an eagle.

As strong as her personal qualities were, she did bring with her one advantage from her family that had impeded her in so many ways: she belonged to the highest circle of society. One cannot imagine a mere middle-class woman attracting enough attention to present her views. But Flo Nightingale could not be ignored.

The ultimate adversary in her efforts was the army she encountered in the Crimea – not the Turkish army, but the British army. England at this time was a world of men; no institution fortified the world of men with such unyielding determination as the British army and its champions in the government. Although she was fortunate when her friend Sidney Herbert held the office of Secretary of War, she found a challenging opponent when Herbert was replaced by Lord Panmure. In her efforts to persuade Lord Panmure to appoint a Royal Commission to investigate the system and provide recommendations for reform, we see Miss Nightingale persisting in her attempts to get him to do something, describing her frustrations with the imposing figure of "The Bison" to her friends, but developing a relationship of playful familiarity with Lord Panmure himself.

She developed a strategy that worked. She discovered he could be bullied. His hide was tough, but his spirit was malleable. One thing he feared above all else was the force of public opinion. At the first hint of an appeal to the public, he would make any concession. Knowing this, Miss Nightingale kept this threat in reserve. Even the War Office could do nothing to save The Bison from Miss Nightingale. She prevailed.

Her strategy in dealing with Sidney Herbert was a different one. He was a faithful disciple, but he found the price of discipleship to be high. Exhausted in her service, he died of Bright's Disease, but not before being scolded for his exhaustion. In a letter quoted by Strachey:

> *"Beaten! (she exclaimed). Can't you see that you've simply thrown away the game? And with all the winning cards in your hands! And so noble a game! Sidney Herbert beaten! And beaten by Ben Hawes! It is*

a worse disgrace ... (her full rage burst out at last) ... a worse disgrace than the hospitals at Scutari."

In her later years, she became preoccupied with religious concerns and she sent a copy of her three-volume "Suggestions for Thought to the Searchers after Truth among the Artisans of England" to her friend John Stuart Mill, who confessed he wasn't altogether convinced by her proof. She couldn't believe it. Her proof of the existence of God was impeccable. She had expected better from Mr. Mill.

Her unusual pattern of life reminds today's reader of the life of Charles Darwin, who retired to his bed in the country while incubating *The Origin of Species*. It is as if the two revolutionaries were reluctant to stand in public to face the opposition and so they retreated from the world. Whatever her diagnosis, she found as she recovered from her illness that a complete recovery wasn't really necessary and might actually be inconvenient. A Victorian woman's access to political activity was indirect, as described by Anthony Trollope in his political novels. Powerful women expressed their views through their influence on men, and Florence Nightingale excelled in this art. Newly appointed viceroys to India, for instance, routinely visited the bedside of this woman who had never been there, to receive their education about India before sailing. Never active in the cause of feminism, she saw little need to embrace the more direct approach of the feminists. She achieved her success in the old-fashioned way.

When dealing with patients, I was always reluctant to use the terms "manipulative" and "secondary gain." These words seldom lent themselves to a productive assessment of undiagnosed illness, but in considering Miss Nightingale, these terms do come to mind. Whatever her methods, her contributions to the profession of nursing were revolutionary. Less well known but also revolutionary, her efforts to reform sanitation and living conditions for soldiers undoubtedly saved many lives.

There have been many biographies of her; those of Lytton Strachey and Cecil Woodham-Smith are not definitive. Strachey's is concise, less iconoclastic now than it was intended to be in 1918, and it entertains with a touch of light irony. Woodham-Smith's excellent account makes good use of Miss Nightingale's correspondence and other private papers, many of them newly available in the 1940s. The many-sided genius of Florence Nightingale is difficult to encompass in one volume, but these two are enough to leave the reader standing in slack-jawed amazement at this lady who had seen hell and was set apart.

"THE CHIEF"

THE LIFE OF SIR WILLIAM OSLER
By Harvey Cushing

WILLIAM OSLER: A LIFE IN MEDICINE
By Michael Bliss

A sick but smiling little girl is lying in her bed surrounded by
four dolls in a painting reproduced for an advertisement by a
large pharmaceutical firm. Just peeping over the side of her bed
is a balding, smiling man with a bushy white mustache, playing
the puppeteer with a hand on each of two dolls. This was Sir
William Osler, Regius Professor of Medicine at Oxford. The year
was 1918 and the little girl's mother wrote, "He visited our little
Janet twice every day from the middle of October until her death
a month later... There would be a little tap, low down on the door
which would be pushed open and a crouching figure playing
goblin would come in, and in a high-pitched voice would ask if
the fairy godmother was at home and could he have a bit of tea."

This painting is reproduced in *William Osler: A Life in Medicine*
(Oxford University Press, 1999) by Michael Bliss, and it is the
first image that comes to mind if one is attempting to explain to a
layman why today there is an American Osler Society, an Osler
Club of London, an Osler Society of McGill University, and an
Osler website based in Houston; and why William Osler is
sometimes referred to as the Father of Modern Medicine.

Other images can be readily invoked in an effort to explain his
influence: a series of four photographs of Osler at a bedside in
the Johns Hopkins Hospital, entitled, "Inspection," "Palpation,"

"Auscultation," and "Contemplation," during the course of his encounter with a patient; John Singer Sargent's monumental painting, *The Four Doctors*, showing the four founding heads of pathology, surgery, internal medicine, and gynecology, in their academic regalia, at Johns Hopkins Hospital; and the photograph of him in shirtsleeves writing his textbook, *The Principles and Practice of Medicine*, with his caption, "*Parturit Osler. Nascitur liber.*" (Osler in labor. The book is born.)

However, the image that comes to mind from a second reading, some forty years after first encountering *The Life of Sir William Osler* (Oxford University Press, 1925) by Harvey Cushing, is that of the young Professor of Medicine at the University of Pennsylvania entering the morgue at Blockley Hospital on a Sunday morning. Interns would come to watch him work; he started at eight in the morning and performed one study after another all day. Although there were two officially appointed pathologists, Osler was free to do any studies they declined, and he wrote notes on 162 post-mortem studies, forty-eight of which were cases of tuberculosis. This was a relatively low-tech procedure requiring only a stone table and a sharp knife, and the textbook Osler wrote six years later carried an air of authority because the author had personally done so many of these direct studies. He never forsook his preference for information acquired by immediate observation, performing his last autopsy in 1919, at age sixty-nine, on a patient who had died with "influenzal pneumonia."

This is the work ethic that informed the practice of modern medicine. Though surely not the origin or sole causal factor of this ethic, Osler's practice and preaching (in one of his essays, work is the "magic word") cast its long shadow over the wards of the teaching hospitals back when I was a medical student and house officer. Every generation seems to think the younger generation has lost the concept of hard work; it is difficult to believe that it has disappeared, but things are certainly different than they were when Osler's staff of "assistants" lived in Johns Hopkins Hospital. Perhaps we need a "second coming."

Another image appears in the Cushing biography, quoted from an 1888 letter when Osler was thirty-eight years old[6]: "*He dances along the street singing as he goes* – as of old." Having divided his life into "day-tight compartments" – a concept he proposed in one of his "lay sermons," "A Way of Life," delivered to Yale undergraduates in 1913 – he apparently subdivided, or compartmentalized, his days as well, dancing along the street between one serious bit of business and another.

His role in the history of medicine is unique. Bliss addresses this in his preface, stating that the idea that Osler was the greatest doctor in the history of the world was seriously advanced after his death in 1919. He wrote the first great textbook of modern medicine, which was also the last to be written by a single author; he published prodigiously, and although his name is attached to some physical findings and diseases (Osler nodes, Osler-Weber-Rendu disease), he made no spectacular discoveries. He himself considered his greatest achievement to be the promotion of bedside teaching of medical students, as opposed to listening to lectures; his personal influence was astonishing, extending to all he encountered – students, colleagues, patients both humble and eminent (among his patients were the Prince of Wales, Henry James, and Walt Whitman). He was an outspoken advocate of humanism and literature in medicine. Cushing wrote that Osler's advocacy of sanitation and other public health measures saved more lives than any of his other activities.

Osler was the oldest of the four young department heads who began the Johns Hopkins traditions in a newly built hospital: he was thirty-nine; W. H. Welch, chief of pathology, was thirty-eight; W. S. Halsted, chief of surgery, was thirty-seven; and H. A. Kelly, head of gynecology, was thirty-one. Professors and residents all lived at the hospital. A visitor from Boston "likened the life to

---

[6] Among the glories of the Cushing biography are the headings at the top of each page: page number, chapter title, season or month and year, age of Osler, subject of the page, and page number -- here, on two facing pages, 290, University of Pennsylvania, Spring 1888, Aet. 38, The Cerebral Palsies of Children, 291.

that of a monastery, with the unusual feature that the monks did not appear to bother their minds about the future." The *esprit de corps* was surely cemented by the leadership, charismatic personality, and practical jokes of William Osler, "The Chief."

Even after he moved out of the hospital, had his own house, and got married, he continued to be close to his assistants, who were often invited to tea and dinner at "The Open Arms," the nickname given to his residence in Baltimore and later in Oxford.

His bedside manner was legendary, but he doesn't seem to have had lengthy interviews with patients; he dictated the pace, and it didn't permit digressions. Bliss writes that today's doctors talk with their patients more than he did. W. S. Thayer, one of his senior assistants, confirmed this observation, but he said he didn't know how he did it.

He was also quotable. I have two or three collections of his sayings, faithfully assembled by latter-day apostles, on my shelves: "The desire to take medicine is perhaps the greatest feature which distinguishes man from animals." "It is astonishing with how little reading a doctor can practice medicine, but it is not astonishing how badly he may do it." "Although one swallow does not make a summer, one tophus makes gout and one crescent malaria."

Collegiality in the medical profession may be a bit frayed in these latter days, but Osler was its chief advocate in his own time. He participated faithfully in medical associations and was even elected president of a pediatric society. He made no effort to develop a private practice, apparently unique among his peers in this respect, but he saw many of his colleagues and their families as patients. Cushing mentions a sudden trip from Baltimore to Montreal to see an old friend when he learned he was sick – perhaps to consult on the case, perhaps to offer the services of friendship.

A summer vacation in 1898 was interrupted by a long sequence of diversions. First there was a summons to Buffalo; from there he went on to see a patient in Iowa. Soon after his return, he was off to see Captain Arthur Lee in Winter Harbour; while in Maine he was called to Minneapolis to see a recent Hopkins graduate who was seriously ill. He then returned to Canton to see his wife at her mother's home, but he soon had to leave at once for Toronto, where his brother Edmond's son was critically ill. This was before the days of automobiles and airplanes. Perhaps he found his own private vacation space in railroad cars.

He left Hopkins at the peak of his career, at age fifty-five, appointed by the King of England to be Regius Professor of Medicine at Oxford, where he was told he wouldn't be required to be in residence at Oxford more than a third of the time. This was essentially retirement. Doctors in their mid-fifties routinely ask themselves why they are working so hard. There must be an easier way. Osler was in England when the offer was made and he telegraphed his wife about the difficulty of the decision as to whether to accept. Her response was immediate: "DO NOT PROCASTINATE. ACCEPT AT ONCE."

Some ten years later, Osler left an entry in his account book in which he alluded to "substernal threatenings," saying that he was not having as many as he had previously had in Baltimore. Was Osler having angina pectoris? Or did he think he was? Was this something he confided to his wife? His autopsy showed some atherosclerotic narrowing of his left anterior descending coronary artery. This is the only mention of chest pain that I found. He died fourteen years after moving to England. Suffice it to say, he appears to have been carrying an uncomfortably hectic schedule in Baltimore. One is tempted to think he knew he needed to slow his pace to reduce his risk of sudden death.

In a speech just before leaving Baltimore, Osler unwittingly repeated the blunder committed by Anthony Trollope in misjudging public reaction to a bit of whimsy. Trollope had published a science-fiction novel, *The Fixed Period*, exploring the idea that old men were no longer useful or happy. Accordingly, they would be admitted to Necropolis, a college that prepared men for a peaceful and honorable death, at age sixty-seven. One year later they would be dispatched by having their veins opened in a warm bath. Trollope received a bit of criticism for having even mentioned such a thing, but it was nothing compared to the reaction to Osler's speech on retirement from Johns Hopkins, where he alluded to Trollope's novel and reiterated one of his own ideas: that men do their greatest work before forty and are useless after sixty. He was slightly mistaken about a couple of the details of Trollope's whimsy, but he mentioned it, saying that men might be retired at age sixty (not sixty-eight as Trollope said) and might have a year of contemplation before chloroform would be used to make a peaceful departure (not with venesection as in *The Fixed Period*). He expressed some doubt as to whether Trollope's suggestion of a college and chloroform should be carried out, as his own time was getting short.

The first press reports dealt with it as the bit of humor that was intended, but subsequent accounts capitalized on it as a way to sell papers; headlines screamed that Professor Osler recommended chloroform for all at age sixty. To "Oslerize" became a jocular byword for euthanasia, and though he admitted he had been hurt, he did not retract his belief that men should rest from their labors at age sixty.

Busying himself with building up and cataloging his own library, he wrote to a friend saying his literary section would be the most interesting one, with poems, novels, plays, and works either by physicians or portraying the profession in some way. If a definition of the "literature of medicine" is needed, this would be a serviceable one.

The reading world is fortunate that Osler's next-door neighbor in Baltimore for four years was Harvey Cushing, arguably the greatest surgeon of his time. Some six years after Osler's death, Cushing published the monumental two-volume biography that won him the 1926 Pulitzer Prize for Biography or Autobiography. Almost three quarters of a century later, Michael Bliss, a professor of history at the University of Toronto, dared to write another biography of Osler, limiting it to one volume of 505 pages; and in his preface he wrote that he did so to see if Osler had any flaws not mentioned in Cushing's book of praise. "Try as I might, I could not find a cause to justify the death of Osler's reputation. He lived a magnificent, epic, important, and more than slightly saintly life." The two books are complementary to each other: the first by a colleague, neighbor, and admirer; the second by a historian writing at the end of the century. The first is a work of prodigious scholarship, with portions of many letters and other documents including lengthy quotations from Osler's own works, so that it could almost be considered a scrapbook; the second is an effort to be more selective and less repetitious. The first was rich in first-hand recollections; the second had the advantage of many additional sources in subsequent decades, uninhibited by the sensitivities of family and friends.

Lady Grace Osler asked Cushing to write her late husband's biography. Beyond the nearly father-and-son relationship between the two men, Cushing had attended their son Revere in his death on the battlefield, and few stronger bonds exist. He couldn't refuse. The job took five years; chain-smoking as he wrote, he started early in the morning and then resumed his task in the evening after a full day in the operating room.

Those who avoid long books miss many rewards; they miss Dickens' best novels, Marcel Proust, and many biographies that are barely contained within one volume. Cushing's biography is now out of print, perhaps largely because of its length. And indeed Cushing himself admitted that it should have been shorter. But the intrepid reader is rewarded by details such as Osler's impressions of the barren, sandy plain that was the Berlin of his student days; the disgusting odor of the city's uncovered sewers; the German students with long hair and slouch hats, many of them wearing glasses, many with sword-cuts received in duels, smoking so much in the amphitheater that the opposite side of the room could only be seen through a blue haze. In a letter, he alluded to anti-Semitic taunts and actually expressed concern that the authors of some papers would be happy to have all the Jews eliminated by genocide. This was stated with his usual irony; what would he have thought if he could have seen what really happened? He did mention the preponderance of Jews in the medical faculties of the German universities, rendering his personal homage to them for their achievements. This was 1884, fifty years before Hitler began to develop his own plans for the Jews.

Cushing's attention to medical detail includes a description of Osler's own case of smallpox, a mild one with only sixteen pustules, of which only two were on his face.

As the official biographer, Cushing struggled with Lady Grace for permission to use observations from her own correspondence. A number of details were considered too private for inclusion. There was little salacious material, but much about Egerton Y. Davis was omitted. E. Y. Davis was Osler's *alter ego*, a fictitious name he used for his practical jokes. Sometimes when approached by a reporter he didn't wish to see, he would deny he was Dr. Osler, explaining that he was often mistaken for him, but that his name was E. Y. Davis of Caughnawauga.

Lady Grace's reticence must surely have accounted for the lack of information in Cushing's book about how she and "Willie" came to be married. Bliss describes her Boston background, the prosperity of her family's silverware business, and her descent from Paul Revere on the American side and also from a captain of the Royal Navy that had bombarded Boston. She was the widow of Dr. Samuel W. Gross of Philadelphia, and Osler had often been a guest in their home. Her self-assurance is shown in the way she dealt with a "little Frenchman" who followed her while she was shopping one time in Paris. She slowed down, turned around, thrust her umbrella at him, and said, "Shoo!"

Among the sources available to Bliss was Osler's "Inner History of the Johns Hopkins Hospital," only published in 1969 in accordance with his order that it be kept secret for fifty years after his death. Among other things, it described the morphine addiction of "The Professor," William S. Halsted, head of the department of surgery. Only Osler and perhaps Welch knew of this. Halsted had become addicted to cocaine when experimenting with it as a local anesthetic, and although he had used morphine to wean himself from cocaine, he required morphine for the rest of his life, prescribed by Osler. Bliss described Halsted as the most important surgeon in the history of American medicine, due to his advocacy of unhurried, meticulous surgery in order to avoid infection and enhance healing.

Cushing had recently read a biography containing so much material about the author that he resolved to avoid mentioning himself, often identifying himself as one of the "latch-keyers," referring to those friends who were given keys to the Osler house. Such modesty is commendable, but the reader is frustrated at his failure to acknowledge his own presence on the battlefield when the Oslers' only son, Revere, was fatally injured. It was the most memorable passage from my first reading, and I struggled to suppress tears on rereading the account. The Oslers had one son who died one week after birth; Revere was born when his father was forty-six years old, and Sir William had had a foreboding when The Great War began that it would take his only son. Two photographs show them standing together: the young man taller than his father, beaming as an Oxford undergraduate in the first picture; both of them with serious demeanor in military uniform in the second.

Revere sustained multiple gunshot wounds to the chest, abdomen, and thigh. An operation was unsuccessful, and he died before sunrise. Cushing quotes his own diary:

We saw him buried in the early morning. A soggy Flanders field beside a little oak grove to the rear of the Dosinghem group – an overcast, windy, autumnal day – the long rows of simple wooden crosses – the new ditches half full of water being dug by Chinese coolies wearing tin helmets – the boy wrapped in an army blanket and covered by a weather-worn Union Jack, carried on their shoulders by four slipping stretcher-bearers. A strange scene – the great-great-grandson of Paul Revere under a British flag, and awaiting him a group of some six or eight American Army medical officers – saddened with thoughts of his father. Happily it was fairly dry at this end of the trench, and some green branches were thrown in for him to lie on. The Padre recited the usual service – a bugler gave the "Last Post" – and we went about our duties. Plot 4, row F.

The Oslers' reaction was to maintain a stiff upper lip. They immediately cancelled all their engagements, but a Swiss physician failed to get the message, came to lunch, stayed a long while after, and first learned of the Oslers' loss from the chauffeur who drove him back to the station.

"The last picture, 1919," is the caption of a photograph in Bliss' book, showing Sir William in formal dress, leaning back, circles under his eyes as if he had been hit with a fist, a countenance even sadder than usual. Bliss' account of his terminal illness includes reviews of the case by medical experts in the light of today's concepts. He was in bed with pneumonia for two months and he most likely had chronic bronchiectasis resulting from repeated infections all his life. There was no consideration of transfer to a hospital, which was an option only for the indigent in England at that time; no x-rays were done. He had thoracenteses and chest tubes placed, with partial rib resection, draining large quantities of fluid. Postmortem studies confirmed empyema, multiple lung abscesses, and bronchiectasis. The pneumonia was most likely triggered by influenza from the great pandemic of 1918-1919.

Bliss' final chapter, "Osler's Afterlife," summarizes the extraordinary impact of Osler on the field of medicine. Written by a historian rather than a physician, however, it does so with an objectivity rarely found in Osleriana. Though Osler was idolized by earlier generations, present-day medical students are often seen to have blank faces when his name is mentioned.

There was a new surge of interest in Osler in the 1960s, with concern about the neglect of humanity in the rush to use new technology. The American Osler Society was formed in 1970 by a group of North American physicians and others who shared a passion for preserving his memory and the values he represented. I attended a meeting of the American Osler Society at the annual meeting of the American College of Physicians in the early 1970s and heard Paul Dudley White, the famous Boston cardiologist who had cared for President Eisenhower at the time of his heart attack, describe having been at Oxford as a young man and having gone to Sir William's office to meet him. "But I was too shy and I never knocked on his door. I missed my great opportunity."

Bliss, writing as an outside observer of the medical profession, expressed a bit of amused skepticism at the extent of "Oslerolatry" of some of his disciples; and indeed, Osler's essays rest on my shelf, sources to be searched for an occasional phrase, but a bit thick in the Victorian idiom for me to go through as serious devotionals. I sometimes marvel to myself at the devotion to his memory expressed by grown men who should be able to see around corners. But medical students and young physicians, for all their iconoclasm and determination to prove things for themselves, have a certain tendency to search for figures of authority, and to create them if need be, thinking along with Voltaire, "If God did not exist, it would be necessary to invent him." And Osler, as a role model for all "chiefs," fills in very nicely as all that a chief should be. Perhaps he should be held up as the cynosure for newly appointed department heads as much as for young clinicians.

These two biographies are complementary works that do justice to Osler's place in history. Cushing's monumental volumes have served as a standard source for years and they remain a must for true believers. Bliss' more recent study is a bit more balanced, less extensive, and is the more accessible of the two. Let him have the last word.

"No one today would presume to master as much of medicine as Osler reached and grasped," Bliss concludes in his final chapter. "Neither his historical nor his sermonizing essays, most of which were outstanding in their day, now have much appeal, though Osler will always be well represented in dictionaries of quotations and aphorisms, and he may never be surpassed as English-speaking medicine's most inspirational father-figure, mentor, and role model."

THE FATHER OF NEUROSURGERY
(AND HIS THREE FABULOUS DAUGHTERS)

HARVEY CUSHING: A Biography
By John F. Fulton

FROM A SURGEON'S JOURNAL
By Harvey Cushing

HARVEY CUSHING: A Life in Surgery
By Michael Bliss

THE SISTERS: Babe Mortimer Paley,
Betsey Roosevelt Whitney, Minnie Astor Fosburgh:
The Lives and Times of the
Fabulous Cushing Sisters
By David Grafton

"I have decided to be a leper," Harvey Cushing told one of his freshman classmates at Harvard Medical School, thus announcing that he would no longer be the fun-loving lad who had entertained his friends at Yale by standing on the stone steps of the old Medical School, "turning a back somerset, landing on the bare sidewalk with his cigarette still going." (A photograph of this feat is included in John Fulton's *Harvey Cushing: A Biography* (Charles C. Thomas, 1946). He didn't give up the cigarettes, but he did continue to isolate himself in his work, much like a leper's isolation. Years later, when the American Impressionist painter Edmund Tarbell painted his portrait, he observed, "I had never seen anyone work like Cushing before, and found it difficult to believe that he could enjoy life on this basis."

Is it a mark of a trivial mind that it remembers trivia from a book read two decades ago? Cushing had to write to his father for money when he was in his late thirties, and this sticks in my mind. Rereading it now, I notice particularly that he was making $25,000 donations for laboratories and fellowships when he was in his fifties, but that he lost most of his money a few years later when the Boston bank, which handled his investments, collapsed in 1932. (And also, when Cushing was my present age, he was dead, after progressive tobacco poisoning, peripheral vascular disease, and a myocardial infarction.)

Fulton's biography is the "standard" one, written by a faithful disciple who was well known in his own right as a physiologist and medical historian. It is closely modeled after Cushing's Pulitzer-Prize winning *Life of Sir William Osler* (Oxford University Press, 1926), relying heavily on lengthy quotations from original sources such as Cushing's abundant diary entries, letters, speeches, and other writings to and about him. It is complete in only one volume, rather than the two of Cushing's *Osler*, but it still runs to 714 pages. It even copies the same type of page headings, including the page number, year, age of Cushing, and subject of the page, such as, "422 Bombing of Base Hospital No. 5 Sept. 1917 Aet.48 Detailed Case Histories 423" .

The major things to know about Cushing are that he is considered the father of neurosurgery; he performed two thousand operations for brain tumors with a progressively decreasing mortality rate; his name is attached to Cushing's Syndrome, a condition where is too much cortisol in the body, and also to Cushing's Disease, a form of Cushing's Syndrome in which the pituitary gland secretes too much ACTH (adrenocorticotropic hormone), which in turn stimulates the adrenal gland to produce too much cortisol. He also wrote the aforementioned biography of Osler. It is sometimes stated that his greatest achievement was the introduction of blood pressure measurement during surgery. He is credited with having introduced the vital signs chart to monitoring of anesthesia during surgery; he was among the first to use x-rays to diagnose brain tumors; he was instrumental in developing electrocautery to achieve hemostasis with a device developed by W. T. Bovie, a physicist after whom the tool is named; and his training program for neurosurgeons was the leading one in the world in the early decades of the twentieth century.

But in addition to the big things, Fulton recorded a wealth of trivia. H. C. (as Fulton referred to him) spent his working days on the East Coast in Boston and Baltimore, but he remained a son of the Western Reserve, the westward extension of the borders of Connecticut designed to provide living space for the people of Connecticut as it began to fill up. His ashes were buried in Cleveland, where his forebears included several generations of doctors. His father, Henry Kirke Cushing, was a Puritanical and successful doctor who had ten children, Harvey being the youngest, and he provided well for them, "coming out even" when he died with little to spare. Dr. Cushing forbade smoking, drinking, easy virtue, and intercollegiate athletics to his son Harvey at Yale. We don't know about the "easy virtue," but the other injunctions were honored more in the breach than in the observance. H. C. was a bit more lenient with his own son, Bill, encouraging him to play for the Yale baseball team as he had done. However, the letters from H. C. to his father seem to indicate a close relationship, whether or not enhanced by the duties to one's financial benefactor.

We learn that during Cushing's time at Harvard, medical students were assigned to "etherize" the patients undergoing surgery. After one of his patients died during anesthesia, Cushing wrote that he wouldn't study medicine. He was so profoundly affected by this experience that he developed a chart for graphing the pulse rate; this may have been the beginning of the graphic anesthesia chart.

His years at the Johns Hopkins Hospital, where he did his surgical training, included a somewhat stand-offish relationship with William Halsted, "The Professor" of the surgery department. Little did he know that Halsted's behavior was related at least in part to his addiction to morphine, which he had used to rid himself of an addiction to cocaine, acquired during his experimentation with it as a local anesthetic agent. Cushing later wrote in an obituary sketch that Halsted was "something of a recluse, fastidious in his tastes and in his friendships," but that "he nevertheless was one of the few American surgeons who may be considered to have established a school of surgery comparable, in a sense, to the school of Billroth in Vienna." His habits were eccentric: "having little interest in private practice, he spent his medical life avoiding patients – even students, when this was possible."

These samples of Cushing's writings illustrate the skills he acquired and practiced extensively, spending most evenings after dinner writing in his study. He was also a talented artist, illustrating clinic and operating notes and letters with sketches. Having observed the artistic talents of my brother-in-law, a retired cardiac surgeon, I have come to think that surgeons with artistic talent have an ability to visualize a surgical field that gives them a significant advantage at the operating table.

Cushing's introduction to the ways of "The Professor" came shortly after his arrival at Johns Hopkins. Chagrined at not being allowed in the operating room on his first day, he was at a patient's bedside after surgery when Halsted entered the ward. Cushing was ready with the postoperative medications he had used at the Massachusetts General Hospital, knowing how ill these patients always were. Dr. Halsted asked about a syringe in Cushing's hand and was told it was strychnine. Upon being asked what strychnine would do for the patient, Cushing replied only that it would do the patient good. He was then told by Halsted that he should read up on strychnine, and if his reading convinced him that strychnine would be beneficial, he should certainly use it. Needless to say, the strychnine was never given. He also began to understand that Halsted operated in a meticulous fashion, disturbing the patient's tissues as little as possible, so that heroic rescue after surgery was not required. This was the hallmark of Cushing's later success in operating on the brain, working slowly and carefully to avoid excessive bleeding and damage.

Cushing was able to assume more and more responsibility for teaching and surgery owing to the frequent absence of The Professor, who spent his summers in the mountains of North Carolina. In a letter to Cushing from Cashiers, North Carolina, Halsted added a P.S. that he could be reached by a telegram to Hendersonville, with this message relayed by telephone to Brevard, thence by telephone to Sapphire, and finally by horseback to him in Cashiers.

Cushing was well liked by his patients, but he was a trial to the nurses, one of whom wrote this for a Christmas party skit:

> *"'C' is for Cushing*
> *So cussedly clever*
> *He can be polite*
> *But hardly is ever."*

William Osler, Chief of the internal medicine department, was another of Cushing's mentors; they became good friends during a trip they made to Europe in 1900, and Cushing rented the house next door to the Oslers a short time later. Their friendship allowed Osler to address some of Cushing's "little ways" in a note that could be used as a model for similar admonitions which are all too frequently required today, and perhaps too infrequently given:

> *"You will not mind a reference to one point. The statement is current that you do not get on well with your surgical subordinates & colleagues. I heard of it last year & it was referred to by a strong admirer of yours in N.Y. The statement also is made that you have criticized before the students – the modes of dressings, operations &c of members of the staff. This, I need scarcely say would be absolutely fatal to your success here. The arrangement of the Hospital staff is so peculiar that loyalty to each other, even in the minutest particulars, is an essential. I know you will not mind*

this from me as I have your interests at heart. Sincerely yours, Wm Osler"

This was hardly the sort of attention Cushing would have received from his surgical chief; but Halsted was an innovator in the operating room. He introduced rubber gloves to surgery because of the allergies of a nurse, whom he later married; he encouraged Cushing to begin an experimental surgery laboratory; and Cushing, with George Crile of Cleveland, brought blood pressure measurement into surgical use. (Measuring the blood pressure is now such an integral part of patient care that it is interesting to note there was some initial apprehension about its general use. Cushing himself mused that it would significantly increase the number of neurasthenics.)

Cushing was not the world's first neurosurgeon; Theodor Kocher in Berne and Victor Horsley in London were operating on the spinal cord and brain, and Charles Sherrington in Liverpool was studying the monkey brain. Nor did Cushing think he would eventually specialize in neurological surgery when he visited these men in 1900. He reassessed his plan of studying with Horsley after meeting him and accompanying him to an operation at a patient's home. Horsley began operating fifteen minutes after arrival, and although there was blood all over the operative field, Horsley cut the trigeminal ganglion and was back in his vehicle less than an hour after he had arrived.

Introducing a number of technological changes to the operating room, Cushing began to establish the feasibility of operating on the brain. He published a monograph in 1908 summarizing his experience since 1902, thus establishing neurosurgery as "a clear-cut field of surgical endeavor." It has been reported that his first eleven patients with brain tumors failed to survive the surgery, between 1901 and 1904. (A century later, when brain tumors are routinely visualized with CT scans and MRIs, it is interesting to reflect that at this time, the decisions to operate on brain tumors were made on the basis of history and physical examination, with the actual diagnosis made only during surgery.) By 1910, though, he had operated on 180 brain tumors with an operative mortality of less than thirteen percent. In letter to his father in 1909, he appeared to have some pride in the locations his patients had been coming from– Boston, Vancouver, New York, Washington, D.C., South Carolina, New Jersey, Maine, Kentucky, Ontario, Wisconsin, and South Dakota. After going to Cleveland to operate on a patient who died after he left, he resolved not to operate outside his own hospital.

He moved to Boston as head of surgery at the newly built Peter Bent Brigham Hospital in 1910. This was the age of the automobile and he took driving lessons. However, after he was involved in the death of a female pedestrian, though he wasn't at fault, he forsook the driver's seat and employed the services of a chauffeur for the rest of his life.

From a Surgeon's Journal (Little, Brown, and Company, 1934) is an extraordinary account of Cushing's experience in World War I. His close friends the Oslers were now in Oxford, and though Cushing had a number of medical friends in Germany, he was no longer neutral by November, 1914. Like many others who go to war, his own service was prompted to some degree by peer pressure. George Crile in Cleveland had responded to a personal appeal to serve in an American hospital in Paris – the *Ambulance américain* (a French hospital is an *ambulance*). Crile asked Cushing to organize a Harvard unit to relieve his Western Reserve University unit after three months. Cushing was reluctant to interrupt his work and his projects, but there were a number of volunteers in Boston ready to go, and Cushing considered it would have been humiliating to have Crile in charge of the Western Reserve Unit and only a junior man in charge of the Harvard unit. The Harvard unit sailed on March 22, 1915.

I began to understand the short distance between ostensibly normal civilian life and the front lines of World War I on a visit to the museum in Ypres a few years ago, where a hand-made sign beside a wooden walkway in one of the exhibits read, "This way to the war." Cushing reflected on this on his first visit to the American hospital in Neuilly: "Here we are as near the worst affair in history as Boston is to Worcester, and everyone appears to take it as though it had always been so, and always would be, and meanwhile goes about his own little business unconcernedly."

The neurosurgeon's workload in a hospital near the front lines was staggering, of course, and on August 17, 1917, Cushing noted that he and his team had beaten their record with eight cases that day, averaging two hours apiece – all of some seriousness. He then reflected that a single major cranial case at home was considered to be a day's work. Despite his efforts to deal with the load, however, the perception of Cushing's colleagues was that his precision and care, which were the reason for his success, made him too slow. When the chief British surgical consultant asked Dr. Crile about this, Crile advised that it was worthwhile having one such perfect technician on hand as a model. On Sundays, Cushing used his "day off" to change dressings, reluctant to accept the consequences of having the orderlies do it.

Even those whose business it is to save lives got caught up in the business of war. Cushing described his reaction to being where the shells were exploding all around: "The savage in you makes you adore it with its squalor and wastefulness and glorious noise. You feel that, after all, this is what men were intended for rather than to sit in easy chairs with a cigarette and whiskey, the evening paper or the bestseller, and to pretend that such a veneer means civilization and that there is no barbarian behind your starched and studded shirt front."

From a Surgeon's Journal is abundantly supplied with photographs and Cushing's own maps, diagrams, and drawings. None of them are more memorable than that of a gowned figure guiding an enormous barbell-shaped magnet with its tip in the head of a patient on a gurney. The magnet was being used in an effort to withdraw a shell fragment from the soldier's brain, and three tries were unsuccessful.

I had taken off my gloves and put the nail down; but then – let's try just once more! So I slipped the brutal thing again down the track, three and a half inches to the base of the brain, and again Cutler gingerly swung the big magnet down and made contact. The current was switched on and as before we slowly drew out the nail – and there it was, the little fragment of rough steel hanging on to its tip! Much emotion on all sides – especially on the part of A. Kocher and Salomon Reinach, both of whom could hardly bear it.

Cushing didn't escape unscathed from the war and the concomitant great influenza pandemic. On August 6, 1918, he recorded that he had been in bed for three days with what he regarded as the "Spanish flu." He was in bed until August 18, and on October 1 he reported doing a head case, and "with the help of poor eyes did it very badly." Four days later, he noted, "Not being very good on my hind legs these influenzal days." He was considered to have had post-viral polyneuritis and the weakness and visual difficulties persisted after he returned home to Boston.

After the war, he returned to his work with energy, enthusiasm, and creativity. When a visiting professor, Chevalier Jackson, didn't appear at the train station in Boston to deliver a lecture, Cushing's resident Tracy Putnam found himself, on instructions from Dr. Cushing, supplied with a fake beard and being introduced as Dr. Jackson, mumbling replies to dangerous questions and delivering the address of the evening. Only one person reported that he had identified who the "distinguished visitor" really was, but then he dismissed the idea as too fantastic to consider.

But this is the Harvey Cushing story that sticks in my mind: Bill Cushing, the elder son, was killed in a car accident in 1926. The circumstances were unfortunate; two young men, two young women (one of them married), all four dead, all four smelling of alcohol. Dr. Cushing received the telephone call as he was leaving for the hospital the next morning. He gave the necessary instructions on the telephone, called his wife in New York to tell her, went to the hospital and performed his scheduled operation before letting his team know what had happened, and then went to Connecticut to claim the body.

In the years before health insurance, "fee for service" carried a more immediate meaning for doctor and patient. Cushing set his own fees individually, asking each patient pointed questions about their financial status. Those without adequate means paid nothing; one of ample means paid $5,000 for removal of a wen from his neck. Cushing, by now a man of independent means, sent the money to his laboratory fund. He declined to charge the astronomical fees of several times greater than $5,000 that some of his colleagues did.

He completed his surgical career with his two thousandth brain tumor operation and with the subsequent description of the syndrome and disease that bears his name. His health began to fail, he found himself involved more heavily in political wrangling at Harvard, and he didn't contest his compulsory retirement at age sixty-three, though he did take a long time sorting out his options.

His family life had always been a secondary consideration for him. The children grew up with a strict though often absent father; but the girls did find ways to bring their world to him. After moving to Yale to become Sterling Professor of Neurology, he was hospitalized in 1933 for his gastric ulcer and great pain in his feet. His nineteen-year-old daughter, Barbara, appeared in his hospital room one afternoon dressed according to all the suggestions for dress that her father had ever given her: "flat-heeled shoes, long skirt, high-necked blouse, ultra-conservative hat, no lipstick, no rouge, no nail polish, unsmiling and with an air of prim propriety." Except for one very proper smile, she kept a straight face; her father, vanquished, sent her across the hall to see one of his friends there.

During his retirement from surgery, he became more interested in current affairs and was appointed to a Medical Advisory Committee to the Committee on Economic Security in

1934. His charge was "to study practicable measures for bringing about the better distribution of medical care in the lower income groups of the population." Taking a middle ground in this early effort to achieve universal health care, Cushing thought it was inevitable and urged the American Medical Association to cease its opposition to it.

His daughter Betsey married James Roosevelt in 1930, and Cushing and President Roosevelt had a cordial, though hardly intimate relationship. The President appointed a Scientific Advisory Board in 1934, much to the distress of the National Academy of Sciences, which was the official advisory board to the Federal government in matters pertaining to science. They asked Cushing to intercede with the President on its behalf. Although the President listened politely to his son's father-in-law, he did not consult the National Academy of Sciences.

Cushing suddenly decided to go to Washington in April, 1935, mostly for the purpose of visiting a sick friend. He felt unable to make the trip except by air, and after a rather harrowing flight in a private plane, he phoned the White House from his hotel to say he would be coming to tea. This proved to be one of the few occasions when Dr. Cushing wasn't entirely welcome, his companion reported. The Roosevelts had other Easter Sunday plans, but FDR came in and steered the conversation to aviation.

Writing almost sixty years after Fulton's 1946 biography, which includes a frontispiece showing Cushing in a contemplative mood in 1929, cigarette in hand, Michael Bliss, in *Harvey Cushing: A Life in Surgery* (Oxford University Press, 2005), is more explicit in describing Cushing's smoking habit and its consequences. He began having intermittent claudication at age fifty-one, with thrombosis of both femoral arteries, probably superimposed on his post-influenzal polyneuritis, leaving him unable to walk more than one or two blocks without stopping to rest. By 1933, he had gained enough insight to observe that the best national health insurance program would be to cut tobacco usage. He lost his left middle toe because of gangrene, and after the amputation, he noted improvement in his symptoms, which he attributed to three weeks of not using tobacco. He noted that every consultant who saw him reached for a cigarette before examining his foot, and although they all advised amputation of his leg, none said anything about stopping smoking. He vowed to go on the road to lecture about addiction to tobacco. He relapsed, but after more of his toe was removed, he is reported to have stopped smoking permanently for the last two or three years of his life. Better late than never, but his death was due to a myocardial infarction.

Bliss, now a retired professor of history at the University of Toronto, has written a somewhat more concise (522 pages) and also more dispassionate account of Cushing's life. It is comparable to a similar Osler book, Bliss' own *William Osler: A Life in Medicine* (Oxford University Press, 1999), and Bliss writes that one book led to the other because of the many ways in which their lives intersected. Of Fulton's book, Bliss writes,

> *Cushing's friend and official biographer, John Farquhar Fulton, was to an uncanny degree the F. Scott Fitzgerald of American medicine. Unfortunately, by the time Fulton published the 754 pages of* Harvey Cushing: A Biography *in 1946, his talents had been so corroded by drink and other diversions that he was unable to do much more than let Cushing speak for himself in scissors-and-paste chapters. These were mostly assembled by two of Cushing's former secretaries, leading spirits of the group of talented women who worked for both Cushing and Fulton and more or less jokingly called themselves the "harem."*

The story with which Bliss begins his book is that of Leonard Wood, the physician who had served as Army Chief of Staff. He was having severe headaches, he had an unsuccessful and non-diagnostic craniotomy in 1905 by Arthur C. Cabot of Boston, and after Victor Horsley in London declined to operate, he was referred to Cushing in Baltimore. Surgery was deferred, but at Wood's insistence, Cushing performed an exploratory craniotomy in 1910. It turned out to be a meningioma, a benign tumor, and it was removed in two operations in four days. Wood did well for several years. Cushing operated on him for a recurrence in 1927, but Wood died after surgery. The autopsy showed bleeding into the ventricle, and Cushing blamed himself for "attempting to do too much at a single session" and not going back for a second look. He couldn't bring himself to go back to the operating room for two weeks.

There are two lives for a biographer to describe: the public and the private. Fulton's biography provides a wealth of material about Cushing's professional life, but is sometimes a bit frustrating in dealing with personal issues. A biographer who comes along a generation or two later can be more liberal in dealing with details that an official biographer might be apprehensive about disclosing.

Fulton devotes one paragraph to Betsey Cushing's marriage to James Roosevelt, quoting a letter from Cushing to A. C. Klebs: "Our front yard looks like a circus and I feel like Mr. Ringling – the wedding ringling. I have reserved a special tent for myself in which I shall sulk, Achilles-like; 10 cts. extra – peanuts and lemonade and camels (cigarettes)." But there is no mention of the groom's father – Franklin Delano Roosevelt, who at that time in 1930 was governor of New York.

Bliss fills in a few of these blanks in a well-balanced account that also deals adequately with Cushing's professional career, though not attempting the completeness of Dr. Fulton. Bliss acknowledges that Cushing's priorities left his family pretty far down the line, leading his wife Kate to write him a letter in 1919, after he had returned from the war.

> "Don't let me do it – don't kill the love and tenderness that I have always felt for you – We have a great task before us – we cannot do it if we are estranged and out of sympathy. We must live up to it. We must not fail now. It is a critical time in our lives – either we go triumphantly on to the end, or we miserably fail and drag out a miserable and cheerless life. It is for both of us to decide ... I can't say these things to you. You are always too busy or too tired."

Perhaps all hard-working doctors tell themselves that the spouse and children will understand. Perhaps they understand all too well.

Bliss throws in one other detail not mentioned elsewhere: Kate was a half-inch taller than her husband.

Bliss presented lectures on both Osler and Cushing at a recent annual meeting of the American College of Physicians, and after the Osler lecture, I asked how he would compare the two men, since he had written biographies of both. "Osler was the man Cushing tried to be," he replied, "but he never succeeded."

David Grafton's gossipy account of *The Sisters* (Villard Books, 1992) tells how it played out and can be taken as an epilogue to the Cushing story. His epigraph is by John F. Kennedy: "All history is gossip," and the cautious reader must maintain skepticism in tiptoeing through this account. Of course, Grafton summarizes Cushing's professional accomplishments pretty briefly; but there is no reluctance in his speculation about personal affairs. One question the reader of the Fulton and Bliss biographies must ask is, "What's this about a ten-year courtship and engagement?" Bliss provides documentary evidence of their close relationship with extensive quotations from their correspondence; but Grafton goes further, perhaps with no more evidence to go on, writing that despite the "extremely long and not terribly romantic courtship," Kate had made up her mind to suppress her feelings and wait, since Harvey Cushing was the man she wanted to marry.

It can be argued that Cushing was "not in a position" to marry during this time, having to depend on his father for financial support while putting in his time at Hopkins and abroad with only a token salary. William Osler, who was to be his mentor, routinely lamented the marriage of any of his young trainees; Osler himself didn't marry until he was forty-two years old.

Bliss, whose biography of Cushing was written thirteen years after Grafton wrote *The Sisters*, specifically repudiates one of Grafton's main theses, that Kate Cushing trained her daughters and pushed them into marrying for money. Bliss points out that the Cushings had significant wealth from both Harvey and Kate's families. It is of interest, however, that all three girls wound up wealthy by marriage. They had an exclusive girls' school education at the high school level, but curiously there was no apparent consideration of college for any of them, although their brothers went to Yale.

Betsey set the standard for her two sisters when she married the son of the future President; she became FDR's favorite, often serving as a White House hostess during Eleanor's frequent absences. When the king and queen of England visited Hyde Park, Betsey was the star, and the king got out of their car to fetch her hat when it blew off. After Jimmy went off to California with his nurse after a hospitalization at the Mayo Clinic, FDR insisted that his own personal attorney represent Betsey.

Her second husband was John Hay Whitney, a "multi-millionaire playboy;" they later spent four years in London when he was U.S. Ambassador to the Court of St. James; and the marriage lasted. He was listed as one of the ten wealthiest men in the world in the 1970s. He died in 1982 at age seventy-seven. She later died in 1998, leaving an estate of $700 million.

Barbara (always called "Babe"), the youngest, was the most beautiful of the three sisters. She married Stanley Grafton Mortimer, Jr., grandson of one of the founders of Standard Oil; after their divorce, her second marriage was to William Paley, chief executive of Columbia Broadcasting System (CBS). A heavy smoker like her father, she died of lung cancer at the age of sixty-three.

Mary ("Minnie"), the eldest, married Vincent Astor, "the single biggest matrimonial catch in the United States of America," in 1940. They divorced in 1953 and she married James Fosburgh in 1954. She became a well-known hostess in the art circles of New York.

Grafton summarizes their careers:

From the moment the Cushing sisters had set foot in top-drawer American society, they had made headlines

73

> *around the world. Their every move had been immediately chronicled in Cholly Knickerbocker's "Smart Set" column, as well as in myriad other gossip columns. Their names – like it, as Babe did, or not, as Betsey did not – were household words. Changing with the times, the sisters had entered the smart set, made a brief stopover in café society, spent a far longer time as members of the jet set, and had finally settled in comfortable dignity into old-guard New York society.*

Could Harvey Cushing have been as philosophical as was Jane Austen's Mr. Bennett, also a father of eligible daughters in *Pride and Prejudice*, who mused: "For what do we live, but to make sport for our neighbors, and laugh at them in our turn?"

These four volumes are complementary in conveying Cushing's legacy both to medicine and to society. A surgeon in training who wonders why he is having to work so hard doesn't owe it all to Cushing by any means; but the compulsive, obsessive work ethic he personified is the essence of the tradition of striving toward perfection that still characterizes so many of the more highly regarded training programs today. Dr. Cushing set a high standard. And as for his legacy to society: perhaps here we can look to David Grafton.

"DR. MACKENZIE'S INK POLYGRAPH"

SIR JAMES MACKENZIE

General Practitioner 1853 - 1925

By Alex Mair

"Lub-dub, lub-dub, lub-dub," is the sound made by the beating human heart, a sound familiar to schoolchildren. In certain conditions such as heart failure, there may be a third sound immediately following the second sound, soft and low-pitched; and this third heart sound was the object of my research project during a year as a fellow in cardiology at the Brompton Hospital in London, in 1974. At that time, echocardiography was a newly developed tool that allowed one to record ultrasound waves beamed at and reflected from the structures of the heart, much as a fisherman might track a school of fish, or radar might be used to search for aircraft. The movement of these structures could be recorded with simultaneous records of certain pulsations of the heart and blood vessels, which could be seen and felt on the chest and neck; and analysis of multi-channel recordings of these events was a potential source of new insights.

The recording of these pulsations required great care and it was done in a hospital laboratory. It was at this time that I happened to read how similar recordings were obtained by James Mackenzie, a general practitioner in the manufacturing town of Burnley, England, in the last decade of the nineteenth century. He had invented his own device and he was the first to record arterial and venous pulses simultaneously, allowing measurement of certain "systolic time intervals" that could be used to analyze the function of a failing heart. As described by Alex Mair in *Sir James Mackezie, M.D., General Practitioner 1853-1925* (Churchill Livingstone, 1973), he connected a receiver to a tambour and lever with an indiarubber tube. The movements were recorded on smoked paper, which was attached to a revolving cylinder. This sounds rather tricky to me, but it is nothing compared to the challenge of the circumstances when he was studying heart disease in pregnancy. Here is his description:

> *It is impossible for those who have not undertaken this kind of research to understand its difficulties... This meant attending them during labour, taking careful observations during the pains and when free from the pains. These observations were not made in a comfortable ward with plenty of help, but often after a hard day's work, during the night in poor cottages, where I had to do the duties of the doctor and the nurse, give chloroform, apply the forceps, and wash the baby.*

Thus Mackenzie easily qualified as patron saint for my efforts. The techniques he developed were basically an extension and documentation of what could be observed at the bedside, where the routine was "observation, palpation, auscultation, contemplation." First you look, then you feel with your hand, only then do you use your stethoscope, and finally you just stand there and scratch your head. Old masters such as Paul Wood and Joseph Perloff were said to make diagnoses by looking and feeling before they ever used the stethoscope. The diagnostic and research tools I used in my studies in the 1960s and 1970s – the phonocardiogram (for recording and analyzing heart sounds and murmurs) and the apexcardiogram (for the pulsations of the chest) are now obsolete and forgotten; and the physical examination itself has all too often become relegated to a ritual honored more in the breach than in the observance. The echocardiogram and cardiac catheterization now provide such precise information that the nuances of physical examination have become parlor games that the busy doctor has little time for, at least in the minds of many physicians. This, of course, is a scandalous trend; medicine has become depersonalized enough as it is; and the physician who knows what he is looking at and listening to possesses a significant advantage.

Mackenzie was one of those Victorians of enormous energy who figured in many advances in many fields in the decades before World War I. He grew up in Scotland, an ambitious lad despite his unremarkable scholastic achievements. He aspired to devote himself to research, but feeling that his record as a student would prevent him from obtaining a university position, he considered himself suited only for the lowest ranks of the medical profession, thus resigning himself to the field of general practice.

Ironically, it was in this role that he did his greatest research work. He began using his "polygraph" (which was made for him by a watchmaker) to record and identify certain irregularities of the heart rhythm before Willem Einthoven invented the electrocardiograph. In 1890, he was the first to describe ventricular premature contractions. (These are the well-known "VPCs" which a nurse at the bedside may announce as she watches the moving line on the oscilloscope: "Veep. Veep. Veep-veep.")

Mackenzie was the first to use the term "auricular fibrillation." He had noticed on his pulse tracings that the jugular vein lost its atrial contraction wave when atrial fibrillation was present. He mistakenly thought the atria were paralyzed in atrial fibrillation, and he thought the heartbeat originated from the atrioventricular node in this condition; but he later changed his mind when he was shown tracings from the newly-developed electrocardiograph in 1906.

Not that Mackenzie had any use for the EKG: he did not. Having invested so much time and effort in his pulse tracings, he never acknowledged that the EKG could be used as a standard of reference in atrial fibrillation or any other arrhythmia. As it has turned out, the EKG, more informative and much easier to use, is now a standard tool in clinical practice and research, while pulse tracings were relegated to the research laboratory and later to the archives of medical history.

He formed a close friendship with Karel Frederik Wenckebach, who was doing similar work as a general practitioner in Holland. Wenckebach, now famous in medical circles as the discoverer[7] of a form of partial heart block bearing his name, had a warm and uninhibited personality; and he and Mackenzie became collaborators in an "us against the world" campaign to present their findings to a skeptical medical establishment. Mackenzie's self-esteem and confidence in his own opinions must have been enhanced by his experience of obtaining polygraph tracings in the cottages of Burnley, for we find him writing to his brother in 1904 that he was certain no one could assess the living heart with anything close to the power possessed by Professor Wenckebach and himself.

Chapter 26 of Mair's book is devoted to the recollections of D. J. W. Linnell, one of Mackenzie's colleagues, including Wenckebach's recollection of how he became convinced of the efficacy of quinine. He had made a diagnosis of auricular fibrillation in one of his patients, a Dutch sea captain who had spent much time in the East Indies, and Wenckebach was about to prescribe digitalis when the captain told him he could stop it any time he wanted to. He demonstrated this by taking some powder from his pocket and swallowing it with a glass of water. Shortly thereafter, his heart rhythm was regular.

Sadly, this warm friendship grew cold in their later years. Each had become a great man in his own right and perhaps their circles no longer overlapped as they once had. Mair's account of their last meeting is the paragraph I remember most vividly from my 1974 reading. Wenckebach was visiting Mackenzie at his office in the London Hospital. Mackenzie later recalled Wenckebach's lack of attention to his description of his work, going to the window and saying, "You have quite a pleasant outlook here, Sir James."

---

[7]This was reported in 1899, with pulse tracings which he timed with a tuning fork in the days before electrocardiography was available for such purposes.

Wenckebach, for his part, later recalled that Mackenzie had become very opinionated and he found it difficult to discuss some matters with him. Each continued to describe the other, however, as a "great man."

Mackenzie made a name for himself in his eighteen years in Burnley, more so in Europe and America than in England, where it was harder to understand how anything very worthwhile could come out of a small town general practice near Manchester. He moved to London in 1907 and opened a practice in cardiology. He encountered some resistance from the establishment in obtaining a satisfactory hospital appointment, but he was elected Fellow of the Royal College of Physicians in 1909, and in 1915, he received a knighthood and became a Fellow of the Royal Society.

His personal life receives relatively little space in McNair's account. He married a young woman in Burnley shortly after he moved there; they had two daughters, one of whom learned to her surprise that it was her father who had written a serial in one of her children's magazines. His older daughter developed polio at age seventeen months and remained unable to walk, but she lived for seventy-nine years. His younger daughter Jean died at age sixteen of meningitis, which had begun as sinusitis. Despite his heavy work schedule of seeing as many as sixty to seventy patients a day in Burnley, he played golf two afternoons a week.

His successful consulting practice in London included such notables as Henry James, and his publications documented his status as an authority in his field. (A copy of the third edition of his textbook, *Diseases of the Heart*, published in 1918, is on my bookshelf. "Cooper Clinic" is inscribed on the inside cover in the hand of St. Cloud Cooper, who in 1920 founded the clinic where I worked from 1969 to 2003.)

He retired to St. Andrews in 1918, where he founded an Institute for Clinical Research, but he moved back to London in 1924.

Sir James suffered from angina pectoris the last twelve years of his life. He had pain on walking two hundred yards, and when in atrial fibrillation, he could only walk one hundred yards before becoming short of breath. He was stricken with severe chest pain while hearing the bagpipes play at a Burns Night program at the Royal Albert Hall in London in 1925. He died in his sleep the following day.

As a disciple several generations removed, I found Mackenzie's story a memorable one that became embedded in the matrix of my life as a cardiologist. His place in the history of medicine is well documented in this biography, but many readers will probably prefer to skim or even skip long quotations and recollections, which could have been selected and pruned with greater discretion. Similarly, the author's admiration for his subject could have been tempered a bit; surely some of the qualities of his greatness could have been implied rather than repeated and elaborated over and over.

But everyone to his own taste. Oliver Wendell Holmes, anatomist, poet, and autocrat of the breakfast table, was sometimes heard to complain that he didn't hear a compliment very well and would often ask for it to be repeated. On the other hand, after one of my friends attended a funeral that featured several lengthy eulogies, he told me, "For mine, just say, 'Birdies on Eighteen and Four, eagle on Twelve -- that's it."

Which would Dr. Mackenzie have preferred? Perhaps the latter; after all, he was an enthusiastic golfer; but after his long struggle for respect in London, who can be sure?

THE PROBLEM OF SHERLOCK HOLMES

ARTHUR CONAN DOYLE

A Life in Letters

By Jon Lellenberg, Daniel Stashower,

and Charles Foley

Sir Arthur Conan Doyle, creator of Sherlock Holmes, is also known as the aspiring serious writer who killed off Sherlock Holmes so he could write more ambitious literature. It didn't work, of course. Nobody remembers anything else he wrote; Holmes is immortal and embedded in our popular culture. Charles Dickens could have told him to stick with his success; it is interesting that Dickens and William Shakespeare wrote for the popular taste, not for "serious lit." Neither of them had a serious education. Dickens put a lisping speech by a circus performer in *Hard Times,* which may be taken as a close approximation of his credo: "People mutht be amuthed. They can't be alwayth a learning, nor yet they can't be alwayth a working, they ain't made for it."

It is tempting to classify Arthur Conan Doyle as we find him in *Arthur Conan Doyle: A Life in Letters* by Jon Lellenberg, Daniel Stashower, and Charles Foley (The Penguin Press, 2007): a Victorian prototype. Ambitious, energetic, serious, with a consumptive wife and a young mistress (though it was only a "platonic relationship" until his wife's death), he fit the mold in many ways.

Conan Doyle's creation, Sherlock Holmes, has become more famous than the author himself. Holmes has entered into the immortality of an icon in our popular culture. It is a curious phenomenon. The creation took on a life of its own. Despite this, one is tempted to say that Conan Doyle wasn't really a great writer. His name isn't found in many lists that include Dickens, Jane Austen, and George Eliot; and yet he created Sherlock Holmes.

The irony is that Conan Doyle aspired to be known as one of the immortal writers of serious literature. Sir Walter Scott was his specific model, and his great ambition was for his historical novels to be appreciated in the same way as *Ivanhoe*. And now, Sir Walter Scott may be a more familiar name than Arthur Conan Doyle, but Sherlock Holmes would certainly be more readily identified by the public than Ivanhoe.

The introductions and commentaries in this collection of letters are more interesting than the selections themselves. No one pretends that letters show the complete and whole writer; in this case we see the fussbudget side of Conan Doyle, obsessed with his efforts to make ends meet. Most of his correspondence went to his family, particularly his mother, who was his principal confidante until her death in 1920; about a thousand letters to her have survived. They are remarkable in that they are so frank, affectionate, and appreciative. Although there is little evidence of communication with his alcoholic father, he withheld little from his mother, even giving her full disclosure about his love for a younger woman for several years before his wife died. He even enlisted his mother as a chaperone for some of his meetings with Jean Leckie.

Other entertaining details do, however, emerge from the letters. As a member of a band at a German school, he found himself playing the "Bombardon," a giant tuba-like instrument. Its measured rhythm, he said, "sounds like a hippopotamus doing a step-dance." On one occasion, he wasn't able to get out a note because his fellows had put his sheets and blankets in it. German student customs would be shocking to a Briton, he added, alluding to the quantities of beer and wine they were able to put away.

The young lad then attended medical school at Edinburgh University, giving some insights into such contemporary debates as the merits of the germ theory, which was no open-and-shut case based on early results. Some opponents of the germ theory achieved better results than the Listerians did. Conan Doyle later recalled a warning by a sardonic professor of the old school to shut the door or the germs would get in. Observing surgery by one of the Listerians, on the other hand, was made difficult by the clouds of carbolic steam put out by the "Puffing Billy."

Conan Doyle made some extra money as a medical student by sailing as ship's surgeon on a whaling ship. There he saw a giant pack of seals in a solid mass on the ice, about fifteen miles by eight miles in size. The bloody work of slaughtering them had its dangers; on one occasion while killing a seal, he fell over the side of a piece of ice and only managed to save himself by grabbing the hind flippers of the seal and pulling himself up, while the seal somehow managed to stay on the ice and not join him in the sea.

His efforts to begin his practice were discouraging. His mother supplemented his income and he appears to have spent more time writing stories while waiting for patients to appear than actually seeing patients. There was an occasional windfall, as in the opportunity to treat a fifty-five-year-old man who called him at 2:30 in the morning because of a hernia. The young doctor was unable to reduce it. Later in the morning, he consulted a colleague who also failed. Another colleague attempted unsuccessfully to reduce it under chloroform at 3:30 P.M. In desperation, Conan Doyle began an operation while his colleague administered ether. The operation, which took an hour and a half, was successful, and the young doctor basked in the blessings of the patient's family and friends, anticipating that the boost in his reputation would be worth more to him than the fee.

His marriage to "Touie" occurred during a period when little correspondence is available, so we learn little of the courtship. He persistently sent short stories for publication, finally getting some accepted, and his modest earnings from his stories brought him about as much income as his medical practice.

The attribution of Sherlock Holmes's character to Dr. Joseph Bell, one of Conan Doyle's professors in medical school, is well known. Dr. Samuel Clark, one of my microanatomy professors at Washington University, told us in one of his lectures how Dr. Bell emphasized the importance of observation. Dr. Bell told his students they should pay particular attention to the urine; its smell (he sniffed it), its color (he held it up to the light), and its taste (he dipped a finger in the urine and then put a finger in his mouth). He then passed the container of urine through the class, with instructions to make the same observations he had made. The poor students all tasted the urine and then Dr. Bell showed them that he had put his index finger into the urine, but it was his little finger that had gone into his mouth.

After only a few Sherlock Holmes stories, the author decided that Holmes was distracting him from his efforts to write great historical novels. We learn little of this. His attempt to deal with this issue was described in only two words in his notebook: "Killed Holmes."

Conan Doyle had a series of favorable events in 1890: he sold *The White Company*, his great historical novel, for two hundred pounds; *The Sign of the Four* came out as a book; he received letters in praise of Sherlock Holmes from Lawson Tait, who had revolutionized abdominal surgery, and from Baron Coleridge, nephew of the poet and Lord Chief Justice of England; and he traveled to Berlin to learn about the work Dr. Robert Koch (who was to win a Nobel Prize) was doing with tuberculosis. He described this as an event that changed his life, where he spread his wings and began to feel he had untapped powers.

On this wave of euphoria, he decided to close his practice in Portsmouth, move to London and become an eye specialist. He spent a couple of months in Vienna studying ophthalmology and he maintained an office in London for six months before deciding to abandon medicine altogether and earn his living by writing.

By 1899 he began to change his mind about Sherlock Holmes and he resumed his career as the creator of the great detective. A stage play was proposed to him, and William Gillette offered to write the script. This suited Conan Doyle very well; he wrote his mother that he hoped the play would make a fortune for all the family. It did indeed. William Gillette also played the role of Sherlock Holmes, and in doing so, he put his own stamp on the dark, thin, brooding detective with the deerstalker cap. He played to large audiences in England and America, and to the extent that money can bring happiness, Conan Doyle was now happy.

He served in the Boer War as a civilian doctor in Africa, from 1899 to 1902, and he eagerly wrote his accounts of the war for the newspapers in England. His wife Touie died of tuberculosis at the age of forty-nine. Conan Doyle wrote that although the long fight had ended in defeat, the fort had been held for thirteen years after experts had despaired. Touie supposedly didn't know of her husband's long "platonic affair;" but her daughter Mary later said that Touie had told her Jean Leckie would be her future stepmother.

Conan Doyle had two children with Touie, three with Jean. His oldest son, Kingsley, was injured in the Great War, but he recovered and returned to the front. He was later recalled to complete his medical studies; but two weeks before the Armistice was signed, he died of influenza in London. His only brother, Innes, who had lived with him in Portsmouth, also died of the influenza epidemic in February, 1919. Kingsley's death is reminiscent of the death of Revere Osler, only child of Sir William Osler, in this war. The death rates were horrible, both from combat and from the influenza epidemic.

Sir Arthur Conan Doyle had become a believer in Spiritualism by this time and was delivering lectures on the subject and attending séances.

He died in 1930 at age seventy-one after "frequent bouts of angina." His wife Jean, Lady Conan Doyle, survived him by ten years. None of his children had children of their own.

One of the authors, Charles Foley, is the great-nephew of Arthur Conan Doyle. All three authors are members of the Baker

Street Irregulars, a club of Sherlock Holmes enthusiasts. They have handled the correspondence well. It was a good Victorian life; the many Sherlock Holmes enthusiasts are indebted to them.

THE ICON

THE HORSE AND BUGGY DOCTOR
By Arthur E. Hertzler, MD

I knew that there was no longer any such thing when I checked out Arthur Hertzler's *The Horse and Buggy Doctor* (Harper and Brothers, 1938) from my high school library. I knew that the horse and buggy had been replaced by a black Plymouth coupe and that it was driven by Dr. H. T. Smith, who was much older than my father and never turned his head when Taylor waved to him from the Second Street sidewalk. And when North Third Street was covered with water from a big spring rain, Dr. Smith drove the Plymouth coupe to get across the street from his house to our house to see my sister when she had the measles.

My sharpest memory from my first reading of the book is of the two line drawings, one of the gangly young doctor carrying a bag in each hand as he walked along a country lane, entitled, "The Stork." (Did this refer to the walking figure or the purpose of his errand?) The caption read, "When the horses and mules gave out the country doctor walked." The second showed a pair of long legs protruding from the buggy as the horse walked along, eating weeds. "Sweet rest, balmy sleep," this caption read. "Sometimes for many nights the buggy was the doctor's only couch." There was also a sketch of the buggy on the cover, showing a barren tree and flecks of snow.

Dr. Hertzler and Dr. Smith may have had some influence on my initial plan, on entering medical school, to be a general practitioner in a small town. I modified that objective a bit, but after I had started in practice in cardiology, I spotted a copy of *The Horse and Buggy Doctor* in a second-hand bookstore and bought it. It has been on my shelves for forty years, and now, seven years after retirement, I have revisited *The Horse and Buggy Doctor.*

I've always known that I lived a sheltered life, but Dr. Hertzler reminded me just how sheltered it was. I was in private practice in cardiology for thirty-four years, and for all except two or three of those years, I was on call regularly, every other to every fourth or fifth night, Most nights I had to put on my pants and go into the hospital one to three times to see a patient; I usually stayed on the third trip. My greatest fear was that my home phone would ring and a nurse would say, "Dr. Prewitt, that patient that I called you about an hour ago has just coded." My resolution may have been a modest one, but it was that no patient would be admitted to my care and die before having been seen by me.

Dr. Hertzler wrote that he called for a fresh team of horses when he drove into a livery stable after midnight one night, after having been on the road sixteen hours a day for weeks. Spotting a bunk and unable to resist, he lay down and woke up at four o'clock. In the next room, he found the livery boy who told him, without turning his head, that he had lied for him. Two people had been there looking for him, and he told them the doctor wasn't back yet. He explained that if their folks were worse off than the doctor, they were dead anyhow and didn't need a doctor.

The only other car on 74th Street at seven o'clock one morning, when I was driving fifty miles an hour to the emergency room, was a city police car that crested the hill just as I did. I saw him turning around and turning on his lights, but I was almost to the hospital and I used my parking pass to get into the parking lot and went straight on into the emergency room. The police officer soon followed me there, carrying with him the barrier he had driven through in hot pursuit.

So much for my pace. Dr. Hertzler wrote that he lived to see automobiles become available to country doctors, who drove them at reckless speeds. He recalled riding with a doctor who drove seventy-five miles an hour on a road with seven curves to the mile. Doctors drove too fast even in horse and buggy days, he contended, saying that seven miles an hour was good time in cold weather with good roads. Three miles an hour was customary on muddy roads, and a mule would walk two and a half miles an hour if unmolested. If urged, he would slow down to two miles an hour and if urged too much, he would stop completely and look back over his shoulder to ask what you were going to do about it.

I did make house calls at night, even carrying a sick man out to my car one time and driving him to the hospital, but at no time did I drive a buggy through a driving snowstorm, as Dr. Hertzler did when he had a twenty-mile drive in the face of a driving blizzard, with sleet and snow coming horizontally into the horses' faces, as well as his own. He carried wire cutters to get through fences when drifting snow took the roads out of the equation, and he had to shoot a dog with his six-shooter as he was diving for his throat. But it wasn't all hardship. When the weather was nice, he used his pistol to shoot jackrabbits.

During long nights at the hospital, I would sometimes find a vacant patient room or go to a doctors-on-call room to rest for an hour or two. Dr. Hertzler sometimes stayed in hotels when traveling for a consultation. He slept in his overcoat in the worst hotel he could remember, which he reached after driving five hours behind unwilling mules in a sleet storm over rough frozen roads. A bundle of rags was used for a broken window, and the room seemed even colder than the outside temperature, which was far below zero.

I did visit a woman who had a large pericardial effusion (a collection of fluid around her heart), in her home one snowy day, and I drove her back to the hospital in my four-wheel drive vehicle. Dr. Hertzler recalled one trip in an open car with no top, fenders, or windshield, with ineffective protection using just blankets and lap robe. A northwest wind was blowing snow and sleet into his face in sub-zero weather for the entire seventy-five mile trip. If he had had car trouble, he thought an old-timer's prediction might have been correct: "All hell won't stop Doc but, by crickey, I'm afeard he may land there tonight." The doctor urged his driver to slow down after he narrowly missed hitting some cows, but he was told that the gas wouldn't shut off and he couldn't reach the brakes because his feet were bundled up in an old buffalo robe. After making the seventy-five miles in three and a half hours, he met the local doctor and went sixteen miles further, where he drained a brain abscess.

Having discovered that I needed one more year of cardiology fellowship before I could take my subspecialty board examination, I took a year off from my practice in 1974, took my family with me to England, and spent a year doing some clinical research at the Brompton Hospital in London. Here, very little happened before late morning; accordingly, my routine was to take the train after the morning rush hour, leaving my local station at 9:15 and arriving at the hospital a little before 11. I also waited after the evening rush to return, leaving the hospital around six and getting home a little before 8.

Dr. Hertzler, having heard of the opportunities for study in Germany from one of his medical school teachers, resolved to spend two years there before he was thirty. He couldn't afford to go to Germany after medical school, so he saved money during his four years of general practice, then took his family with him to Berlin, where he registered for lectures and laboratory experience in all phases of medicine, including ophthalmology, dermatology, and also the history of religions. He spent several hours in the dissecting room before the morning university work began, and during vacations he sometimes devoted as many as ten hours a day to his cadavers. In a special course in ear, nose, and throat under Professor Janzen, all forty-six students except Hertzler and his pal were specialists. All the specialists failed to use Janzen's technique properly, so Hertzler and his friend obtained a set of the professor's instruments, bribed the night watchman to let them into the deadhouse, and practiced doing several hundred tonsillectomies on the cadavers. When their turn came to do the procedure on real patients in the class, they showed themselves to be so proficient that the professor proclaimed them to be natural throat specialists.

He taught gross anatomy in Kansas City after his return, driving back and forth from Halstead, Kansas, where he practiced and operated. In his early years, almost all his surgery was done in the home. An elderly woman in my examination room once told me about one time Dr. Cooper, founder of the clinic where I worked, had driven out to Sallisaw, some thirty miles from Fort Smith, and done a gall bladder operation on her mother in the kitchen. I'm sure my mouth fell open; if I had remembered Dr. Hertzler's chapter on kitchen surgery, which I read when I was in high school, I would have understood it better.

All that is required for aseptic surgery is reasonably clean skin, clean tools, and an operator who knows what he is doing, Hertzler maintains. Although he doesn't say so specifically, it appears that kitchen surgery allowed avoidance of hospital-borne infections, as long as the operator could keep his own hands clean; Hertzler says it is essential to keep the hands out of infectious material for twenty-four hours, citing the example of a friend who operated for necrosis of a jaw, and his subsequent five laparotomies became infected. The other factor for success in the kitchen: prompt performance of the operation (the biggest factor in aseptic operating).

A photograph in the book shows a parade in which "Kitchen Surgery – 40 yrs. ago" is portrayed on one of the floats: the bearded surgeon (no mask) seated at the side of the kitchen table where the patient lies, his overalls drawn down below his knees and hanging over his feet. Lanterns are placed on the china closet and the kitchen table. The assistant stands at the patient's head to administer anesthesia. Clean, rapid surgery is far more effective in avoiding infections than all the face masks ever made, Hertzler declares; he does concede, however, that rubber gloves greatly helped to improve hand sterilization. He considers sterile drapes to be an unnecessary addition; just keep the instruments away from the unwashed skin – and always put the instruments back into the dishpan after use. Gall bladders and appendices were not removed in the kitchen; they were merely drained when a proper operating room wasn't available.

Preparations included boiling the instruments, removing furniture and pictures, scrubbing the walls and floor, and nailing sheets on the windows to keep the neighbors from peeping in. The advent of the motor car permitted use of its headlights, with the car driven up to the window of the room where the surgery was to take place. Someone was delegated to hold up a mirror to deflect the light onto the operative site. Hertzler strongly preferred the assistance of a nurse; the local physician usually assisted and was more often a hindrance than a help.

Hertzler concluded that he had done every type of surgery in the kitchen, from in-grown toenails to Gasserian ganglions. "I was not afraid then. I would not consider tackling such things under those circumstances now."

This was just before the introduction of antibiotics and the drainage of pus was one of the major functions of the doctor. On one occasion, he drove through the mud for three hours to find a fourteen-year-old boy, cyanotic, sitting up in bed. His skin was grayish-blue, his chest was heaving, his mouth was open, and his eyes were bulging. Throwing down his instrument roll, he sat down on the floor with his legs spread out under the bed. A quick stab with the scalpel – he was too near death to need an anesthetic – produced a stream of pus that struck the doctor in the neck and drenched him. He then placed a drain in the opening, wrapped his own pus-soaked body in a blanket, and made the three-hour journey home. "The patient promptly recovered and is now a useful citizen in his town and recently voted for Landon, but I have never recovered from the memory of that pus bath. Bah!"

Historical exhibits often show early hospitals that appear to be large residential houses. Why didn't they look like hospitals? Hertzler's chapter on his hospital outdoes any exhibit in explaining how they worked. He confesses that he thought he could build up his surgical practice if he had a hospital, as many other doctors were doing. A hospital was a place for the surgeon to operate. Non-surgical cases were treated at home; hospitals were thought of as places where sick people went to die.

Most hospitals began in a private residence. The doctor and his family lived downstairs and the wife did the cooking for the patients as well as for her family. There were usually only five or six hospital beds. The cook's room was often used as the operating room; heat for sterilization came from the kitchen stove. The doctor, accordingly, was obliged to eat an early breakfast so the stove could then be used to prepare for surgery. These arrangements were considered to be only a minor modification of kitchen surgery in private homes.

His hospital was built to provide five rooms on the second floor for the surgical patients and five on the third floor for non-surgical patients. It so happened that Dr. Hertzler built a larger hospital later, and finally, in 1933, he sold it to the Sisters of St. Joseph for one dollar. Like the owner of a boat, it appears that the two happiest days of the owner are when he buys it and when he sells it.

A doctor who has braved the snows of the Kansas prairie in a horse and buggy, operated in Kansas farm houses, built and sold his own hospital, and maintained his own private practice, may understandably become a bit opinionated. Dr. Hertzler used this book as a bully pulpit for his views and practices.

Some of these are fundamental and coincide with my own. In describing his childhood fascination with a local physician who "was never sober" and died after falling out of his wagon into the creek and catching pneumonia, but who "lived for his patients, like all country doctors," Hertzler writes, "Yet with this hardy man a spirit died, the spirit of service, a service done without thought of reward either here or hereafter... To my small mind there was something heroic about him. He was not afraid of mud, high water or the devil." The wilderness and the frontier required pioneers with a special brand of courage, fortitude, and persistence. When the spirit of service was added to these virtues, it could shine so that an idealistic young lad could identify it and adopt it for his own.

The horse and buggy doctor knew that the greatest service he could render for most of his patients was pain relief , for which he used morphine then, and for which we use morphine now, though we also have other agents and delivery systems. His effectiveness was enhanced because he stayed by the patient's bed for many hours if necessary, until the discomfort was relieved.

I always felt obliged to stand by the emergency room gurney of a patient with the pain of acute myocardial infarction until I was satisfied the morphine I was ordering had done its job. But it didn't require hours.

"No reproach attaches to the practice of masterly inactivity," is one of Dr. Hertzler's "pearls," the term residents use for succinct observations delivered on rounds. A patient told me one time that she had consulted me because when her father was sick, one doctor tried to do one thing, and another tried to do another, "but you didn't do anything" – a strategy that must have been interpreted as masterly inactivity.

"Just plain advice never was productive of revenue unless fortified by a few pills." Early in my practice, I learned the importance of not sending the patient out the door without something in hand. Sometimes masterly inactivity is appropriate, sometimes not.

The doctor stayed with the dying patient until the end, ensuring there was no suffering, an obligation rendered not so much to the dying as to the living. Of course there is a duty to relieve suffering, but there is also a duty to those who are grieving. This is the physician's last duty, and it is one he neglects at his peril.

As an afterthought to a discussion of counterproductive colleagues, the author adds that the priests would always stand in the background and encourage the patient, often saying that the doctor knows best. Hertzler claimed that sometimes this was right, but the affirmation increased his own efforts to prove them correct. As a Protestant working in a Catholic hospital, this was my experience. The Protestant preachers were a mixed lot; but the authoritarian Catholic priests and nuns backed the doctor every step of the way.

Dr. Hertzler unburdened himself of a number of other strongly held opinions. In many of them, he was a creature of his time. He had little use for the examiners who visited his hospital and questioned the policies he had put in place. He maintained that the people of Kansas had adequate medical care, if they wanted it, no matter whether they could or couldn't pay. And in another context: "Modesty forbids me to extol further the superiority of Kansas."

In his preface, Hertzler writes that he protested bitterly when his editor asked him to make his book more personal; he did insert a number of cases, but he stubbornly repeated that it is in no sense an autobiography. I share the editor's frustration. The book is dedicated to "Agnes Helen and Margaret, my daughters," yet there are only a few allusions to them. There is also a reference to the death of a daughter. But nowhere is there any mention of a wife! Surely there was one. Did she die giving birth to the third child? I tried looking it up, but without success. He doesn't have a Wikipedia entry.

A rewarding book is one that describes familiar circumstances and explains them. As a young man in practice, I was so preoccupied with the effort of establishing my footing that I had little interest in the historical foundation I was standing on. Such insecurity diminishes a bit with time, so that eventually one looks around and behind with a bit more interest. A second visit to *The Horse and Buggy Doctor* leaves little doubt that there were giants in those days. Every one of my stories can be easily trumped by Dr. Hertzler. Every age does have its trials, and I have had all of them I wanted. But I never drove a buggy through the snow.

THE SIMPLE LIFE

SCHWEITZER: A Biography
By George Marshall and David Poling

ALBERT SCHWEITZER: A Biography
By James Brabazon

OUT OF MY LIFE AND THOUGHT
An Autobiography
By Albert Schweitzer

How many degrees of separation is this? I spent an hour with a lady who had spent an hour with Albert Schweitzer. That is about as close as I'm likely to come to sainthood. My wife and I were in England in May a few years ago, spending a fortnight in a rented cottage in Great Shelford, near Cambridge. Our policy of embedding ourselves in the community included attendance at the local church, where we met an elderly (older than we were) lady named Ann Elliott, and she invited us to come round for tea on the following Wednesday afternoon. At the appointed hour, a young woman who introduced herself only as a friend opened the door and this bright but nameless soul did all the honors of serving tea and chocolates and running little errands for Ann, who was eighty-two and had two artificial knees. Another neighbor named Val was also there.

We all gathered in the living room, and after a few pleasantries, Ann asked her young friend to show us the Albert Schweitzer picture; it was a small framed print of Schweitzer making rounds at his African hospital in Lambaréné, and there was a two-line inscription to Alan (her late husband) and Ann with his signature. So how did she know Schweitzer, we asked. She and her husband had been traveling in Europe at a time when they knew Schweitzer was home from Africa for a visit to his native village of Günsbach in Alsace-Lorraine. En route to Strasbourg, she looked at the map and told her husband that they were only a few miles from Schweitzer's village. They made a short detour and stopped in the local bistro. It turned out that a man at an adjoining table was a carpenter who lived next door to Schweitzer and was working on his house. As they were talking about him, the carpenter looked out the window and said, "Oh, there he is now. Would you like to meet him?" Of course, so they went out and met him. Dr. Schweitzer invited them to his house, which Ann said was very plain indeed, and they visited for an hour. She asked him if he had any advice for her, and he replied, "Be yourself." Before they left, he asked if they would like for him to play for them, so he went to his organ and played something by Bach.

Albert Schweitzer was a complex man, a many-sided genius who resolved early to abandon the joys of scholarship, musical genius, and organ building in order to pursue one very simple goal: to help others. He elected to do this by becoming a doctor and going to darkest Africa to heal the sick. It turned out that simplicity wasn't so easy to achieve, and when he did achieve it, his altruistic mission didn't escape criticism.

His background was mixed in several ways. He was born in 1875 in Alsace-Lorraine, which had been part of France until 1871, when it became German by the fortunes of war. He grew up speaking the Alsatian dialect of German, but he also knew French. His father was a pastor in the Lutheran-Evangelical church, but the parish church was also used for Catholic services. His father's religion was one "which men could understand with their minds and could then affirm with their hearts," according to George Marshall and David Poling in

Schweitzer: A Biography (Doubleday and Company, 1971). At age ten, however, he was sent to live with his uncle and aunt, and when at age fifteen he was examined for confirmation, he couldn't agree with Pastor Wennagel that faith took precedence over reason. He did succeed in becoming confirmed so he could play the organ in the church, but he persisted in his rational approach to religion all his life.

He went on to study philosophy, theology, and music in Paris, Berlin, and Strasbourg, where he received his doctorate in philosophy in 1899. During this time, he spent six years writing a pamphlet on Bach and became one of the world's great organists. On one occasion, he failed to appear for a reception prior to a recital. It was thought the concert might have to be cancelled and the minister happened to enter the chancel, where he discovered Dr. Schweitzer among the organ pipes. He had arrived on time, had tried out the organ and found it out of balance, and had spent the rest of the afternoon tuning the organ, rearranging the stops and pipes, and adjusting the mechanism with the expected improvement in the organ's sound at the evening concert.

The book that established his reputation as a world-class theologian was *The Quest of the Historical Jesus*, published in 1906 and translated into English in 1910. His conclusions were contrary to many religious teachings and provoked some hostility. He summarized his views on Jesus in a few chapters in *Out of My Life and Thought: An Autobiography* (Henry Holt and Company, Inc., 1933), attributing all Jesus' words and actions to His anticipation that the world would end soon. He emphasized Jesus' gospel of love and reminded the reader that knowledge of spiritual truth is not dependent on further understanding of world history and ordinary life.

He had promised himself at the age of twenty-one that he would devote his life to the direct service of humanity, but not yet. After devoting his youthful energies to scholarship, he shocked his friends by renouncing it all and announcing on his thirtieth birthday that he would go to medical school and subsequently to Africa as a missionary. Life was too good, he had decided, and he was enjoying the scholar's life too much. He must pay life back for all its goodness.

He had tried doing some volunteer social work for paroled prisoners and derelicts in 1903, but it had not worked out well. Fund-raising was a nightmare and the prisoners had not responded to his efforts. But then in 1904 he had happened to see an article, "The Needs of the Congo Mission," in a missionary magazine the librarian had purposely set out so he would see it. He later defended his decision as a completely rational one, not the result of having heard the voice of God. As for those whose lives had been determined by such a call, Schweitzer only said that their ears were sharper than his.

Part of the appeal of the Congo was that it would give him an opportunity to do things the way he wanted to, without being required to collaborate. This is much like when I sometimes perversely enjoyed being the only doctor in the hospital in the middle of the night because I was, by default, the boss. Schweitzer maintained he was prepared to subject himself to some organization if necessary, but he really hoped to make a place for himself where he could conduct his mission just as he liked.

Furthermore, he would escape the theological bickering and criticism of his rather heretical views, saying that being a doctor would permit him to work and not be obliged to talk. The result of this outlook was the rather paternalistic and dictatorial role he was to play in his hospital in Lambaréné, where he concentrated on his work at hand as an individual doctor taking care of one patient at a time, with little regard for public health measures that would have required more coordination with others.

He thought of his role as one of atonement for the wrongs done to underdeveloped people by Christian white men. This need for atonement, he thought, was in itself a justification for missions.

The story of Schweitzer's relationship with Hélène Bresslau has only recently been elucidated by the publication of their correspondence, as described by James Brabazon in a revised edition of *Albert Schweitzer: A Biography* (Syracuse University Press, 2000). Their daughter Rhena stumbled upon these letters when going through her parents' possessions in the 1980s. In these letters, we find that their relationship, though not a physical one in the ten years before they married, had been more intimate than had been supposed. Hélène's father was a professor of history at Strasbourg. A Jew, he had rejected the Hebrew tradition and all religious institutionalism. Albert and Hélène were both members of a social service organization in Strasbourg, and a small group of these young people went on bicycle jaunts to the country on picnics. Hélène, at eighteen, five years younger than Albert, was determined to devote herself to social service, and she had already worked in a state orphanage and helped manage a home for unwed mothers. They subsequently observed a bicycle trip to the countryside on March 22, 1902, as the beginning of their friendship, the time when they began exchanging frank and open letters, and also keeping the intimate nature of their relationship secret from everyone else.

Theirs was a curious relationship, Brabazon says, one that wasn't normal, and was based on renunciation. That it could survive at all was extraordinary in itself. Albert may have been using her as a sounding board for his innermost thoughts, perhaps as a substitute for his Aunt Mathilde, in whom he had confided before she died. At times, he wrote that he didn't want to stand in the way of her happiness and urged her to marry if she should meet some man who might make her happy. This relationship may have been summarized in a 1905 letter in which he reminded her of a promise that she would call him if she should ever want someone. He had made a similar promise to her, and he told her that he guarded her promise as a jewel to call upon.

Hélène started to train as a nurse in January, 1904, before he thought of becoming a doctor; at this time his idea of service was to adopt and raise a number of abandoned or orphaned boys. This turned out to be a mismatch, and several months later he saw the magazine article that inspired him to become a doctor to the Congo.

His letters to Hélène reveal the inner conflicts behind his outward resolve. He became impatient with the life of abstract thought and longed for action. *"I believe because I act."* He may well be called an existentialist who preceded his nephew, Jean Paul Sartre, whose existentialism was of a more pessimistic sort.

Medical school was a challenge for Schweitzer. The German academic system made no provision for a faculty member to attend classes and receive another degree. Somewhat surprisingly, a compromise was reached where the governing body decreed he could sit for the examinations on the strength of certificates stating that he had attended the lectures, issued by the professors. The professors agreed that, as a colleague, he could attend their lectures without paying fees.

He felt that he couldn't give up his pulpit and he continued to preach on Sundays during his first few years in medical school. He played organ concerts to meet his expenses. The demands of a scientific discipline were different from the humanities, and he discovered that as a thirty-something, he couldn't memorize facts as easily as he had done in his twenties. Not only that, but he said that he had "stupidly" decided he would study pure science as an end in itself, rather than preparing for his tests. Wiser heads prevailed, however, and he allowed himself to be persuaded by his classmates to join a cramming club in order to pass his exams. Exhausted by his busy schedule, he studied while his feet were immersed in a basin of cold water to stay awake.

He did find satisfaction in plunging into scientific subject matter. In the humanities, he had come to think that an opinion could prevail as accepted truth on the basis of its presentation. But now he was in a world of facts, which he welcomed as important for his intellectual development.

Preparation for what was to be the role of a latter-day saint involved other lessons, and he learned some of these by living in the home of Frederick Curtius, president of the Lutheran Church of Alsace. There, he often played the piano for the aged Countess of Erlach, whose health prevented her from going outdoors. It was she whom he credited with rounding off some of the hard angles in his personality. She also cautioned him never to go outside bareheaded after sunset in the tropics in order to avoid malaria. This injunction he faithfully followed, even though he doubted that it had anything to do with his not getting malaria.

The clinical years of medical school were more congenial than the study of the basic sciences. Schweitzer wrote his doctoral thesis, *The Psychiatric Study of Jesus*, in which he responded to claims that Jesus had an unbalanced, neurotic personality by showing that each of the four gospels, written by different persons, showed different aspects of his personality. He followed his regular medical school curriculum with postgraduate training in tropical diseases, in Paris and Berlin.

Hélène developed tuberculosis at some time, possibly in 1908 when she had a stretch of overwork, and a few months later, she sustained a back injury while skiing.

One gets the impression that early in their friendship, he envisioned a role so all-consuming that he would have no time for marriage. Perhaps Schweitzer was in no position to offer marriage, since he was still a student on the way to becoming a triple doctor in philosophy, theology, and medicine. In December, 1911, he wrote that he was constantly thinking about announcing their decision to marry, but that he wasn't yet sure. And yet on that day he did compose and send a formal letter to Hélène's father requesting a serious interview about marriage.

His social skills were challenged in the process of gaining sponsorship for his proposed mission to Africa. The Paris Missionary Society, which had published the magazine article calling for volunteers to go to the Congo, refused to sponsor him because of his liberal theology, including such opinions as his view that the Gospel of John, which he knew to have been written in the century after Jesus' life, might not have been written by the Apostle John. So he and his wife set about raising the money from private sources (a strategy frequently employed by missionaries to this day), a sometimes disagreeable and humiliating experience, but a successful one. He then applied again to the Paris Missionary Society for sponsorship, with the conditions that he had secured his own funding, and that he would be *"muet comme une carpe* (mute as a fish)" on his theological views, which might have confused the missionaries. He declined to appear before the board to be questioned on his beliefs; instead he called personally on each board member. He promised that he would function only as a doctor, and with this understanding the Society agreed to sponsor him, with only one member resigning from the board in protest.

It turns out that Schweitzer had other options besides the Paris Missionary Society and could have obtained sponsorship from a more liberal mission organization. But he was just stubborn enough to try to bend the Paris Missionary Society to his proposal. He didn't believe that a missionary society could refuse to send a doctor to serve the suffering natives in its district because they didn't think his theology was sufficiently orthodox.

Albert's mother, not reconciled to his having renounced his brilliant career in Europe, didn't wave when his train pulled out of Grünsbach. He and Hélène sailed for Africa in April, 1913, encountering a three-day storm just after leaving Bordeaux. On board, the African natives taught him about African fruits and vegetables, and they showed him their personal charms and amulets. He got his first intimation of the challenge from the Islam religion from a French lieutenant, who told him that the native African would be a good servant, soldier, and guide, unless "infested" with Mohammedanism. In that case, no amount of good works, such as railways, canals, or irrigation projects, would make any impression on him, since he was "absolutely and on principle opposed to everything European."

He expected to find his hospital ready when he arrived at Lambaréné; instead, he was angry to find that the site hadn't even been selected. He refitted a chicken coop to get started. He found himself treating patients in what he called "the fellowship of those who bear the mark of pain." In describing a man with a strangulated hernia, he wrote that he was the only person in hundreds of miles who could help him, and that he would not merely save his life. Ultimately, all die, but this man could be saved from days of torturous pain. "Pain is a more terrible lord of mankind than even death itself."

Hernia surgery was perhaps his most dramatic and most frequent surgical operation. The basic health problem he encountered was malnutrition; the jungle was no cornucopia. Manioc, yams, and bananas were the staple foods; eating dirt was a common manifestation of starvation. The commonest diseases he encountered were skin conditions, malaria, sleeping sickness, leprosy, elephantiasis, heart disease, osteomyelitis, and dysentery.

He encountered the same ambivalence about native religions that so often occurs when Christianity is introduced to a culture with its own traditional religion. His orderly, Joseph, explained why he couldn't speak against local practices, including human sacrifice: nobody knew who the medicine men were and they would never forgive.

Schweitzer also learned about the "cleavage of communal life" that so often occurs in these situations when "things fall apart". A secret organization, called the "Leopard Men," was formed to terrorize those who accepted the Christian way. When the government arrested ninety men on suspicion in an effort to eradicate the Leopard Men, they all gave each other poison in prison and died. Perhaps as a result of such occurrences, Schweitzer never made a vigorous effort to convert his patients to Christianity, and he ran his hospital as if it were a non-sectarian enterprise.

He learned of the Great War, which was to have such a profound effect on his life and work, on the morning of August 5, 1914. On that same evening he became a prisoner of war, taken by the French, apparently because he was an Alsatian. He was kept under house arrest for three months and was then allowed to resume hospital activities, although he had to restrict himself to contact with the African people only. With more spare time, he wrote his *Philosophy of Civilization,* in which he developed his concept of "Reverence for Life," a principle that forbade the unnecessary taking of the life of any living creature.

The last year of the war found him being transported to France as a prisoner of war. On his departure, he gave his manuscript of *Philosophy of Civilization* to an American Presbyterian missionary, who "would have liked best to throw the heavy packet into the river, because he considered philosophy to be unnecessary and harmful." He spent some time in a French concentration camp until he was released in a prisoner exchange. He returned to his home in Günsbach, where he learned that his mother had been crushed to death when a German cavalry officer, galloping out of control, ran over her in the road. His father's parsonage had been commandeered by the German officers and his father had been reduced to serving as a house boy. Schweitzer sank into a deep depression. Hélène became more unstable and fearful; it was said that she would never fully recover, and that "her partnership in marriage would be restricted in every way."

When Schweitzer developed a painful rectal abscess from his dysentery, he dragged himself six kilometers toward Colmar. He subsequently had successful surgery in Strasbourg, but his depression remained, and he took up the therapeutic activity of rebuilding old organs. He also had psychoanalysis. An opportunity to play organ recitals in Sweden helped, but his recovery took five years.

The birth of their daughter Rhena in 1919 failed to overcome the growing separation between Albert and Hélène, and she urged her husband to return to Lambaréné without her. It was no longer possible for her to be in the tropics during the rainy season because of her tuberculosis and her young daughter.

Thanking her for the sacrifice of allowing him to return to Lambaréné, he arrived there in April, 1924, at age forty-nine, to find the hospital in shambles. "It might be the Sleeping Beauty's place of concealment." After a year of work rebuilding the hospital, he had an extended period of fatigue and loss of energy. Perhaps remembering the Countess' admonition to keep his head covered, he attributed his relapse to sunstroke from a sunbeam coming through a hole in the roof and striking his head.

This was followed by a blow for freedom, however, when in 1927 he opened a new hospital, the Albert Schweitzer-Bresslau Hospital, which was independent from the Paris Missionary Society. At this time he began to have hospital staff. First to arrive were Dr. Fritz Trenz and a nurse, Martha Lauterburg. Dr. Trenz distinguished himself by isolating a member of the cholera bacteria family. Since he didn't have the facilities to study it in Lambaréné, he had to transport it back to Europe. But it was illegal to take an infected animal into Europe, so he himself drank a vial of the bacterial culture just before boarding the ship. He had fever and dysentery, but when he arrived in Strasbourg, he extracted very satisfactory specimens of the bacteria from himself.

By now, Schweitzer was famous not only for his hospital, but for what he had given up to serve in it. This was the story that brought money to the hospital, and he found himself obliged to play the role of the jungle doctor whom the world knew in order to keep the money coming. He lectured in England and Europe in 1928 and 1929, and Hélène returned to Africa with him, leaving Rhena with friends. Hélène's tuberculosis flared into a febrile episode on the voyage, but she refused to turn back. They returned to a well organized hospital with over 250 patients and a staff numbering thirty-five. Doctors came and went. He didn't succeed in retaining a doctor who would stay and become an heir apparent to his duties there.

Schweitzer tried to develop native physicians, but they rarely returned from Europe, so he began encouraging bright young men at the hospital to become male nurses. Although he thought about establishing a branch hospital, he allowed himself to be so busy at Lambaréné that this never happened.

He made four trips to and from Europe between the wars to see his wife and daughter. The marriage, however, suffered. "This was *not* a case of a beautiful marriage wrecked on the harsh shores of ambition," Brabazon writes. "It was a case of a partnership of idealists that for practical reasons became a marriage and then through nobody's fault became unworkable." The work came first.

He offended the Nazis in 1932 with a speech in Frankfurt when he said, "Remain men, in possession of your own souls;" and he decided never again to enter Nazi Germany. After all, since Alsace had become French again after World War I, he was no longer a German national, and his wife was Jewish. Neither was he comfortable with the French, and after a twelve-day visit to Europe in February, 1939, he returned to Africa. Hélène went to Lambaréné in 1941. Some friends she had met in America formed The Albert Schweitzer Fellowship, and its financial support was crucial for his hospital's survival during the war.

Hélène returned to Switzerland in 1947 because of her health; Schweitzer visited her in 1948 and saw his grandchildren for the first time. Although he never learned to fly an airplane or drive a car, he did visit America in 1949. He was acclaimed by *Life* magazine as "The Greatest Man in the World." He received the Nobel Peace Prize in 1952. He became concerned about the nuclear arms race, joining other men of science in urging an end to nuclear testing. The Eisenhower administration, however, feared his opposition would strengthen the Russian hand and attempted to discredit him. Lewis Strauss, head of the Atomic Energy Commission, asked Herbert Hoover, head of the FBI, to investigate whether the Albert Schweitzer Fellowship in New York might be an anti-American organization. But Hoover found nothing out of line.

Hélène died in 1957, at age seventy-seven, ten days after leaving Lambaréné to return to Europe. Her autopsy showed evidence of "several slight heart attacks" and severe lung disease with scarring from tuberculosis.

Brabazon defends Schweitzer vigorously against attacks made against him in his last years. "To itemize the inaccuracies, false insinuations, and out-of-context quotations in (Gerald)

McKnight's book (*Verdict on Schweitzer*) would take a chapter in itself." McKnight had called it a "jungle sore suppurating into the fresh body of emergent Africa, hampering the advance of clean, clear-minded and progressive Africans who are now building modern and fully equipped hospitals in the vicinity... in a word Schweitzer's hospital is redundant... an old man's private dream-world overtaken by realities he refuses to accept."

Schweitzer did indeed go deep into the jungle so he could do things his way. He had no love for administration. Like Paul Farmer today, who resembles Schweitzer in many ways, Schweitzer preferred to deal with patients one at a time rather than organize public health projects. The American cardiologist Dr. Paul Dudley White challenged Schweitzer in 1963 to do more in regard to preventive medicine, saying that such fundamental public health projects as draining the swamps and getting rid of malaria-transmitting mosquitoes would decrease Dr. Schweitzer's work by half. But at this time, Schweitzer was eighty-eight years old.

In view of charges that Schweitzer was a paternalistic and dictatorial relic of the colonial past, it is of interest that in 1959 the new state of Gabon asked him to represent the African states on the French delegation to the United Nations Commission on the Rights of Man.

He walked through his orchard at Lambaréné on April 27, 1965; on the following day he went to bed, and on April 29, he was semi-comatose. His death on September 4 was attributed to cerebral vascular insufficiency, uremia, and pneumonitis.

Its website states that the Albert Schweitzer Hospital in Gabon states had 35,000 outpatient visits and more than 6,000 hospitalizations annually, and that two surgeons perform close to 2,200 operations each year. It is said to be one of the five leading facilities in Africa studying malaria.

After all is said and done, Albert Schweitzer succeeded in what he deliberately set out to do: serve human beings one at a time with humility, albeit with a rather domineering personality. Though he made every effort to make his mission a simple one, he was clearly a complex and many-sided person, as shown in his thoughts for publication in *Out of My Life and Thought*, and in his secret thoughts in his letters to Hélène, which were never intended to be published. The biographies by Marshall and Poling and by Brabazon are both books of praise, but they convey the many facets of his life with clarity and credibility. The more recent book by Brabazon is a bit more specific; for example it mentions "rectal abscess" rather than "infection", and it deals with the marital relationship more openly; it also has the advantage of the availability of the premarital correspondence and some papers dealing with the Eisenhower administration's opposition to his efforts to promote nuclear disarmament.

What better evidence can there be of a determination to demonstrate humanity and humility than his willingness to spend an unscheduled hour with Ann Elliott and her husband, who happened, on the spur of the moment, to make a detour to see the village of the great man?

THE SILVER SPOON KID

THE WAY IT WAS
Sex, Surgery, Treasure, & Travel 1907-1987
By George Crile, Jr., M. D.

"Another one of those silver spoon kids, eh?" The foreman at our neighbor's ice cream plant failed to conceal his skepticism when my teenage son turned up to work, broom in hand, one summer morning. Silver spoon? Perhaps, but silver spoons are relative, and one can imagine few spoons more silver than that of George Crile, Jr., who admitted as much in the last chapter of his memoir, *The Way It Was: Sex, Surgery, Treasure, and Travel 1907-1987* (The Kent State University Press, 1992): "The silver spoon that my mother put in my mouth is still there." Consider his gifts: son and namesake of a world-famous surgeon who was the principal founder of the Cleveland Clinic; raised in grand style in a home where his father dressed in a tuxedo for dinner; and childhood vacations sailing off the Florida Keys and canoeing in the Canadian forests. He became an end on the Yale football team; he was a member of *Skull and Bones*, the not-so-secret society at Yale; and he graduated first in his class at Harvard Medical School. When he applied for a surgery internship at Barnes Hospital in St. Louis, Dr. Evarts Graham, one of the early giants of thoracic surgery, sent a telegram to Dr. Crile, Sr., asking if the new intern was his son. Upon receiving the affirmative reply, the appointment was made. What more could a young lad want?

Having been raised in a stable, loving, and supportive family, he married Jane Halle, daughter of Cleveland wealth, whose photograph in the book shows her in the cockpit of a small airplane with her dog. Capable and strong, her death from breast cancer after twenty-eight years of marriage was the one tragedy of "Barney" Crile's life. An entry in her journal written shortly before she died gave an enviable summation of their marriage: "Our life was good. Everything, but never too much of anything."

Perhaps you can't tell a book by its cover, but the dust jacket of this one is of interest. The photograph shows Dr. Crile, Sr., performing his twenty-five-thousandth thyroidectomy in the Cleveland Clinic, assisted by his son, the author. You can't get around Dr. Crile, Sr. He was known as a great man, and it's difficult to think about Barney Crile without thinking of him as Dr. Crile's son. The dates on the cover indicate that the book was written by an eighty-year-old man. A memoir, of course, includes only what the author remembers, and he acknowledges several gaps; in this case, his recollections are all too amply supplemented by correspondence and clippings, particularly those preserved by his mother for a scrapbook of his college years.

And then there's the first word on the jacket, the first word of the subtitle: sex. What's sex got to do with it? Not all that much, it turns out. One suspects he used the subtitle purely as an attention-getting device. Barney and Jane, both of whom had majored in English in college, took a course in journalism at Cleveland State University's night school when they decided to write a book about their treasure-hunting adventures. Their unnamed professor, besides emphasizing that they should use simple words instead of complex ones, added that they should include lots of facts, particularly any that had to do with sex. In this book, any readers looking for explicit or graphic material will be disappointed, even though the author seems to go out of his way to allude to a few personal matters, which many readers would prefer to assume rather than read about.

Few physicians raise a child who follows them into medicine, in the same field of medicine, and even into the same practice, as George, Jr., followed his father. But every son asserts his independence in his own way. Barney, in assisting his father in surgery during his residency at Cleveland Clinic, began to doubt the value of some of his father's operations, especially those related to ideas he developed in his later years about the "radio-electric theory of life." Dr. Crile Sr. thought that an excess of nervous energy, governed by the adrenal glands and the autonomic nervous system, accounted for a number of diseases. He thus performed many operations to remove the celiac ganglion (a nerve plexus deep in the abdomen) and to denervate the adrenal glands in largely fruitless attempts to cure such diseases as epilepsy, hypertension, and "neuro-circulatory asthenia." (Some hypertensive patients did achieve better blood pressure control after celiac ganglionectomy.) George Jr. soon learned that discussion of these issues with his father only led to discord, but his skepticism on this issue led him to question other dogmas and established surgical practices.

Dr. Crile Jr. was best known for his campaigns against radical operations when they were not supported by follow-up studies, becoming a forerunner of those who now advocate "evidence-based medicine." His *New York Times* obituary stated, "Dr. Crile's battle against unnecessary surgery affected the lives of uncounted people in this country, but particularly women stricken with breast cancers."

He was among the first to question the necessity for radical mastectomy, a disfiguring operation leaving many women with arms swollen by lymphedema. His iconoclasm made him a pariah among established surgeons, and he was once even reprimanded by the Cleveland Academy of Medicine, saying that he lacked concern for his patients and that patients' confidence in their surgeons would suffer as a result of his statements.

He was a loyal assistant to his father, particularly after Dr. Crile Sr.'s eyesight became so bad that he could no longer read for himself. He then resorted to removing overactive thyroid glands by feel rather than by sight, leaving the responsibility of stopping the bleeding to his assistants.

The surgery for Dr. Crile Sr.'s glaucoma was kept a secret so as not to damage his reputation, and it was thought that the Cleveland Clinic would not have survived the Depression years without the income from Dr. Crile's thyroidectomies. During these procedures, Dr. Crile Jr. said that he became an expert in tying bleeders. During one operation for thyroid cancer, he cautioned his father that he was too close to the carotid artery. The anesthetist became concerned as the senior surgeon continued undeterred, and as she looked over the drapes, she was hit in the face by blood from the severed carotid. Fortunately, in this case the patient had collateral blood supply from the other side and escaped death or paralysis.

Dr. Crile Jr.'s career in surgery took him through a time of major changes. Until the appearance of medications such as propylthiouracil and radiation therapy with radioactive iodine (which Dr. Crile advocated), the treatment for hyperthyroidism was surgical. When it was learned that thyroiditis could be treated medically, thyroid surgery began to disappear from the Cleveland Clinic, decreasing from 2,700 cases a year to less than fifty. What would his father, with his 25,000 thyroidectomies, have thought?

Crile also helped to simplify management of peptic ulcer disease, advocating a less radical operation than the standard practice of removing part of the stomach. He improved drainage of the stomach with a procedure that placed an opening between the stomach and the intestine, nearer the end of the stomach where it empties into the duodenum. These changes in general surgery became apparent to me in the 1970s when I realized that I wasn't doing preoperative assessments for subtotal gastric resections so often, nor was I seeing patients who had had them recently. New and effective medical treatment for ulcer disease appeared and the operations quietly disappeared. Radical neck dissections and radical mastectomies also faded away, and again, Dr. Crile was among the critical thinkers responsible for these transformations. Other big operations appeared, but these did not escape caustic comment. Visiting the Phoenicians' shaft tombs in Lebanon, Barney Crile deplored the practice of penetrating seventy feet of rock for a king's burial: "Yet today we still do the same sort of thing. We spend $100,000 on a heart transplant and usually, from the standpoint of the Welfare of Society, it is just about as productive as the shaft tombs were."

Antibiotics had a major effect on surgery, eliminating the rationale for "prophylactic appendectomies" and allowing less rush and urgency for suspected appendicitis. Barney himself had two personal encounters with life-threatening infections before antibiotics became available. The first was lobar pneumonia as a college student, when his parents rushed to his bedside; he came through his febrile "crisis," which was often fatal, with only a bit of bronchiectasis to show for it. The second was a streptococcal infection of his hand and arm, acquired when he plunged his ungloved hand into the drain hole of a postoperative patient with a hemolytic streptococcal wound infection and a hemorrhage. Barney became comatose and required surgical drainage, but he survived.

Among the medical historical trivia is the interaction between the families of George Crile, Sr., and Harvey Cushing. They were old friends, having grown up in old Cleveland families, and they served together in World War I. Barney later spent some time at the Cushing house when he was a medical student at Harvard and Cushing, the Professor of Surgery, became a "foster father" to Barney. Dr. Crile described Cushing as "intense, meticulous, and brilliant," but each of them had his own ego. As recorded in Michael Bliss' *Harvey Cushing: A Life in Surgery*, Cushing was grief-stricken after the death of his brother Ned, a physician in Cleveland. A note written by Harvey Cushing expressed his hope that Ned's physician's "touch" would pass on to his son Pat, adding, "[George] Crile doesn't have it – fine as he is and fond as Ned is of him."

No less fascinating than the medical and surgical trivia are the personal bits. The Great Depression had a devastating effect on the Criles' financial assets, but they kept up appearances for several years, continuing to host parties in their ballroom, which was in demand for society events, and continuing with their travel and vacations. Dr. Crile Sr. seemed not to worry about their financial situation as long as he could work, but after his death, his 2,500-acre farm was sold for its lumber when the estate was declared bankrupt.

George Jr. dealt with the problem that faces sons of great men all his life: it's a tough act to follow. What can you do for an encore? He summarizes this problem in his last chapter, assessing himself as one who had never been able to stick to an interest for more than five years at a time.

He and Jane found a sunken treasure ship in the Caribbean while vacationing in the Florida Keys in 1948, and after diving to inspect it, they created movies of their findings. On a trip to the Middle East four years later, they turned their attention to a certain area of the island of Crete, which corresponded to their reading of Homer's account of the Trojan War. After finding three ancient shipwrecks there, they presented their findings to the National Geographic Society and wrote a book, *Treasure-Diving Holidays: An American Family's Adventures on the Floors of Three Seas.*

Another book, *More than Booty*, was published after Jane's death in 1962. He was devastated by her death, but he soon sought female company; and his "Widow of the Week" venture was suspended when Jane's sister introduced him to Helga Sandburg, the gifted daughter of another great man, Carl Sandburg the poet. When the justice of the peace performed an official ceremony, he asked if they wanted the regular service or the special one. Barney asked for the best ceremony he could perform, saying that she had already had two husbands and he wanted this marriage to last. It did, and indeed they lived happily ever after. Helga was a poet and author in her own right, a woman who, according to Barney, could do anything better than any other woman.

The Way It Was leads us through some of the significant changes in medicine and surgery, and also in our society, in the twentieth century. Those of us less gifted (which must comprise about ninety-nine percent of us) can read about the activities of this stratum of the world's talent with great interest. For my taste, the account could have omitted many of the scrapbook excerpts and long letters that are quoted verbatim. It is also unfortunate that his unnamed professor of journalism didn't cure him of his penchant for the unnecessary last sentence that concludes too many paragraphs. Examples from the first chapter are: "Nor have I been able to ever since!" "That's the last duel I ever fought." "Never before or since have I so regretted performing an absurd act."

George Crile, Jr. died of lung cancer in 1992 at age eighty-four, perhaps related to the smoking habit that he triumphantly discontinued after sustaining chest injuries in a motor vehicle accident at age fifty-eight. Two of his three daughters married surgeons, and the third, an artist, married the chancellor of City University of New York. His son, George Crile III, had a successful career in journalism and wrote *Charlie Wilson's War*, the book later made into a movie about the war in Afghanistan. *Wikipedia*, for what it's worth as an indicator of worldly fame, includes entries about George Crile, Sr., and George Crile III. If for nothing other than his contributions to making some operations less extensive and less frequent, Barney deserves an entry of his own.

THE THRILL OF THE CHASE

FOR THE LOVE OF ENZYMES
The Odyssey of a Biochemist
By Arthur Kornberg

I heard Arthur Kornberg, Nobel Prize winning biochemist and author of *For the Love of Enzymes: The Odyssey of a Biochemist* (Harvard University Press, 1989), give a guest lecture at Washington University School of Medicine when I was a student. Although I remember hardly anything of it, I am sure it was a recounting of his work with DNA, which had led to his Nobel Prize in 1959. He had been Head of the Department of Microbiology at Washington University until 1959, the year I arrived as a freshman medical student. Some fifty years later, the term "DNA" has now entered our slang in such phrases as, "It's in our corporate DNA." I cringe when I hear this, indignant as usual when it dawns on me that a new word or phrase has entered our popular culture, being used in an inaccurate way by people who have only the haziest idea of what it means. In our microbiology course, we heard the DNA story from almost every lecturer, who probably had no idea what the other lecturers were talking about. We heard it so often that I was astonished at one of the questions asked on a test: "What is DNA?" Naïve as I was, I could hardly believe that this was a serious question. "DNA is a celebrated macromolecule," I wrote, learning later to my dismay that the question was indeed a serious one. I received no credit for my answer. Don't overestimate the teacher, I learned. Play it straight. Don't be funny. Keep your game face.

But Arthur Kornberg, who had radically reorganized the microbiology course at Washington University to emphasize the basic science of genetics and biochemistry rather than the identification of bacteria for clinical purposes, was a formidable figure who could hardly be overestimated. During his lifetime, he was at the center of research into the hottest story in medical science: the genetic revolution. He received the Nobel Prize in Physiology or Medicine in 1959 for the discovery of DNA polymerase, the enzyme required for the synthesis of DNA.

DNA polymerase was one of his thirty favorite enzymes that he discovered, he relates in *For the Love of Enzymes: The Odyssey of a Biochemist* (Harvard University Press, 1989). The title is not misleading; the book really is about enzymes. "I never met a dull enzyme," Kornberg declares. And it is not a dull book. The reader is carried along through his early years by the enthusiasm and energy of youth. He appears to have carried these qualities through to his old age, but the clock does tick. Kornberg displays the tricks that make a book about an esoteric subject understandable and interesting to the reader who refuses to be intimidated. Words are defined when first introduced; history and personal interest are included; analogies are thrown in; the illustrations are simple drawings conveying the action; and the importance and relevance of the subject are emphasized. This isn't a history of science, but there are many stories that leave the reader with a nodding familiarity with beri-beri, scurvy, pellagra, and rickets; Lavoisier and Pasteur; Vitamin K, rat poison, and the dicumarols; Koch and his postulates and tuberculosis and cholera; Watson and Crick and the structure of DNA; and Kornberg's own role in the ongoing history of how DNA works.

There is a frustrating lack of personal details; Kornberg did have a personal and family life, though he admittedly spent long hours in the laboratory. His wife Sylvy was a distinguished scientist in her own right and collaborated with him on a number of projects. Her famous comment on learning of her

120

husband's Nobel Prize was, "I was robbed!" When the reader first meets Sylvy, they are moving from apartment to apartment in New York, waiting for their rental to become available. Who is this? When and how did they meet? What about their wedding?

Sylvy interrupted her career for motherhood, at least for a while, and Kornberg tells us that the boys often spent time playing with the graduate assistants in the laboratory, having such a good time that Roger, when asked what he wanted for Christmas, said, "A week in the laboratory." Kornberg usually took one of the boys on his lecture trips. And all three sons have had distinguished careers, the two older sons in their father's own field of biochemistry, the youngest in architecture, specializing in laboratories. Roger, the oldest son, won the Nobel Prize in 2006 for his work in describing the physical structure of RNA polymerase. His father was in Stockholm for the presentation. (How many fathers-son pairs have won the Nobel Prize? Six. And one mother-daughter pair, the Curies, who also count as a father-daughter pair.) The middle son, Thomas, gave up a career in music because of occupational trauma to his left index finger and then went on to become professor of biochemistry at the University of California in San Francisco. When his finger forced him to give up music, he was taking a course in biology at Columbia and was distressed when he heard some disparaging comments about DNA polymerase, an enzyme that his father had discovered. There was a missing polymerase that led to some skepticism. Tom wasn't sure he was prepared to address this issue, having had no laboratory experience. His father dismissed these concerns (so much for prerequisites for advanced courses), telling him that one of his colleagues, despite his expertise and experience, had been working on the problem without any success. So Tom obtained space to work in a laboratory in the Biology Department at Columbia; within three weeks he found a DNA polymerase in *E. Coli* cells that was different from the one his father had discovered. He presented these sensational findings at a meeting of the International Congress of Biochemistry in Switzerland, as a rookie who had first worked in a research laboratory only three months earlier.

If anything can be more gratifying in life than winning a Nobel Prize, I should guess that it would be seeing your child win it; and perhaps even more, having all three children turn out well. After all, these kids grew up in Silicon Valley during the social revolution of the sixties. Kornberg, father of eight grandchildren, which he doesn't mention in his book, limits his reflections about his family to recalling that he and his wife had completely trusted their children, allowing them access to the family bank account when they entered college, and speculating that this mutual sense of trust might have helped them avoid the pitfalls of the drug culture of the sixties and seventies. As in other close families, there was also a league of sibs who were intensely loyal to one another.

Arthur Kornberg himself was one of the highly gifted cohorts of first and second generation Jewish immigrants from central Europe who grew up in New York City and contributed so much to our culture and our society. (How many were there? Start with Einstein, Oppenheimer, and George Gershwin. It is a staggering list.) But it wasn't easy. Kornberg devotes four pages of his last chapter to "the virus of anti-Semitism," in which he relates that ninety percent of the students at City College of New York, which has produced nine Nobel laureates, were Jewish; and all but five of his two hundred premed classmates were denied admission to medical schools. He was one of the quota of two Jews to be admitted to University of Rochester Medical School.

Things improved in subsequent years; about a third of the students in my entering class of eighty at Washington University School of Medicine in 1959 were Jewish. I was interested to read that Carl Cori at Washington University was one of those who "bravely rejected discrimination." Dr. Cori was Arthur Kornberg's mentor at Washington University from 1953 to 1959. I remember him as a stone-faced lecturer, first making me think that it was sometimes better to hear the disciple than the prophet. His wife Gerty, also a biochemist, was Jewish, and they emigrated to the U.S. from Germany in 1922. They collaborated in the laboratory, but she didn't receive a faculty appointment at Washington University until they both received the Nobel Prize in 1947, when she was made a Professor of Biochemistry.

Names of immigrants from Eastern Europe often underwent transformation. The Kornberg name was adopted before Arthur's father left. Since the army draft was "a fate no orthodox Jew could contemplate," he took the name of a man named Kornberg, who had already done his service. They left Austrian Galicia (now part of Poland) in 1900; if the family had stayed, most likely they all would have been killed in the concentration camps. His father, who spoke six languages, operated a sewing machine for thirty years and then opened a hardware store; his mother learned English at age fifty-four to do the family correspondence when his father lost his eyesight.

Kornberg came to basic science from the practice of medicine during World War II when he was transferred from being a ship's surgeon in the Navy to the National Institutes of Health because of some research he had done on Gilbert's Disease as a medical student. (This is a benign increase in serum bilirubin, resulting from an inborn error of metabolism, which he discovered in himself in medical school. I discovered the same elevation of serum bilirubin in myself as a medical student, presumably from the same benign cause, never clearly defined. Benign syndromes don't attract much research attention.)

The NIH, now a giant in the world of medical research, though at the mercy of stingy Congressional appropriations, was only a collection of a few small buildings when Kornberg was there in the 1940s. The enthusiasm and energy of the young researcher are captured in his description of the results of a lab accident when he was working with Severo Ochoa, with whom he would later share the Nobel Prize. Ochoa discovered the accident and called Kornberg before he got home an hour later, to be sure he was safe. The next morning, Kornberg glanced at the last fraction of supernatant fluid that had been separated. Instead of dumping it out, he had happened to store it in a refrigerator at minus fifteen degrees Centigrade. Noticing that the fluid had become slightly turbid, he decided to sort out the solid material with the centrifuge and analyze it. "Holy Toledo!" This fraction contained most of the enzyme activity, much purer than any of their previous preparations. So an accidentally broken cylinder had led to a step that became part of the procedure they subsequently published.

We've all experienced lucky accidents. The one I remember best is a flub that my father loved telling about for years. We were planting sweet potatoes and my job was to sit on the planter behind the tractor and stuff the little potato slips into the furrow. After one or two rows, I had used up all my supply of potato slips, planting them far more liberally than I was supposed to. But when we harvested the crop, my two rows had the best yield. Farmers often notice a few rows in the field are different from the others, some better, some worse, owing to some random variation in the equipment settings, and they make use of this information. It sounds more sophisticated when laboratory scientists do the same thing, but it's all basically the same process.

Every laboratory seems to have some serendipity stories, but one must not forget the first five letters in "laboratory." Another story, describing a Japanese colleague, is one I remember most from my first reading of the book about fifteen years ago. In purifying an enzyme, Reiji Okazaki used a heating step where he held ten milliliters of the enzyme in a test tube for five minutes at seventy degrees; then he centrifuged the solution to remove the coagulated impurities. But when he needed to produce several liters of the product, he simply repeated his original procedure several hundred times. Kornberg said he was embarrassed to report such an unsophisticated procedure in his publication, but he then realized that Okazaki had preferred not to waste time and material in learning how to do the procedure in a large container. Kornberg found himself recommending variations of the "Okazaki procedure" to his students, finding that it consistently yielded the desired results. Attempts to do one big step rather than many little steps sometimes resulted in products that couldn't be used.

An incidental rule of life: A good story is one that conveys a rule of life. And a good book is not without a few little rules of life. Arthur Kornberg has demonstrated in this volume that the prophet himself can tell his own story and do it very well, providing immediacy and credibility that a journalist may lack. The thrill of the chase is not limited to deer season or the fox hunt.

TO THE LEAST OF THESE

MOUNTAINS BEYOND MOUNTAINS
The Quest of Dr. Paul Farmer,
A Man Who Would Cure the World
By Tracy Kidder

Tuberculosis could be treated much more cheaply in Haiti than in Boston, I heard Paul Farmer say in an interview on National Public Radio, shortly after the appearance of Tracy Kidder's biography, *Mountains Beyond Mountains: The Quest of Dr. Paul Farmer, A Man Who Would Cure the World* (Random House, 2003). He could treat an uncomplicated case of tuberculosis in Haiti for $150 to $200, compared to the usual cost of $15,000 to $20,000 in the United States.

Farmer is one of those rare individuals who blossoms from an unlikely garden: his father was a feckless soul who raised his family on a houseboat. Paul was an intelligent lad who learned the importance of hard work and went to Duke on a full scholarship. While a student, he spent some months in Paris, where he learned French. He returned and developed an interest in medical anthropology, adopting as his hero Rudolph Virchow, who had stated a fundamental law: "If disease is an expression of individual life under unfavorable conditions, then epidemics must be indicative of mass disturbances of mass life." Farmer attended a vigil at Duke Chapel, protesting the murder of Archbishop Oscar Romero in El Salvador, and this ignited his interest in liberation theology. He met a Belgian nun who took him on a tour of North Carolina tobacco plantations, where he met Haitian migrant workers. This led him to write a long article, *Haitians Without a Home,* and after graduation from Duke, he went to Haiti in the spring of 1983. In the fall of 1984, he enrolled in Harvard Medical School on scholarship, and from then on, he balanced his life commuting between Harvard and Haiti.

Balancing a life between Harvard and Haiti: that means that at thirty-five, with an MD and a Ph.D. from Harvard in anthropology, he was working in Boston four months a year, living in a church rectory in a poor neighborhood, and spending the rest of his time working without pay in Haiti, mainly treating peasants who were dislocated by a hydroelectric dam. And he was quite happy with his life in medicine: "I don't know why everybody isn't excited by it."

His day job in Boston was as professor of both medicine and medical anthropology at Harvard Medical School, where, outside the door of the social work department at the Brigham and Women's Hospital, the following message was unsigned:

JOE

OUT	IN
cold	warm
their drugs	our drugs
½ gal vodka	6 pack bud

Below this message, someone else's scrawl says: "Why do I know Paul Farmer wrote this?" This message is pretty quickly deciphered by anyone familiar with day care shelters (to one of which Joe was being sent), which rarely allow the use of alcohol (such as a six-pack of Budweiser) by their clients. Farmer's cryptic but pragmatic appeal was to allow Joe some beer so he would be warm and take his medications.

It is difficult to keep from thinking of Farmer as a latter-day Albert Schweitzer. Like Schweitzer, he is a multi-faceted genius, with great energy and the discipline to focus his efforts. He has expanded the scope of his work beyond the confines of the mission field he has chosen, and he selected associates whose interests and talents complemented his own. One of these was Jim Kim, who was more inclined to take a global perspective on things. At one point, they needed money to meet their obligations, and here Jim "had an alternate vision." He had been courting the Gates Foundation and they discussed how much money to ask for. Paul suggested two to four million dollars. "No," Jim said, "We're going to ask for forty-five million."

They did receive the larger sum, which was used to combat tuberculosis resistant to multiple drugs (MDR-TB), through programs in Peru, Haiti, and the former Soviet Union. But Farmer pursued his work among the poor with his own vision. His religion is said to be a bit unorthodox, but the nature of his work requires strong beliefs. While driving by the poor people of Haiti on a dirt road, Kidder said, "If you've done it unto the least of them, you've done it unto me." Farmer identified it as Matthew twenty-five, quoted the entire passage, and added, "*Then* it says, Inasmuch as you did it *not*, you're screwed."

Like Sir William Osler, Farmer is eminently quotable, and Kidder has transcribed many memorable lines. Like some chief residents I have known, he had his own collection of sayings. "*Love, ID*," ("ID" is medical slang for the subspecialty of Infectious Disease) is used as a tag line to end a consultation with a difficult suggestion, and also to punctuate "hard sayings" in conversation. "O for the P" is an abbreviation for "Options for the Poor" (who need more options). Kidder relates, "A young assistant of his once said to him, in exasperation, that he had no priorities. That wasn't true, he replied. Patients came first, prisoners second, and students third." (This almost sounds like Jesus replying to one of his questioners.) In watching nuns doing menial chores for migrant laborers, he said, "A reluctance to do scut work is why a lot of my peers don't stick with this line of work." In discussing some of the many frustrations involved in taking care of the poor in Haiti, he said, "I have fought for *my whole life* a long defeat... I'm not going to stop because we keep losing. Now I actually think sometimes we may win. I don't dislike victory." And Kidder comes up with a few quotable lines himself: "Farmer wasn't put on earth to make anyone feel comfortable, except for those lucky enough to be his patients."

Another of his abbreviations is WL, meaning "White Liberal," and he uses it in the same way that Martin Luther King, Jr., alluded to the white moderate in his letter from the Birmingham jail, saying the greatest stumbling block for the Negro was not the member of the White Citizens' Council or Ku Klux Klan but the white moderate, who was more devoted to order than to justice.

Farmer maintains that he loves WLs, even though they think that all the world's problems can be solved at no cost to themselves. He counters that there is much to be said for sacrifice, remorse, and pity. "It's what separates us from roaches."

As active as he has been in public health issues, Farmer's preference has been the treatment of individual patients; but individuals sometimes provide the incentive to address general problems. Multiple-drug-resistant tuberculosis posed a problem in Peru in the 1990s, exacerbated by the refusal of government health officials to admit the problem existed. Father Jack Roussin, a friend of Farmer's and a member of the board of directors of Partners in Health, left Boston to serve a parish in Carabayllo, on the outskirts of Lima, and he encouraged his friends to start a project in his new parish. There didn't appear to be a problem with tuberculosis, because of a new TB control program assisted by the World Health Organization. But Father Jack became ill and died a month after being transported back to the Brigham at Boston, where tuberculosis was diagnosed and then treated with the standard program of four first-line TB drugs. Shortly after his death, culture and sensitivity tests showed that Father Jack's tuberculosis bacilli had been resistant to all four drugs. Since he had never been treated for tuberculosis before, the only way he could have contracted such a resistant bug was to have caught it from someone else, apparently in Carabayllo.

But the official party line was that there were no treatment failures in Peru on the standard program. Farmer worked through a local project director, who visited government clinics to ask about resistant cases, and he was sometimes told they had things that would interest him, but which couldn't be shown to him. Charts would be opened in front of him, but not shown to him, so he learned to read them upside down. He then located ten patients and obtained sputum specimens. But he couldn't get cultures done in Peru, so Farmer carried them back to Boston in his suitcase and got the cultures done at the Massachusetts State Lab, using his position on the state tuberculosis commission to label the specimens, "Paul Farmer, TB commissioner."

All ten specimens showed resistance to all five first-line drugs. Drug resistance had usually been due to development of resistance to drugs one at a time when patients failed to take their full prescribed dose; but Farmer determined that these patients had been compliant with the World Health Organization's DOTS (directly observed treatment of short-course chemotherapy) and had then been retreated with the same regimen, going from having organisms resistant to one or two drugs to having formidable bugs resistant to all five first-line drugs. Under these circumstances, more expensive second-line drugs are indicated; but the WHO policy was to "prioritize" its resources; in other words, discontinue all treatment for those with resistant organisms.

Here, Farmer and Partners in Health found themselves pitted against the system; the Peruvian government was heavily invested in the DOTS program and it was reluctant to acknowledge a problem that would call for more resources. As it turned out, Farmer and his associate Jim Kim each worked in his own way: Farmer consulted on the management of one particular patient – the daughter of one of the Peruvian TB doctors – who had multiple-drug-resistant TB and recommended a combination of second-line drugs. Kim focused on the big picture, utilizing what Farmer called, "The big-shot strategy." He began to lobby WHO for the inclusion of second-line drugs on the official list of essential drugs. Then he was able to get generic drug manufacturers to produce and sell the drugs at lower prices. And they made progress. Kim and Farmer worked together, but one observer said, "It was eighty-five percent Jim."

One wonders how such focus on his mission could be reconciled with a personal life. First, there is the story of Ophelia Dahl, who declined his proposal of marriage. She first met Farmer when she was a volunteer for Eye Care Haiti, staying a week at Eye Care house in Mirebalais, Haiti. She was from Buckinghamshire, England, the daughter of Patricia Neal, the movie actress who won an Oscar for her role in *Hud*, and Roald Dahl, author of *Charlie and the Chocolate Factory*. After trying to make a phone call to her father, she spotted a pale young man on the balcony of Eye Care House and then, doing "what any well-bred English girl would do," she stepped up and introduced herself. She was eighteen, he was twenty-three, and when she left to return to England, she said she would go into a pre-med program. As it turned out, she and Farmer became two of the founders of Partners in Health, the organization through which they work to deliver health care to the poor throughout the world. She is now the Director of PIH. She and her domestic partner, Lisa Frantzis, have one child.

Paul Farmer eventually married a Haitian anthropologist, Didi Bertrand, "the most beautiful woman in Cange," in 1996, in front of a crowd of four thousand people. They now have three children, two of them adopted. They have recently moved to Rwanda because they considered Haiti to be unsafe for raising a family.

They have had a complicated life. Five years after publication of *Mountains Beyond Mountains*, he and his wife were spending half the week in Kigali, where their daughter was in school, and half the week in the staff quarters of the Rwinkwavu Hospital in Rwanda. They know many aspects of complexity, one of which was explained by a woman in Haiti who was one of the subjects of a study to determine whether compliance was determined by beliefs. In a study group of one hundred Haitians, it was found that whether they thought tuberculosis came from germs or sorcery made no difference as to whether their tuberculosis was cured. One elderly woman told him that she wasn't stupid and that she knew that coughing up germs caused tuberculosis. But she also said that she believed in sorcery, she knew who had sent her sickness to her, and she was going to get her back.

In response to this paradoxical announcement, she was asked why she continued to take her medicines if she believed someone had used sorcery to cause her illness.

"Honey," she replied, "are you incapable of complexity?"

And finally, Kidder used the following lines from T. S. Eliot's "The Dry Salvages" as one of his two epigraphs:

> *...And right action is freedom*
> *From past and future also.*
> *For most of us, this is the aim*
> *Never here to be realized;*
> *Who are only undefeated*
> *Because we have gone on trying...*

Paul Farmer continues to go on trying. As of 2009, Partners in Health had 11,000 employees in forty-nine health centers and hospitals in eleven countries, with adequate funding for the first time, proving that such "untreatable" diseases as multiple-drug resistant tuberculosis and AIDS can indeed be treated effectively. If it can be done in Haiti, it can be done anywhere.

NONFICTION

Should this section be titled, "Essays"? Some of the books are collections of essays originally published in magazines and journals. Others are lengthier and might be referred to as "History." Others are just lengthier for good reasons. It is a pretty grab-bag lot. I have no fondness for a word like nonfiction, which describes by exclusion, and I would welcome a better one. In the meantime, there is a rich field to survey.

Essays themselves are so well accepted in the literature of medicine that a recent anthology, *The Best American Medical Writing 2009* (Kaplan Publishing) limited itself to essays, describing many aspects of contemporary medical care and concerns. The essays reviewed in this collection are limited, rather arbitrarily, to collections of essays; and they validate the inclusion of various forms of nonfiction among the works generally considered as imaginative writing in the world of literature.

Quite a few collections of essays that might be described as medical detective stories are to be found in a recent glance at the "Medicine section" of one of the book store chains. I counted some two hundred titles in one such section of a fairly representative store recently, indicating what must be quite some popular interest in reading about medicine. This collection of reviews includes a prototype of the genre, Berton Roueché's

The Medical Detectives, and a more recent example, written by a physician, Lisa Sanders' *Every Patient Tells a Story: Medical Mysteries and the Art of Diagnosis.* Dr. Sanders' background in television broadcasting and writing for the *New York Times Magazine* gives her a unique perspective and forms a counterpoint to Roueché's stories from previous generations.

Lewis Thomas set a high standard with the appearance of his *Notes of a Biology Watcher* in the *New England Journal of Medicine* in the 1970s. Whenever I spotted one of these essays, I read it first, and not surprisingly, they were quickly collected into a few books. He ventured beyond the essay form with some autobiographical recollections, *The Youngest Science: Notes of a Medicine-Watcher,* providing an authoritative perspective on recent medical history.

The diagnostic challenges of neurology serve as a springboard for essays that Oliver Sacks continues to write in the *New Yorker. The Man who Mistook His Wife for a Hat* is an early and classic example of his ability to bring to the lay reader the fascination of a field that attracts physicians to its intellectual puzzles.

Beginning to publish in the *New Yorker* while still in surgical training, Atul Gawande has emerged as an energetic and articulate interpreter of current developments in medicine to the general public. Having started with his first collection of reviews, I had a difficult time ignoring either of his subsequent collections; so I included all three. He lends first-person authenticity with his personal accounts of practice in surgery, but he also plays the reporter, as in his travels in India, where he seized the opportunity to describe the immunization campaign that is attempting to eradicate polio.

The more general field of genetics and its implication for medicine and the world is explored by Philip R. Reilly in *The Strongest Boy in the World: How Genetic Information is Reshaping Our Lives.* Some of the essays might seem a bit removed from the world of medicine until one reads in the account of the genetics of rice that the recent definition of the rice genome might be "the most important advance in human health in history." Board-certified in internal medicine and clinical genetics, Dr. Reilly is also a member of the Massachusetts bar. Having served as CEO of Interleukin Genetics Inc. and also on the Harvard faculty, his eclectic background gives the reader an opportunity to take the long view and make some new connections.

Some subjects permit more leisurely, book-length treatment. Among these is the Civil War, represented in this collection by one selection of diary entries by a surgeon in the Confederate Army. It isn't the most dramatic of Civil War accounts, but even one of the less disruptive and bloody war experiences is enough to convince the present-day reader that this war was one we would rather read about than live through.

One of the major figures in both literature and medicine in the nineteenth century was Oliver Wendell Holmes. His account of his visit to England in his later years is a minor piece, admittedly an indulgent name-dropping piece, but one that allows the reader to accompany the genial autocrat of the breakfast table on a triumphal tour of a part of the old world, picking up a couple of honorary doctorates on the way. In these latter days of more convenient travel, many of us, including myself, can compare notes with Dr. Holmes on his procession.

Books on the shelf sometimes take on a life of their own. I bought a used 1935 edition of *Rats, Lice and History* by Hans Zinsser in 1976, recognizing it as a classic and intending to read it directly. And for thirty-five years it sat on my shelf; my familiarity with the spine of the book almost led me to think I had actually read it. Finally, in collecting these reviews, the time had come. Never too late. Its whimsical approach calls for leisurely enjoyment, though not necessarily with such a lengthy incubation period. In consideration of books on the shelf: somehow I have two copies of the 1896 edition of Oliver Wendell Holmes' *Medical Essays*; in reading through one of the copies while thinking about Dr. Holmes, I discovered that I had to use a sharp knife to cut several of the folded pages of *Medical Essays* in order to read them in 2010. Again, better late than never. Let no published page go unread, or at least unskimmed.

DNA appears prominently in at least two reviews, those of James Watson and Arthur Kornberg, both Nobel Prize winners for their discoveries of what Watson's colleague Francis Crick pronounced as "the secret of life." If a previous generation of physicians had the privilege of working through the discovery and implementation of antibiotics, my generation could be termed the "DNA generation." These books are meant more for entertainment than the lectures on the subject were; perhaps in the books we can round out a few points we may have missed.

The enthusiasm that almost all readers have had for Anne Fadiman's *The Spirit Catches You and You Fall Down: A Hmong Child, Her American Doctors, and the Collision of Two Cultures* has left me feeling like a skeptic among true believers. One's personal experiences can mar an appreciation for certain subjects; I wouldn't feel particularly comfortable at a malpractice plaintiff attorneys' meeting. But this is my problem. The book is a good one and it merits its acclaim, but I was on the side of the unfortunate pediatrician all the way.

One of my mentors used to quote a line he attributed to W. C. Fields: "I know that the doctors and the undertakers are in cahoots. But it hurts my feelings when they wink at each other." So instructed, I have always been discreet in my greetings to funeral directors. Thomas Lynch, an Irish poet and a Michigan mortician, reminds us that if doctors and undertakers are not in cahoots, they do share a number of professional concerns. If we don't wink, we should at least nod.

In the current climate of tell-it-all journalism, Cole Porter's wry observation that "anything goes" seems to take on more and more meaning. Fewer stories go untold. There are exceptions. The story of the Great Influenza Pandemic of 1918-1920 was suppressed to the extent that it is still not represented in our collective consciousness in proportion to its impact on our world. As an example, my parents were about seven to ten years of age at the time, but they never talked about it to me, except to mention a familial fear of pneumonia. Among the recent efforts to give this story its due is John M. Barry's *The Great Influenza: The Epic Story of the Deadliest Plague in History.* To my mind, this account is less focused than it might have been, but it tells a number of dramatic stories we need to hear.

Essays both short and long seem to proliferate in spite of concerns about the lack of literacy in our culture, not least in the field of medicine. The works reviewed in this section, though only a sample of this genre, indicate its popularity. Perhaps this is surprising but it is also gratifying.

ONE MAN'S CIVIL WAR

I ACTED FROM PRINCIPLE
The Civil War Diary of Dr. William M. McPheeters,
Confederate Surgeon in the Trans-Mississippi
Edited by Cynthia Dehaven Pitcock
and Bill J. Gurley

The first image of the Civil War surgeon that comes to mind may well be that of a bearded man wearing an apron, wielding a bloody meat cleaver with unwashed hands, amputating the limb of a screaming soldier being restrained by others, in the midst of other victims. The photograph on the cover of a recent diary, *I Acted From Principle: The Civil War Diary of Dr. William M. McPheeters, Confederate Surgeon in the Trans-Mississippi*, edited by Cynthia Dehaven Pitcock and Bill J. Gurley (University of Arkansas Press, 2002) shows us that Dr. McPheeters was bearded. As for the rest of the picture of a Civil War surgeon at work: gloves weren't used; instruments were probably wiped and washed and/or rinsed, but certainly not autoclaved. Chloroform was generally available, and Dr. McPheeters alludes to its use elsewhere; screams were emitted before or after being chloroformed, sometimes on learning of the amputation. Restraint was often required for induction of anesthesia. For the most part, Dr. McPheeters spares us these assaults on our senses. He did have field hospital experience and the day of his first exposure to battle (The Battle of Helena, July 4, 1863) is described in what for him was a lengthy entry of two pages, in which he simply states that his first amputation was the left arm of a young man from Little Rock, and that he was thus engaged for the duration of the battle, subsequently attending to the wounded until 2 A.M., finally retiring "tired and sick at heart."

Ten days after the battle, he reported amputating a man's leg above a knee that had been shattered by the screw cap from a shell; the man died two days later, and in the absence of a minister, Dr. McPheeters read him passages from the Bible, trying "to point him to the Lamb of God as best I could. Another patient also died. Two young ladies from Helena came out and took dinner with us."

Not all injured limbs were amputated. On July 21 he treated a compound fracture of the upper third of the femur with a "double inclined plane."

Who was Dr. McPheeters and what was his background? The editors dug through a number of libraries to present a biographical introduction to the diary, which began June 1, 1863. (This is one of my books where the notes in the back are underlined almost as heavily as the main text.) He grew up in North Carolina, received his undergraduate degree at the University of North Carolina in Chapel Hill, and then his MD degree from University of Pennsylvania College Medicine in Philadelphia. After a year of residency at Old Blockley Hospital in Philadelphia, he traveled by riverboat to St. Louis, where he opened an office and waited about two months before he saw his first patient; a desperately ill but penniless boatman. On October 15, 1842, he recorded having been practicing medicine in St. Louis for one year, booking four hundred and seven dollars, and receiving only thirty-eight dollars, but also receiving more in furniture.

He joined the Medical Society of Missouri, attended lectures at the Medical Department of Kemper College while waiting for patients, and joined the Presbyterian church downtown on Eighth and Pine Streets. He helped establish the first free clinic for the poor west of the Mississippi. (There were a number of opportunities for historic firsts at this time.) He circulated in local society and met, among others, Miss Julia Dent, who was later to be Mrs. U. S. Grant, who would prove to be a useful connection. He married Miss Pink Seldon, who died in childbirth ten months later. He remarried in 1849, forming a union that was to last fifty-five years until his death. Sallie Buchanan was a proud and spirited beauty; their wedding was hailed as one of the most important of the social season.

In advancing his practice, he had become coeditor of the *St. Louis Medical and Surgical Journal* and had helped form a statewide medical society. He and his coeditors addressed the problems of tuberculosis and cholera. They suggested that the city's polluted drinking water might be due to the lead pipes and they called for drastic measures in public sanitation in a city with no sewer system and few paved streets. There were about fifty physicians in St. Louis when McPheeters arrived; ten years later, the city's population had tripled to seventy thousand with the arrival of Irish and German immigrants, whom he described as "poorly nourished, filthy, and poverty stricken." He remained in town to treat cholera when a quarter of the city's population fled the epidemic, which took 8,108 lives in 1849.

He became professor of pathology, anatomy, and clinical medicine in the Medical Department of St. Louis University in 1849; served on the City Board of Health; and became director of the Marine Hospital in St. Louis, all while continuing his now prosperous private practice.

The issue of slavery divided the city in the 1850s. Although many wealthy St. Louisans had household slaves, the McPheeters' did not; they hired two live-in Irish women and a German manservant. However, he failed to conceal his sympathy for the Rebel cause and in 1861, he was arrested and required to sign an oath of allegiance to the U.S. government. He refused, knowing that this refusal would eventually lead to his imprisonment. There is no more frightening account in the book than that of the entry into his house of Federal agents, in the middle of the day, to loot its contents – including over two thousand dollars worth of furniture – when one of his children was critically ill. There was a second raid on February 19 and everything else was taken, leaving only the bare walls. Between the two raids, the young son had died.

"I acted from principle," Dr. McPheeters wrote. After a second arrest he again refused to sign an oath of allegiance. He left his family, leaving a note for the dean of the medical school, which was read to his anatomy class the next morning, and he escaped into the night, riding horseback to Richmond, where he joined the army of the Confederacy and was sent to Mississippi and then to Arkansas. On what principle did he act? He cited the right of states to secede peacefully from the union, for whatever reason. But the fact that he was from North Carolina cannot have been irrelevant, nor, indeed, the plundering of his house.

Dr. McPheeters' wife, Sallie, and his children stayed in St. Louis almost until the end of the war. She visited him in the summer of 1863 to tell him of the death of one of their sons, traveling by boat on the Mississippi River. Here she was, alone among the women from the North. But one of them was Mrs. U. S. Grant, who was told of the "ostracized rebel woman on board."

Having asked the captain to send Dr. McPheeters' wife to her, Mrs. Grant introduced herself and asked the Confederate wife to join her. Remembering Dr. McPheeters as a bachelor in the St. Louis scene, she told Mrs. McPheeters not to let the women annoy her. She would see that Mrs. McPheeters wouldn't be molested, and on arrival in Vicksburg, she would see to it that General Grant would take her to her husband in his buggy.

General Grant may have been otherwise engaged, but Mrs. McPheeters did indeed find her husband at his duties outside Helena. This was some two weeks after the battle and Dr. McPheeters himself had had several personal encounters with the Yankees. Two days after the battle, a squad of federal cavalry came to his hospital, which had been left behind by the retreating Confederate troops. Col. Powell Clayton[8], in charge of

---

[8] Col. Clayton remained in Arkansas after the war and became governor and then U.S. senator from Arkansas. His brother William Clayton served as U.S. Attorney for the Western District of Arkansas when Judge Isaac Parker was on the bench; and it is his home in Fort Smith that is now open to the public as the "Clayton House."

the cavalry squad, asked why a white flag had been raised, and Dr. McPheeters replied that the yellow flag hadn't been honored and he wanted to prevent injuries. After a parley, General Ross offered to send provisions and to forward a letter to his wife. There was some conversation and some whiskey was drunk before the Yankees departed. Two weeks later, Dr. McPheeters was captured by a Federal scout and taken to his colonel, who promptly released him when he learned who he was.

Dr. McPheeters had requested that he be attached to the service of General Sterling Price in the hopes that he might make his way back to Missouri. The remainder of the war found Price's division marching down to southwest Arkansas, into Louisiana and then back north through Arkansas to Missouri, then back south to Texas, finishing up in southwest Arkansas. There were battles at Mansfield, Louisiana; Pleasant Hill, Louisiana; Jenkins Ferry, Arkansas; Pilot Knob, Missouri; Westport, Missouri; Mine Creek, Kansas; Newtonia, Missouri; and various other skirmishes. The battles all required the surgeon's services: amputations, setting fractures, and elevating depressed skulls. His reflections on these occasions were generally brief, but similar to other historical accounts that have come down to us. At Jenkins Ferry, April 30, 1864, he rode over the battlefield, which was a rain-soaked quagmire extending for miles along the Saline River valley. Thinking it incredible that men could wade and fight in such mud, he found it a dreadful sight, riding among men, both dead and dying, whom he had seen and talked with only a few hours before. "War is a dreadful thing."

His diary ran from June 1, 1863, to June 20, 1865; during these two years his battlefield surgery and attendance may have totaled thirty days, depending on how it was defined. Most of the time, however, was spent accompanying the army on the march, with long stretches in camp with nothing much to do except read, smoke, and make conversation. In camp near Camden, Arkansas, June 6, 1864: "A dull, disagreeable day in camp." That day, he "ate, smoked, slept, and read, finishing the *Last Days of Jesus* and commenced Cummings' *Great Preparation*." He visited

145

with some officers, and then after finishing his tea, he paid a visit to Mrs. Churchill and spent an hour with her.

Disease killed more soldiers in the Civil War than did combat wounds, but the diary tells relatively little about mortality from disease. Perhaps this was because surgery was something he did and disease was something he mostly just watched. One wouldn't expect a scholarly analysis under these conditions. There is no evidence of a running log or statistical report.

His wife and two surviving children, Maggy and Sally, joined him near the end of the war when his wife Sallie (mother and daughter had different spellings of their names) was banished from St. Louis. She wrote a rather spirited cover note to go along with a letter to her husband in December, 1864, addressing the commander of the Federal Department of Arkansas as someone whom her husband had held in the highest regard. She added that she hoped the war hadn't changed him, as it had changed so many other gentlemen to fiends, asking further that he forward any return letter her husband might send her. For this, he would have the thanks of a Rebel "though she be."

Perhaps she was "going for a 'T,'" as basketball coaches will sometimes deliberately incur a technical foul. In any event, she was imprisoned for two days and then banished on a boat down the Mississippi, with her two daughters, to Gaines Landing, from where she travelled west to Monticello, Arkansas, then met her husband a few miles farther on in Warren.

At the conclusion of the war, the family travelled by boat from Camden to New Orleans and then back home to St. Louis, where they stayed for a short time in a hotel and then in the home of a friend who was away in the country. They then reoccupied their old home on Tenth and Pine.

Dr. McPheeters resumed his distinguished career, teaching at a medical school until he took a position as full-time medical examiner for the St. Louis Mutual Insurance Company. He and Sallie commemorated their golden wedding anniversary with a "celebrated affair" in their Pine Street home. (They had now moved out to 3452 Pine Street.) The St. Louis Medical Society

146

honored him and three other elderly doctors in a banquet at the Planters House Hotel in 1903 when he was eighty-eight years old. He died of pneumonia two years later and the St. Louis Medical Society remembered him in a memorial addresses as a "superbly trained physician, an innovative editor, a medical educator, and a tireless public servant."

He was also recalled as a faithful wartime diarist and a disciplined soldier in a lost cause, but his service in the Confederate army was only mentioned "with great tact."

Those with an interest in the Trans-Mississippi Department of the Confederate army, Civil War medicine, and the medical history in St. Louis, are fortunate that an account such as Dr. McPheeters' has been preserved and presented with such skill and care. (One fears that the complete unedited transcript might be as tedious as the long months he spent in winter quarters.) Such historical records are all the more important in view of the lack of much in the way of surviving landmarks. The tracks of the army of the Trans-Mississippi were hardly more permanent than were the teepees of the Sioux. And a recent visit to St. Louis confirmed that the city grew far too fast for anything to remain of Dr. McPheeters' house, or the hospital where he worked, in what is now downtown St. Louis. But we do have these pocket-sized pages, sewn together, inscribed in miniature with a steel pen, now transcribed and edited with scholarly care. We're lucky.

THE AUTOCRAT IN ENGLAND

OUR HUNDRED DAYS IN EUROPE
By Oliver Wendell Holmes

Dedicated bookworms know that a book transcends social, economic, professional, and temporal barriers. Having spent some time in England, I can compare notes with the nineteenth-century Autocrat of the Breakfast Table, Dr. Oliver Wendell Holmes, as though we were old friends, comparing his travels with mine a century later. Not only that, I can close the book any time I wish without appearing to be impolite. My wife, Mary, and I spent a year in England in our youth (age thirty-six, in my case) and returned thirty-three years later for a less extended stay. *Our Hundred Days in Europe* (The *Physician Travelers* series, Arno Press and the New York Times, 1971) describes Holmes' return in 1887 after his first visit fifty years earlier. We visited many of the same sites. The major differences were 121 years between his return visit and ours; and his astonishingly busy schedule of visits with the great people of literature, medicine, and public life in England. And the purpose of his visit was to receive honorary degrees from Oxford and Cambridge.

Holmes was best known as a poet and author, and many of his poems are American classics: "Old Ironsides," "The Deacon's Masterpiece, or The Wonderful One-Hoss Shay," "The Chambered Nautilus." His essays collected in *The Autocrat of the Breakfast Table* are perhaps more famous than read nowadays. But he was also a distinguished professor of anatomy at Harvard Medical School. In his 1843 essay, "The Contagiousness of Puerperal Fever," he stated, "The disease known as Puerperal

Fever is so far contagious as to be frequently carried from patient to patient by physicians and nurses." He and Ignaz Semmelweis in Europe were the early proponents of physicians' washing their hands before delivering a baby, a practice that saved many lives but was not generally accepted for several decades.

Holmes was a good entertainer and he knew it and loved it. He was one of those who makes the appropriate gestures of self-deprecation without expecting them to be taken seriously. Nobody cared – almost.

My introduction to Dr. Holmes, many years ago, was in Catherine Drinker Bowen's *Yankee from Olympus*, a biography of his son Oliver Wendell Holmes, Jr., an associate justice of the Supreme Court. It was apparent to this young reader that Wendell Jr. had a daddy problem. The Dr. Holmes who sticks in my mind is the father who receives a telegram that his son had been shot through the neck, but the wound wasn't thought to be mortal. Dr. Holmes then sets out on a search for his son that is to last eight days, going from one war scene to another. He finally finds him on a train, and he and his son exchange polite greetings, calling each other "Wendell" and "Father."

Much to Wendell's embarrassment, his father writes an article for the *Atlantic*, "My Hunt after the Captain." To Wendell, the war was too horrible to talk about. To his father, it was interesting material for his public to read about: "For this our son and brother was dead and is alive again, and was lost and is found... Lay him in his own bed, and let him sleep off his aches and weariness."

The article concluded with a melodramatic account of their greeting, calling each other "Boy" and "Dad." Wendell's reaction on reading this was that never in his life had he been called "Boy" by his father.

So I was prepared to take *Our Hundred Days in Europe* with a raised eyebrow. I was also prepared to grant a distinguished senior celebrity a bit of license. Although I sometimes fail, I think I have generally been polite, patient, and attentive to my elders; but I have always been quite aware that I was doing it. That said, it was worth the slight effort to follow Dr. Holmes' flowery style. "People,--the right kind of people,--meet at a dinner-party as two ships meet and pass each other other at sea," he wrote. "They exchange a few signals; ask each other's reckoning... [but] one or both may remember the hour passed together all their days."

Of course, Holmes is indebted to Henry Wadsworth Longfellow's lines from *Tales of a Wayside Inn*, published in 1873, which I learned to quote even before I read *Yankee from Olympus*:

> *Ships that pass in the night, and speak each other in passing,*
> *Only a signal shown and distant voice in the darkness;*
> *So the ocean of life, we pass and speak one another,*
> *Only a look and a voice, then darkness again and silence.*

Far be it from me to begrudge a senior author from a previous century a bit of indulgence; would that I could indulge myself, as I do in these reviews, half as gracefully as the famous Autocrat.

Holmes traveled with his daughter Amelia; it is a testament to his stamina that he managed the social schedule he describes: engagements for breakfast, luncheon, tea, and dinner, day after day. Of course, he throws in in a bit of name-dropping, but I am interested to see whom he met: Dr. Priestley, Sir James Paget, Sir William Gull. Priestley is credited with the discovery of oxygen, Paget gave his name to Paget's Disease (a disorder leading to dense, brittle bones), and Gull first identified hypothyroidism, so all three are well known to the present-day physician. A bit more familiar are Robert Browning and Oscar Wilde.

The people Holmes encountered are long since gone, but the places are still there, relatively unchanged. Having recently visited Bath, I was interested in Holmes' surprise to find how deeply old civilizations tend to be buried. "Everyone seems to have lived in the cellar," and it's hard to believe that the cellar floor was once the surface of the earth.

One envies Holmes' visit to Salisbury with an English friend as his companion and guide. They took a room in Salisbury Close for a week and made excursions from there. He is frank in his admiration, considering Salisbury Cathedral to be the apple of the eye of England, with Salisbury Close the white of the eye. As at Stratford, he wrote, it was difficult to awake each morning and find that he wasn't dreaming.

Even with a hundred-day trip, Holmes lamented the lack of time for his visit, and his description of museum fatigue – a visit to the Louvre being more tiring than spending the same amount of time walking the wards of a hospital – corresponds with my own experience.

We recently spent some time standing in front of the reproduction of Trajan's Column in the Victoria and Albert Museum. I was interested to see that Dr. Holmes gave first place among his recollections of the "South Kensington Museum" to the long array of soldiers portrayed in their march around the circumference of this column.

Who would not envy Dr. Holmes this trip? It was surely an ego trip for one who made only a token effort to conceal his high tolerance for flattery. Compliments and pleasant journeys are blessings to be enjoyed at the time; Holmes knew how to enjoy them. Like Ecclesiastes, he appears to have believed that "every man should eat and drink, and enjoy the good of all his labor, it is the gift of God." His wife died after he returned, and then his daughter and traveling companion Amelia also died. But he enjoyed his trip to England in 1886. His account wasn't one of his more significant works. But it succeeds in conveying the *joi de vivre* that he maintained into his later years. Today's reader can take it as a pleasant conversation with the old master.

HISTORY, AS SEEN FROM THE HEALTH DEPARTMENT

RATS, LICE AND HISTORY
By Hans Zinsser

Typhus is one of those diseases that medical students today will read about but, unless they venture far afield, they will never see it. And that is a good thing. The sum total of human misery and loss caused by its epidemics of the past five centuries staggers the imagination. Should any movie director present a realistic depiction of its horrors, it would be unbearable. A detailed written description of case after case, epidemic after epidemic, war after war would soon numb the reader beyond the point of comprehension. And so it is that a book written in 1934 and still in print in 2010 delivers a story that the reader can absorb. The archaic wit of Hans Zinsser's *Rats, Lice and History* (Little Brown and Company, 1935) makes it a unique work among the histories of disease. Consider the subtitle of *Rats, Lice and History: Being a Study in Biography, which, after Twelve Preliminary Chapters Indispensable for the Preparation of the Lay Reader, Deals With the Life History of TYPHUS FEVER.*

This isn't the prose style of 1934. It is closer to the style of the eighteenth century, consciously modeled after *Tristram Shandy*, by Laurence Sterne. But *Tristram Shandy* wasn't even a typical example of the writing of its day. An unsigned reviewer wrote in 1760 that it "affects (and not unsuccessfully) to please, by a contempt of all the rules observed in other writings, and therefore cannot justly have its merit measured by them."[9]

The reader must be prepared for digressions and discursions. Ostensibly a biography of one particular disease, this biography doesn't appear until the last third of the book. The reader can take the entire work as a history of disease in general, though the writer disclaims any responsibility for being systematic or comprehensive.

The preliminary digressions cover several prerequisites to a consideration of typhus: the concept of parasitism; the association of wars with disease; the nature of viruses and viral diseases as they were understood at the time; the louse, which is infected by the virus and transmits it to man; and the rat, which may also harbor the virus and carry its virus-infected fleas to man. And finally, the last few chapters deal with the disease itself. But though the self-deprecating author declares this a digression – he only wrote this to "suit his fancy" – it is actually the outline for a systematic and comprehensive review of the disease that was his major professional preoccupation.

The preface includes an assertion of the versatility of the human mind, protesting the current bias against a specialist having any interest beyond his chosen field, and acknowledging that writing this book would expose him to the risk of being considered less of a bacteriologist. But since one can only work ten hours and sleep eight out of a twenty-four day, he deemed it worth the risk.

As would be expected, the scientific aspects of a work written in 1934 are a bit dated. Zinsser himself had just recently established that Brill disease is a recrudescent form of epidemic typhus; but it wasn't yet known that murine typhus is a different disease and has a lower mortality rate than epidemic typhus. And, of course, antibiotic therapy was unanticipated in 1934.

But the history of the disease is told with just enough irony to be accepted as the all-seeing eye of the senior investigator, not

---

[9] From an unsigned notice in the *Royal Female Magazine,* I (February 1760), 56, cited by Howes A. / *The Critical Heritage.* NY: Routledge, 1996, p.53

the smart-aleck humor of the insensitive. Humor is a risky tool, but by and large, it comes off well three quarters of a century after publication. The footnotes are often humorous ones, and they are sometimes lengthy, but they do tread the margin. For "pure saprophyte" he notes that if the reader doesn't understand this word, it is too bad. And in another place, he appends a two-page footnote in German, untranslated. One of his most risky entries is his footnote on epidemic disease in war, where he declares that war is now, as ever, seventy-five percent a problem of engineering and sanitation and less than twenty-five percent military. And then, having served with distinction in the Spanish-American War and World War I, he adds that the apparent courage of the American soldiers in World War I was due not so much to the knowledge that the German troops were in front of them, but that the surgeons of America, with their sleeves rolled up, were behind them.

Though he maintains that typhus didn't appear in epidemic form until 1489 and 1490, when soldiers brought it from Cyprus to Spain during the fight for Granada, he surveys the earliest history of bacterial diseases, asserting that they have always attacked the higher forms of life. Evidence is cited of chronic osteomyelitis of the spine of a reptile that lived 21 million years ago; the finding of tuberculosis in the Egyptian mummies is also mentioned. Of course, there were the Biblical plagues. What were the diagnoses? So uncertain is our historic data and so primitive were early diagnostic methods that we may never know.

The Unitarian theory of disease doesn't go much further in analysis of historic epidemics than it does in today's geriatric practice. When the "triple scourges" of war, pestilence, and starvation were unleashed, nothing was pretty or simple. During the horrible Thirty Years' War in that "most miserable century" for man, the seventeenth century, typhus was the predominant disease in the first part of the war, and bubonic plague was more prevalent in the latter years. Accompanying these, however, were dysentery, typhoid fever, diphtheria, smallpox, scarlet fever, and others that may have been a bit less deadly. Sieges were a catalyst for the spread of disease, and in the siege of Montpellier in 1623, a contemporary description was clearly that of typhus – red or black spots like flea bites from the fourth to the ninth day, covering the body but especially the loins, chest, and neck.

Numbers, though by no means precise of course, were overwhelming – for instance, 60,000 deaths in Lyons just in 1628. For sheer numbers and for various reasons, Russia was the site of enormous casualties on both sides in the Napoleonic invasion; and from 1917 to 1921 there were at least 25 million cases of typhus alone, with perhaps three million deaths.

The story of lice necessarily reminds us of the relatively recent triumph of personal hygiene. The fact general lousiness was inevitable in the Middle Ages comes as no great surprise. But some of us need reminding that Samuel Pepys described in his diary how his wig had to be cleansed of its nits. And George Washington included among the "Rules of Civility" which he copied in his fourteenth year, that one shouldn't kill fleas, lice, or ticks in the sight of others.

Zinsser adds that the louse has now been banished from polite society, and even if a motor car may not be in every garage, there is always a bathtub in every residence. I usually skip over lists, inventories, and catalogs. But the amazing variety of blessings brought to the New World from the Old merits citation: "Culture and smallpox, the Christian religion and measles, rum, European quarrels, scarlet fever, sparrows, horses and donkeys, Anglo-Saxons, Irishmen, Jews, Negroes, trousers, influenza, wheat, brotherly love, gunpowder, and tuberculosis." In return, the Old World received gold, tobacco, syphilis, potatoes, and Indian corn at first. Later, America received even more bounty from across the ocean: "Industry, politics, capitalism, Communism, alcoholism, methodism, baptism, free verse, free love, psychoanalysis, educational systems, journalism, philanthropism, the camera, science, art, literature, football, rats, remittance men, gypsy moths, Russian princes, starlings, macaroni, Wiener Schnitzel, labor troubles, bankers and brokers, and so forth, and so forth." America has given in return:

"High tariffs, peanuts, phonographs, chewing gum, moving pictures, breakfast foods, heiresses, Christian Science, cocktail shakers, efficiency methods, and the boloney dollar." Here, he apologizes for the digression.

Could this provide the outline for a course in western civilization?

That typhus is a less prevalent and deadly scourge in the twenty-first century is due to many factors, among them, improved hygiene and sanitation, the availability of vaccines and antibiotics, and improved food production and nutrition. World War II and subsequent conflicts haven't been marked by the epidemics of previous wars. Zinsser foretold some of these advances after the effects of World War I with his observation that no one won that war except medical science. Although the gain wasn't worth the loss, mankind did retrieve significant knowledge about sanitation and medical science from this catastrophe.

Hans Zinsser was born in 1878 in New York to an affluent family of German immigrants; only German was spoken in the home until he was ten years old. His father was a manufacturing chemist, and the family also had a country home in Westchester, where Hans became an excellent horseman. His early education was in the home. He made annual trips to Europe until he was twenty years old, and he enrolled at Columbia at the age of seventeen. He initially studied literature and later switched to biology and then to medicine. After graduation from Columbia, he practiced medicine for a short time and then entered full-time academic work, teaching and doing research at Columbia, Stanford, and finally Harvard. In addition to his medical publications, he wrote articles for *The Atlantic Monthly* and also published a volume of poetry. He was a strong advocate of including science in a liberal arts education. He lived a little over two years after learning he had leukemia and he died at age sixty-one in 1940.

His textbook of bacteriology went through eight editions, and his textbook on immunology went through five editions. His two non-medical books were his autobiography, published in the year of his death, and *Rats, Lice and History,* in which, with a fine contempt of the rules of scientific writing, he has left us a classic in its own right. We will always have rats and lice with us; may typhus soon be consigned to history.

DETECTIVE STORIES

THE MEDICAL DETECTIVES
By Berton Roueché

EVERY PATIENT TELLS A STORY
Medical Mysteries and the Art of Diagnosis
By Lisa Sanders

"Mad Tom" was what we called one of our fellow interns who stubbornly persisted in maintaining a positive outlook in clear defiance of all the unwritten rules of doctors in training. When one of us would sign out to him on his night on call and wish him good luck, which meant having no admissions, he would respond, "Thanks. I hope I get some great cases!"

"Great cases" are what's fun about medicine. This is where "*æquanimitas*" kicks in. Illness and injury are unhappy events by definition, and the doctor who fails to understand their patients' distress is unfeeling. But the doctor who trudges to work feeling only the discomfort of the patients will become too depressed to function well. Call it equanimity, compartmentalization, or what you will, but the doctor who relishes the intellectual stimulus of the game is the one who will have more fun. Leaving home in the morning, I often asked myself, "How will I be entertained today?" A pharmaceutical representative told me one time about a rural family practitioner who played chess with the drug reps. Between exam rooms, he would pause briefly at the board, move one of his pieces, and disappear into another room to see his next patient. Needless to say, the doctor routinely won.

TAYLOR PREWITT

Diagnostic challenges have been celebrated in a spate of medical mystery books in recent years. Berton Roueché set the standard for this genre with his *Annals of Medicine* series that appeared in *The New Yorker* from the 1940s to the 1980s. These were collected into two volumes, *Medical Detectives* (Pocket Books, 1982) and a sequel, *Medical Detectives Volume II* (Pocket Books, 1986). Currently available is a 1991 version, which adds three previously uncollected stories to the twenty-two tales of the first volume, published by Plume, another division of Penguin Books. Roueché's term of office began about two decades before mine, so his accounts deal with medicine as I was supposed to know it. Re-reading them in retirement, there is often the pleasure of recollection, sometimes a better-late-than-never feeling of, "So that's what it was all about."

Many of Roueché's stories follow the pattern of the murder mystery with investigations of mysterious epidemics. The title of the first story, "Eleven Blue Men," recalls such Sherlock Holmes titles as "The Adventure of the Dancing Men," and "The Red-Headed League." In this case, the New York Department of Health was called in when several derelict men all became ill and cyanotic in the same New York City neighborhood within a matter of hours. All had become ill within thirty minutes of eating oatmeal in the Eclipse Cafeteria between seven-thirty and ten-thirty on the same morning. Food poisoning? Gas? Dope? A careful investigation disclosed that some of the oatmeal had inadvertently been salted with sodium nitrate, not sodium chloride (table salt), and the sodium nitrate had included small amounts of sodium nitrite, which can be poisonous. Like many murder mysteries, this one concluded with the detective's retrospective account of how he unraveled the case, saving the best for the last as Dr. Morris Greenberg addressed the question of why the men had used so *much* salt. He remembered having been told that they were all heavy drinkers, and he recalled clinical studies that had shown alcoholics have a low serum concentration of sodium and chloride. Any mammal, including man, with a deficiency of salt tries to obtain more of it. And, just as with Agatha Christie or Dick Francis, everything is tied up in a bow.

The sudden flash of intuition that solves a murder mystery or a medical mystery is the moment of drama in many stories, but the truth is more often found by painstaking attention to the routine of touching all the bases. In "A Rainy Day on the Vineyard," an outbreak of four cases of an undiagnosed febrile illness in the same house party is investigated by the Epidemiology Intelligence Service: Samples of pond water, the rotten log, and the earth at the septic tank were all obtained. Similarly, a complete set of "febrile agglutinins" – serological tests for various antibodies – was obtained. To the investigators' surprise, the only positive result was for tularemia. The investigator concluded that they were all astonished by the results. Tularemia wasn't really expected. But that was what it was.

Having been trained in the game of always proposing a diagnosis, like betting on a horse, I was interested in observing that the experts I consulted, and whom I respected and relied upon, rarely bothered with playing the game of betting on one specific diagnosis. Just as the director of the cardiac catheterization laboratory at St. Louis Children's Hospital in my medical school days, Alex Hartmann, sometimes became impatient with debates about the subtleties of the heart murmurs I had been recording – "Oh hell, let's just go to the cath lab," – so other consultants just wait for a definitive procedure or test, such as gastroscopy for a source of upper gastrointestinal bleeding. And so I often found it more expedient to tell a patient and family that we would just have to "wait and find out" what a coronary arteriogram would show.

The diagnosis of tularemia in this account is followed by a history of our knowledge of this disease. I wonder whether some of these chapters might provide better textbook descriptions for medical students than those of more pedestrian writers. "There is nothing natural about the transfer of the rabies virus," Roueché writes in "The Incurable Wound," his story of a case of rabies. "It wrings collaboration from its carrier hosts by torturing them into a homicidal fury."

Chapter 14, "The West Branch Study," is a story I first heard from Gene Page, whom I knew in Memphis in the late 1960s when we were both officers in the U.S. Public Health Service, fulfilling our two-year military obligation at the Memphis-Shelby County Health Department. (This two-year interval of military service has almost disappeared from doctors' resumés since the draft was discontinued in 1979.) Gene was in the Epidemiology Intelligence Service, which figures in many of Roueché's stories; I was in the Venereal Disease branch of the USPHS. Gene, a blonde-haired Floridian just under six feet tall, had played fullback for the Florida Gator team that had beaten Baylor in the 1960 Gator Bowl. On returning to Memphis after having been sent to West Branch, Michigan, to investigate an epidemic of hepatitis A, Gene showed us his series of slides. The pay-off slide showed a little man in a bakery, with his arms in a bucket of glaze, "up to his elbows," preparing to put the icing on doughnuts that would spread the hepatitis virus throughout the community. One of the other investigators sat and watched the icing process and reported that instead of using a pastry tube, he just used his bare hands after using them on the fried cakes, squeezing a handful of icing through his fingers. "It was horrifying. Page and I could hardly keep from shouting."

As in the case of the eleven blue men, some of these stories date back to the 1940s and 1950s, describing diseases now considered historical in the United States: typhoid, hookworm (trichinosis), and (with one notable recent exception) anthrax. Much of this material represents what I was supposed to have learned in medical school, reminding me of how dated my formal schooling has become. In discussing the hepatitis outbreak investigated by Gene Page, Roueché writes that though we have vaccines against smallpox, polio, and measles, it is far from certain that a vaccine against hepatitis will ever be developed. The first commercial vaccine against hepatitis B was introduced in 1982; a vaccine against hepatitis A, in 1995.

Dr. Ben Saltzman is a legendary figure in Arkansas medical history, having been a family practitioner in Mountain Home and, later, director of the Department of Health. He was called "the father of rural medicine in Arkansas" by Dean Thomas Bruce when a professorship at the University of Arkansas for Medical Sciences was named after him. He was chairman of the Rotary 3H Program, out of which grew Rotary's Polio Plus Program, with the goal of worldwide eradication of polio. His name appears in Chapter 6, "The Liberace Room," an account of a mysterious epidemic of a febrile disease diagnosed, through the efforts of the Public Health Service, as histoplasmosis. The PHS investigator came into the case when there were thirty-six cases out of three hundred eighty-six students in the school. But what depressed him most, he said, was Dr. Saltzman himself, who was far from being the slow-witted country doctor he had hoped to find. On the other hand, he appeared to be so sharp that if he hadn't solved it, the investigators were going to have a hard time.

As it turned out, the hard work led to the attribution of the outbreak to *Histoplasma capsulatum* spores in the dust from a truckload of coal from a strip mine near Fayetteville, dumped into the school's coal cellar on January 29.

If Berton Roueché's medical detectives are a reminder of the state of medical diagnosis fifty years ago, Lisa Sanders' *Every Patient Tells a Story: Medical Mysteries and the Art of Diagnosis* (Broadway Books, 2009) brings us up to date. Her credentials are not irrelevant. She left a career in television to attend Yale University School of Medicine, motivated, as she tells us in the introduction, by the potential for medicine to transform the lives of those it touches, as opposed to television, which may reach millions but touch only a few. She writes a monthly column for *The New York Times Magazine* and serves as technical advisor for the popular television show, *House, M.D.*.

How diagnoses are made receives more emphasis than the final answer, though she does tell us about a few rare conditions. The book is organized around the primary elements of diagnosis: history, physical examination, diagnostic studies, and analysis of the data. Remember Osler's four steps at the bedside: observation, palpation, auscultation, contemplation. Willis Hurst, professor and cardiologist at Emory University, preached about the "five fingers": history, physical exam, chest x-ray, electrocardiogram, and lab studies. And Martin Winckler organized *The Case of Dr. Sachs,* his novel about a French physician, into Presentation, History, Clinical Examination, Further Investigations, Diagnosis, Treatment, and Prognosis. System is important, and Sanders' four-part classification is useful in describing the high-tech focus of today's medical system.

The lack of attention to physical examination in recent years, if not its actual demise, is confirmed by this recent medical school graduate, along with appropriate sentiments of regret. Among her personal anecdotes is a story of a missed diagnosis of mitral stenosis, finally made when her "asthma" patient was hospitalized for severe shortness of breath, and a senior internist in the hospital heard the murmur of mitral stenosis; the diagnosis was confirmed by echocardiography.

The murmur of mitral stenosis is a low-pitched rumble that can be extremely difficult to hear and I missed my share of them. I developed my own little drill, which I surely must have developed from the teaching of some of the old masters of cardiac diagnosis, and which I later preached to students. "The murmur is the last thing you listen for when you're looking for mitral stenosis (and the trick is to be looking for it). A loud first heart sound, a loud pulmonic component of the second sound, and an opening click are all easier to hear than a soft diastolic rumble." Never miss a chance to do something the easy way. Sadly, however, more murmurs are missed these days because the stethoscope is around the doctor's neck, not in the ears. Such tricks of the trade may have gone the way of the village blacksmith and the shoe repairman.

My faithfulness about the physical examination was renewed when it dawned on me, soon after going into practice, that my patients were actually paying money for their visits to me. When they got my bill, I reasoned, I wanted them to have a recollection of something that I had actually done. In my zeal, I had my nurse ask the patients to disrobe to the waist and put on an examination gown before I came in. In retrospect, this may have been a bit much. It wouldn't have taken that much longer for me to step out for a moment before beginning my exam, and everyone would have been more comfortable.

The disappearance of the autopsy is also appropriately observed. CT scans, MRIs, and other powerful diagnostic tools have resulted in less uncertainty about cause of death. Of course, we lose much information that we used to obtain about unsuspected conditions that were found at autopsy, but after all, it is a labor-intensive exercise, and labor isn't free. A request for an autopsy inserts a discordant note into the discussion with the family at a time when the doctor wants peace and harmony above all else. A family with no interest in an autopsy is unlikely to be interested in a malpractice suit, and the doctor is reluctant to interrupt the momentum that may be developing toward an amicable ending to a conversation that everyone wants to conclude. Accreditation agencies no longer require certain percentages of autopsies, so everyone just lets the matter drop.

The discussion of diagnostic tests is limited to one chapter about testing for Lyme Disease in an area of Connecticut where the diagnosis is so common that one doctor is described as limiting his practice to Lyme Disease. The point is made that one must be skeptical about test results, a principle that first became part of my thinking when I was recording heart murmurs with phonocardiograms as a summer project after my junior year in medical school. In discussing one case, the intern based his diagnosis on what the phonocardiogram was reported to show. "Wait a minute," I thought to myself, "I'm just learning how to do this. I'm not sure it's right. Is he really taking this seriously?"

Of course, we assume that lab technicians take their work seriously, but we also learn that mistakes can happen. When the data doesn't fit, "somebody must be lying," and it often turns out to be one of the test reports. "When you land in enemy territory," a commander once told his soldiers who were about to parachute behind enemy lines, "you may sometimes find that there is a discrepancy between your map and the ground. In such a case, you may take it as a general rule that the ground is correct."

A good bit of space in medical journals these days is taken up by papers not about medical science itself but about how well doctors perform in one way or another. This is important information and Dr. Sanders reviews a number of these studies, such as a study showing discrepancies between autopsy findings and clinical diagnoses in twenty percent of cases. If this is disturbing, and it should be, some slight comfort can be found in the finding of another study reporting that the likelihood of an important diagnostic error has declined twenty-five percent in every decade since the middle of the twentieth century.

There is ample evidence that the public is curious to know what really happens behind the doors that say, "Medical Personnel Only." The medical detective books that have become so popular recently provide a peek behind the closed doors, and these two books spanning the past sixty years are responsible efforts to satisfy such curiosity.

THE SECRET OF LIFE

THE DOUBLE HELIX
A Personal Account of the Discovery of
The Structure of DNA
By James D. Watson

It was a rainy night in Cambridge a few years ago when my wife and I followed our guide from one college to another, stopping to dry out at The Eagle, a pub made famous as the hangout of the American pilots stationed there during World War II (where they wrote their names and division numbers on the ceiling). But The Eagle was also the watering hole James Watson and Francis Crick went to for refreshment and discussion of their project to determine the structure of DNA (deoxyribonucleic acid), the molecule that contains and transmits genetic information. And it was here that Francis Crick appeared one day to announce to all that he and Watson had discovered the secret of life.

The Double Helix: A Personal Account of the Discovery of the Structure of DNA (Simon and Schuster, 1968) is James Watson's account of what has been called the most important scientific discovery of the twentieth century. It is a controversial account because his two chief collaborators, Francis Crick and Maurice Wilkins, disputed parts of it and objected to its publication. It is such a breezy account that no reader could mistake it for a balanced summary of how it happened. Watson's characterizations of the other workers are basically generous, but it is a frank and unguarded account. Of Crick, he wrote, "He talked louder and faster than anyone else and, when he laughed, his location within the Cavendish was obvious. Almost everyone enjoyed these manic moments." And of Wilkins, he wrote, "Maurice continually frustrated Francis by never seeming enthusiastic enough about DNA. He appeared to enjoy slowly understating important arguments." The famed English reticence surely recoiled at such personal observations.

"You've gotta cooperate to graduate" is a useful motto for college students, but it also applies to scientific research. Science advances more quickly by collaboration and also by competition. All this personal interaction generates results, but it also spins off gossip, intrigue, and all sorts of personal understandings and misunderstandings. I was vastly entertained by all this in the cardiology department of the Brompton Hospital during my year in London in 1974. When an American encounters a little subset of the English intellectual community, its quaint little ways stand out more sharply than they might to the English who grew up with it, though the English are by no means unaware of its features, which provide provender for much lunchtime and evening pub conversation.

Jim Watson clearly found all this fascinating. He was a boy wonder – literally a Quiz Kid who had appeared on the NBC radio show. He enrolled at the University of Chicago at age fifteen, graduated four years later, and completed his Ph.D. in zoology at the University of Indiana at age twenty-two. He was twenty-four when he did the work that resulted in a Nobel Prize for himself, Crick, and Wilkins.

Not one to get bogged down in details, Watson hoped he could solve the problem of the gene without having to learn any chemistry. He had been mostly interested in birds at the University of Chicago and had tried to avoid the difficult courses in chemistry and physics. One gets the impression he arrived upon the scene in England and observed that there were several gifted people working on their own little projects, each of whom had only limited interest in the big picture. And if he could just get the required information from each of them, he could put it all together.

He framed it as a race to be the first to determine the structure of DNA, with Linus Pauling in California as the competition. The prize for winning this big a race would surely be a Nobel Prize itself. Pauling, who was to be a multiple Nobel Prize winner, had used molecular models to demonstrate the helical structure of proteins, and he was working on the structure of DNA. However he had other fish to fry, so he may not have been as focused on DNA as was Watson, who looked on it as his passport to fame and success. Coincidentally, Linus Pauling's son Peter was in England at the time and was a good friend of Watson's.

Watson described it as a matter of five people: Maurice Wilkins, Rosalind Franklin, Linus Pauling, Francis Crick, and himself. Rosalind Franklin, who died of cancer at age thirty-seven, worked at King's College in London with (as she thought of it) or under (as he thought of it) Maurice Wilkins. It was she who provided the famous and crucial "Photo 51," showing the crystallographic properties of DNA; or perhaps we should say, refused to provide "Photo 51," which Wilkins obtained anyway and showed to Watson. Watson portrayed her as a private worker, protective of her own domain, and vicious when approached. Once the problem was solved, however, she appeared as generous and gracious. She didn't live long enough to receive a Nobel Prize along with the others, and she has been lifted up as the unsung and underappreciated hero of the quest. A Jewish woman fighting to break through the glass ceiling, she has become a symbol. The Chicago Medical School has appropriated her name and is now The Rosalind Franklin University of Medicine and Science.

Watson described her as a woman with strong features who might have been "quite stunning" if she had paid any attention to her appearance and her clothes, which she did not. Maurice Wilkins was impeded in his effort to work with Watson and Crick on DNA because Rosy (they didn't call her this to her face) refused to think of herself as an assistant to Wilkins. She claimed that DNA was her own project. The great climactic scene, which could have come straight out of P. G. Wodehouse, occurred when Watson visited Wilkins at King's and, finding him to be busy, pushed open the door to where Franklin was working. Watson showed her a copy of Pauling's paper suggesting a helical structure for DNA, but she "became annoyed" and said that there was no evidence that Linus Pauling or anyone else could use to support a helical structure for DNA. She told him to look at her X-ray evidence. Watson, who already knew about her X-ray evidence because Wilkins had shared it with him, raised the possibility that she might not be competent in the interpretation of X-ray images.

Watson then claimed that Franklin came out from behind her bench. Afraid that she might hit him, Watson grabbed the Pauling manuscript and went back to the open door. But his exit was blocked by Wilkins, who was just arriving in search of Watson. Jim Watson, making an excuse that he was just finishing a conversation with Franklin, tried to ease past Wilkins, leaving him face to face with Rosalind Franklin. She made an about face and shut the door on them.

Walking back down the hall, Watson told Wilkins that his arrival might have saved him from being assaulted by Rosalind Franklin; Wilkins agreed and said she had made a similar lunge toward him a few months earlier in the course of an argument in his office. She had blocked the door and only at the last moment had she given way.

It was on this occasion that Maurice Wilkins went next door and picked up a print of a new configuration that they called the "B" structure. Watson reports that when he saw it, his mouth fell open and he felt his heart racing. The pattern showed an "X" pattern indicating a helical structure of DNA. Watson and Crick later obtained Rosalind Franklin's experimental data, not directly from her, but through committee reports of research that were circulating through the institutions.

It is to be remembered that the discovery of the structure of DNA wasn't a day job for Watson and Crick. Crick was supposed to be working on hemoglobin, and Watson on myoglobin and tobacco mosaic virus; and they had to obtain permission from

Sir Lawrence Bragg, Director of the Cavendish Laboratory, to continue their work with DNA. One gets the impression of a couple of naughty boys sneaking out of school and peeking into the results of others. Many of their ideas arose from long walks along the banks of the Cam River, and Watson repeatedly alludes to his difficulty in making progress in Frick's absence.

Another schoolboy aspect of the project had to do with the molecular model that was the tool for determining the configuration of DNA. Pauling had introduced the concept of using a three-dimensional model to demonstrate molecular structure, and Watson and Crick relied on the machine shop at Cambridge to provide the metal components. Their own cardboard cutouts were too floppy, and when they got the metal parts, they were able to be more precise about the relationships of the various components, and to build the now-famous model of the double helix of DNA.

It is surprising how quickly it all came together. Watson and Crick worked on the problem for about two years, less time than it takes most people to earn a Ph.D. Their careers then parted and they each went on to a successful career in science. Their work was published in *Nature* in 1953, and the Nobel Prize was awarded in 1962, by which time Watson was thirty-four and Crick forty-four. Rosalind Franklin died in 1958 of ovarian cancer, which may or may not have been related to her X-ray exposure in the laboratory.

It is gratifying to read that the players in this drama of discovery met amicably and rejoiced among themselves at its conclusion. Pauling came to visit his son Peter in Cambridge and reviewed their data. He was said to be genuinely thrilled by the elegance of their solution.

Rosalind Franklin astonished Watson with her instant acceptance of the model, showing no signs of the fierce annoyance she had previously displayed with him and Crick. Watson concluded with a testimonial to Franklin's honesty and generosity, admitting that they had not appreciated the struggles that a woman was obliged to face in order to be taken seriously in the scientific community. She didn't live long enough to receive the Nobel, but she did have a medical school named after her.

OBITER DICTA

THE LIVES OF A CELL: Notes of a Biology Watcher

THE MEDUSA AND THE SNAIL: More Notes of a
Biology Watcher

THE YOUNGEST SCIENCE: Notes of a Medicine-
Watcher
All by Lewis Thomas

"Notes of a Biology Watcher" began to appear in *The New England Journal of Medicine* in the early 1970s, written by Lewis Thomas, who at the time was president of the Sloan-Kettering Cancer Center in New York. These little essays quickly attracted attention, and several collections were published over the next two decades; indeed, the first of these, *The Lives of a Cell: Notes of a Biology Watcher* (Viking Press, 1974) is eleventh on the Modern Library's list of the best 100 nonfiction books of the century. The charm of his vision lies in his ability to stand back from the living world and see it afresh, as when he looked down, apparently from his room in a tall hotel, on the groups of medical scientists gathering for the annual meetings in Atlantic City, seeing them as social insects forming little subgroups. "There is the same vibrating, ionic movement, interrupted by the darting back and forth of jerky individuals to touch antennae and exchange small bits of information." He half-expected to see them putting together some sort of nest.

His point was that the achievements of science are those of a community, not of individuals; and this arrangement could well

TAYLOR PREWITT

provide a model for building information in other human systems. Scientific publications each present fragments of work, much as termites working together to build a nest. We like to think of scientific investigation as the work of lone individual thinkers, he mused, and lone scientists may not have the greatest of social skills; but these lone workers do extend their antennae and make contact with others. He didn't come out and say that we are all just parts of an ant hill or a flock of birds or a school of fish; but when we look at our communities from a "suitable height," we get the idea.

In the first essay in his first book, *The Lives of a Cell,* he delivered his view of our planet as sharing many characteristics of the single cell. He saw the cell as pretty complicated, with components that have their own existence – such as the mitochondria, the little engines of energy generation, which entered the ancient precursors of our own cells and stayed there as "stable and responsible lodgers." In this, as in his other essays, Thomas the scientist found himself so astonished at the beauty and complexity of how we are made that he wanted to share this insight with the general reader. Most general readers, I suspect, have not taken the prerequisite courses to engage these subjects comfortably. This is unfortunate and doesn't reflect well on general education in our society. Now it may be that education has improved enough that young students of today acquire this sort of information as readily as they learn computer skills. As a matter of fact, these terms turn up in my grandchildren's homework. In any event, such information can be conveyed to the world at large. Television shows are illustrated well enough to convey these concepts. But one fears that the technology of communication isn't being put to its best use. If we fail the test of following the reflections of Lewis Thomas, we have a bit of catching up to do.

Besides the mitochondria, there are other components of cells that have their own separate identity. The chloroplasts of the cells of green plants are also "separate creatures with their own genomes, speaking their own language." Even our own DNA,

174

which we claim as our very own, may have entered in some ancient fusion of cells. And viruses come and go, "passing around heredity as though at a great party."

Hence his epiphany while driving through the woods at night: the earth cannot be thought of as an organism such as a man or a dolphin. It is too big and too complex; its working parts don't appear to have any connections with one another. "It is *most* like a single cell."

In "Organelles as Organisms," he expanded on these reflections about the cell, repeating that the mitochondria are independent little creatures, living more or less independently within the cells, where they reproduce themselves on their own, independently of the reproduction of the cell. Thomas expressed surprise that this discovery and its confirmation has not "sent the investigators out into the streets, hallooing;" instead there is only careful speculation about the process. Most scientists think the mitochondria were probably eaten up by larger cells more than a billion years ago and have just stayed there.

In "The Technology of Medicine," he used, and may have originated, the term "halfway technology," to describe the treatment of coronary disease at the time, which was almost all technological, such as transplanted and artificial hearts. But when we learn enough about how heart disease really works, we may be able to come up with ways to prevent or reverse the disease process, and the elaborate mechanical techniques will become less important and may even be set aside. This "halfway technology" stands between "nontechnology," which is supportive care, indispensable but expensive; and "genuinely decisive technology," such as immunization against the common childhood diseases that we rarely see any more, such as diphtheria, measles, and mumps. Methods such as immunization, which are based on better understanding of the disease process, are cheaper and more efficient; and this is a good reason to justify more basic research that may not yield immediate results, but that ultimately leads to the best results.

In the years since he wrote this, cardiac revascularization

techniques have continued to improve and are indeed quite costly; public health data have emphasized the importance of risk factors such as hypertension, cholesterol, and smoking; and the once-astronomical rate of heart disease in this country has decreased significantly with some definite improvement in population measures of cholesterol and smoking. More recently, however, a new threat of an obesity epidemic has emerged, threatening to wipe out the gains of previous decades; and decisive technology, analogous to specific hormone therapy for some endocrine disorders, has yet to appear.

Lewis Thomas' genius lies in his whimsy, in the *obiter dicta* (the little opinions of a judge that are not binding) dropped out of the side of his mouth, the playful little speculations that bring us up short when we remember they come from a distinguished senior professor in a white coat, one who was Dean of Yale Medical School and later president of the Sloan-Kettering Institute. In "On Transcendental Metaworry (TMW)" in *The Medusa and the Snail: More Notes of a Biology Watcher* (Viking, 1979) he described man as "the Worrying Animal. It is a trait needing further development, awaiting perfection. Most of us tend to neglect the activity, living precariously out on the thin edge of anxiety but never plunging in."

And in an essay, "Warts," that could stand as a model of nimble organization, he started out with a trivial, homely subject; used it as a springboard to wonder how warts can vanish under the power of suggestion, hinting that it is related to the unknown way the body reacts to the presence of the wart-causing virus; and concluded with a wonderfully ironic plea for a campaign to study these mysteries: "It would be worth a War on Warts, a Conquest of Warts, a National Institute of Warts and All." Even Thomas' whimsy was prescient; there have indeed been further developments in the war on warts, using elegant immunologic techniques which would surely have pleased him. Dr. Sandra Johnson, a local colleague, has told me about the work she did at University of Arkansas for Medical Sciences, achieving a high cure rate for warts by injecting common skin test antigens into the warts themselves. This initiates an immune response by the body leading to the disappearance of not only the injected warts, but also those not injected.

His views in "How to Fix the Premedical Curriculum" coincide with my own, hardened in my case by serving a few years on the admissions committee for our state's medical school.

> *There is still some talk in medical deans' offices about the need for general culture, but nobody really means it, and certainly the premedical students don't believe it. They concentrate on science.*
>
> *They concentrate on science with a fury, and they live for grades. If there are courses in the humanities that can be taken without risk to class standing they will line up for these, but they will not get into anything tough except science.*

He recommended that the concept of "pre-med" should be eliminated, and that such students should take no more of a science curriculum than anyone else. What should they take? He proposed classical Greek language studies as the basic course. Latin should have been learned in high school. Other basic required courses would include English, history, philosophy, and at least two foreign languages, not just their grammar but also their literature. Volunteer work in local hospitals wouldn't be held against them, but neither would it help. Grades cannot be ignored, but grades *in general* should be weighed, not just the science grades. Admissions tests should be eliminated, and medical school admissions committees should rely more on opinions from the colleges as to whom they select. Society would benefit from having doctors who have learned "about how human beings have always lived out their lives."

The Youngest Science: Notes of a Medicine-Watcher (The Viking Press, 1983) is an extraordinary memoir, drawing on the history of his father and mother to describe the life of a doctor in the years before the Great Depression, telling of his own initiation into medicine in the thirties, and then recalling his distinguished career in medical science thereafter. The dust jacket describes it as the third book in a series sponsored by the Alfred P. Sloan Foundation: "books by distinguished scientists, designed to make the process of scientific discovery more understandable, more real, and more exciting to the general reader." In this case, the product succeeds in its purpose.

As a five-year-old boy, Lewis Thomas accompanied his father on house calls in Flushing, New York, when he and people on the streets were wearing gauze masks because of the 1918 influenza epidemic. A major lesson his father intended him to learn was that there were many people needing help, and there was little to do for them.

His prescriptions, "fantastic formulations, containing five or six different vegetable ingredients," were always provided. They were harmless and they gave the patient something to do while waiting for the problem to run its course.

The job description of the doctor under the requirements of "1911 medicine" was one that could be preserved and added as part of a Bill of Rights addendum to the Hippocratic oath for physicians emerging today, particularly in view of the doctor's role in providing a "medical home": "First of all, the physician was expected to walk in and take over; he became responsible for the outcome whether he could affect it or not. Second, it was assumed that he would *stand by,* on call, until it was over. Third, and this was probably the most important of his duties, he would explain what had happened and what was likely to happen."

Thomas' mother, a nurse, had become the chief surgeon's personal assistant, which was the highest honor a Roosevelt Hospital nurse could obtain. She would go a day ahead to the homes of patients scheduled for surgery, to prepare for the operation that would be performed there, usually on a kitchen table.

Hans Zinsser, a recognized authority in infectious disease and, later, the author of the classic history of typhus, *Rats, Lice, and History*, was an old friend of Lewis Thomas' father, having been an intern with him at Roosevelt Hospital. Zinsser also admired his mother, Thomas relates, and he reckons that his admission to Harvard Medical School was due to both luck and pull. When he appeared in Boston for his medical school interviews, he was sent to Dr. Zinsser's office, where the interview was brief. Zinsser told him that his parents were good friends of his, and he would help him to come to Harvard because of them, not because of him. Zinsser was good-natured about it, but he made it clear that this was favoritism; it was not really personal.

Reflecting on my own internship, surely the most physically demanding year of my life, it dawned on me, perhaps for the first time, that Thomas' assessment of his own internship as the most rewarding job he had ever had, coincides with my own and may be more widely held than is generally appreciated. Thomas had no qualifications in calling it "the best of times."

Details vary from one generation to another. The details, for all I know, may have changed so that the generalization no longer holds true. In my case, I felt like the moth that had changed into a butterfly by metamorphosing from a trudging medical student to a responsible physician. And this is basically what Thomas described. He listed some of the emergencies he had to face: first, lobar pneumonia, providing a bacteriologist's classic history of the famous "crisis" in lobar pneumonia and its immunologic mechanism; second, diabetic acidosis, which must still require assiduous attention; and third, acute congestive heart failure. Powerful diuretics weren't available for the management of pulmonary edema, and Thomas describes the therapeutic sequence as bleeding, digitalis, and oxygen. These were three of the six components of the MAD TOP mnemonic we used in 1961: morphine, aminophylline, digitalis, tourniquets, oxygen, and phlebotomy. Few accepted indications for therapeutic bloodletting remain nowadays, but this one was effective. Physicians today are incredulous that the "D" didn't stand for "diuretics," but mercuhydrin didn't act fast enough to be useful in an emergency.

Thomas' World War II experience was at the Rockefeller Institute, which was signed up as a navy medical research unit, and from this time on, he pursued research as his first love. His love of the research process was described with a memorable figure of speech as he explained that successful research rarely resulted from a successful prediction of results.

> *It has the sound of an intellectually flawless acrobatic act. The mind stands still for a moment, leaps out into midair at precisely the millisecond when a trapeze from the other side is hanging at the extremity of its arc, zips down, out, and up again, lets go and flies into a triple somersault, then catches a second trapeze timed for that moment and floats to a platform amid deafening applause. There is no margin for error.*

To the contrary, he reminded us, predictions are usually wrong, and we really learn from the errors. And this leads him to a meditation on the Latin root for error, meaning "to wander." And indeed, Thomas wandered through the derivation of this and many other words, pursuing his lifelong fascination with word origins.

Thomas' career took him through service on the New York Board of Health, and he recounted the battle to obtain approval for fluoridation of the city's drinking water, finally succeeding when it was shown it would save the city a lot of money. He was dean of two medical schools, New York University and Yale, leading to reflections as to who should be in charge of a university. The answer, he told us, is no one. A university is a community of scholars and should be "the most decentralized of institutions."

He maintained his research into the nature of inflammation and the body's immune response to injury in addition to all his other duties, paraphrasing Oliver Wendell Holmes to say, "The key to a long, contented life in the laboratory is to have a chronic insoluble problem and keep working at it."

His essays for *The New England Journal of Medicine* led to another career, in writing, of course. After Thomas' death at age eighty from macroglobulinemia, Gerald Weissman wrote that he may have been the only member of the National Academy of

Sciences to win both a National Book Award and an Albert Lasker Award. (The Albert Lasker Basic Medical Research Award honors scientists for work contributing to the elimination of major causes of disability and death. The National Book Awards have become the nation's preeminent literary prizes and are given to recognize achievements fiction, nonfiction, poetry, and young people's literature.)

It is unfortunate that the language and domain of the scientist are more foreign to the layman than those of the artist. Perhaps this is because communication is a basic property of the arts; it is also a basic property of science, but too often the communication is only internal. It is surely no coincidence that Thomas was a protégé of Hans Zinsser, who showed in bacteriology that it was possible to function both as a laboratory scientist and as a respected writer. Each was the spokesman to the world for his generation of biological scientists. Writing from the standpoint of a life devoted to the study of infectious diseases, each was able to use this frame of reference for unique insights into our place in this world, and what we are doing with it. Physician writers such as Abraham Verghese and Atul Gawande have picked up some of the slack in recent years, but medical science could still use a few clones of Lewis Thomas.

MARCHING TO A DIFFERENT DRUMMER

THE MAN WHO MISTOOK HIS WIFE FOR A HAT
And Other Clinical Tales
By Oliver Sacks

Neurology is a different drummer, and those who master its demanding intellectual challenges are at risk of being perceived as marching to this different drummer. The differences may diminish as neurological disorders become more treatable, but neurology has traditionally emphasized clinical diagnosis of disorders for which little treatment is available. Diagnosis requires careful examination and thoughtful assessment of possibilities. Attention to the patient's care and comfort is usually left for the primary care physician, and all too often, the neurologist is set up to be perceived as cold and calculating, not as a warm and caring physician.

It requires a good bit of *aequanimitas* to see the patients in a neurologist's practice and not be overwhelmed by the burden of untreatable tragic conditions, destined only to get worse. The natural response is to retreat to the position of the intellectual observer of human misfortune, analyzing, categorizing, and collecting, but not allowing oneself to become too closely involved. This "scientific" aspect of medicine, which appeals to the natural curiosity of the child in all of us, is one of the chief attractions of the medical profession; I maintained enthusiasm for seeing patients by reading about their diseases and wondering in the mornings, "What fascinating things will come along today to entertain me?" But there is a balance between being a passive observer and an active interventionalist, and it is more fun to intervene.

"In hell you drift," George Bernard Shaw wrote. "In heaven you steer." The relative lack of tools for intervention has more often left the neurologist in the role of the passive observer, though technological advances are beginning to tilt this balance.

The most memorable example of observation without intervention in my experience occurred on a ward of the North Carolina Memorial Hospital in the 1960s. It was an eight-man ward, and one of the patients was discovered by a nurse to be without respirations. She immediately called for emergency resuscitation, which was unsuccessful. The patient in the next bed told one of us, "It was six minutes after he stopped breathing before anybody noticed it. I looked at my watch."

Oliver Sacks, who has been called one of the great clinical writers of the twentieth century, has made good use of his observational and literary skills in embracing the fields of medicine and literature. He has born in England in 1931. Both parents were physicians, and he has been a neurologist in New York since 1966. *The Man Who Mistook His Wife for a Hat and Other Clinical Tales* (Simon and Schuster, 1970, revised 1985), is one of his best-known works, being blessed with a provocative title. (A woman passing by at the swimming pool looked at my copy and said, "Interesting title.") The title story describes a music professor with a curious visual agnosia: an inability to interpret sensory input to the brain. He was seen in consultation by Dr. Sacks, whose observations are described so clearly as to be easily understood without the benefit of medical training. Just as in reading a whodunit, the reader waits for the diagnosis, only to be told that the disease, which was either a large tumor or a degenerative process, gradually advanced, but Dr. P. continued his work as a music teacher until the last days of his life. No diagnosis! This was in the days before computed tomography (CT scans, which were introduced in the mid-1970s) and magnetic resonance imaging (MRI), but surely something must have been discussed and considered. Was he ineligible for surgery for some unstated reason? Harvey Cushing started operating on brain tumors in the early days of the twentieth century. The author told us that after his observations four years earlier, he had never seen him again, and in his postscript, written for the 1985 edition, he wrote of his great regret that circumstances beyond his control prevented him from following the case further.

Here, Dr. Sacks was the passive observer, but we find other stories where there was intervention. Perhaps the best-known of these is his book *Awakenings,* which describes Dr. Sacks' 1969 discovery in a ward in Mount Carmel Hospital, in New York, of a group of unresponsive patients, victims of an epidemic of *encephalitis lethargica,* or "sleeping sickness," fifty years earlier. L-dopa, a chemical that transmits nervous impulses from nerve to muscle, had just recently been discovered. Dr. Sacks tried giving some of them L-Dopa, and they began to wake up! Worth a book, certainly, and also the ensuing movie.

Few interventions are so dramatic or even successful. "The Twins," one of the most astonishing of the clinical tales, describes a pair of identical twins who were already famous when he encountered them, because of their powers of recollection and their ability to say immediately on what day of the week a date far into the future or past would or did fall. This was attributed to their unconscious use of some algorithm that allowed them to "see" the answer. They had no conception of multiplication or division and were variously described as severely retarded, autistic, or psychotic. Dr. Sacks used the proximity of his office to their lounge area to eavesdrop on their private conversations, in which one would mention a six-figure number to the other, who would smile and then reply with another six-figure number. They seemed to derive pleasure from sharing these numbers with each other, and Dr. Sacks copied down the numbers and looked them up in a book at home, where he confirmed his suspicion that these were prime numbers, i.e., numbers which can only be divided by 1 or themselves. He then joined them and gradually began to participate in their conversation, throwing in some eight-digit prime numbers he had brought from home. This resulted in a pause in the conversation, and then, as they both realized that they were prime numbers, they broke into smiles. This stranger was someone who could play with them.

The game went on with the twins eventually raising the stakes to twelve-figure prime numbers, beyond the scope of Dr. Sacks' book, which only went up to ten-figure numbers.

The sequel to the story, provided in his 1985 postscript, is that after ten years it was decided to separate the twins to prevent "their unhealthy communication together." They became able to hold menial jobs and do a few simple tasks; but they lost their genius for numbers, which had been their greatest joy. Sacks' sarcastic conclusion is appropriate: "But this is a small price to pay, no doubt, for their having become quasi-independent and 'socially acceptable'."

Patients such as these are so exotic as to be unknown in a less specialized practice. But some of them are more familiar. Korsakov's Syndrome, described in Chapter 2, "The Lost Mariner," became quite familiar to me in the early 1970s when my practice was less limited to cardiology, and I dealt with a man well known in the local community. He worked at the bus station and had drunk enough in his lifetime to develop the curious amnesia that has been known as Korsakov's Syndrome. Unfortunately, he did not respond to thiamine or anything else.

Older physicians gradually develop one advantage over their younger colleagues in that they develop their own personal experience with many of the conditions they see in practice. I read Dr. Sacks' description of one of his own neurological conditions in *The New Yorker* several years ago: he was hiking alone above a Norwegian fjord when he sustained a serious injury to his leg and subsequently was unable to recognize it as a part of his own body. It is a thrilling first-person adventure story, and it was published as a short book, *A Leg to Stand On*, which is alluded to in the postscript to "The Man Who Fell Out of Bed." One of the challenges of bedside medicine is to appreciate the lack of awareness that a stroke victim may have of a leg and/or an arm; and my own experience of this phenomenon was seeing my own arm after having a brachial plexus block for surgery on my finger. I didn't recognize it as part of me, despite the anesthesiologist's assurance that it was indeed mine.

A similar deficit often seen in those who have had a stroke is unawareness of one side of the field of vision. "Eyes Right" describes "an intelligent woman in her sixties" who couldn't look to her left, so she requested a rotating wheelchair so that she could swivel to her right, through a circle, to find something she knew should be on her left, even though she couldn't see anything on her left side. When she would find the object of her attention, such as a dinner plate, however, she might only see the right half of it, so she would make another rotation, progressively cutting her missing portion in two. But there would always be a progressively smaller missing bit. "It's absurd," she says. "I feel like Zeno's arrow – I never get there. I may look funny, but under the circumstances what else can I do?" (One is hesitant to wonder how many attending physicians would have known about Zeno's arrow.)

The effect of treatment is addressed in "Witty Ticcy Ray," an account of a man with Tourette's Syndrome, whose response to Haldol was a mixed blessing: he became more socially acceptable but less creative and he missed the fun of his Tourette excesses. So he took Haldol on Monday through Friday and left it off on the weekends.

We are strangely and wonderfully made, and the neurologist has opportunities unavailable to the rest of us to confirm this truism. Dr. Sacks has performed a service for the reading public by sharing his observations and insights. The ground rules for revelation of patients' private information are changing, and one wonders how much of this material would have escaped editorial censure today. I called myself being careful about such matters in my own practice, but in retrospect, I don't think I always met today's standards of protection of patients' privacy. I suspect, however, that I may have been overly sensitive about not writing publicly about patients I saw, and I did not want to ask their permission to do so. I didn't want them to think I would use their stories for anything other than their own welfare. I was their doctor, not a writer looking for material for my next book or paper. People do write accounts such as these, however, and the resulting literature has been invaluable to me in maintaining my enthusiasm for dealing with sick folks. Dr. Sacks was criticized by Tom Shakespeare, a British sociologist and geneticist, as "the man who mistook his patients for a literary career," and there may be some truth in this, but his contributions far outweigh the scruples about his methods. *The Man Who Mistook His Wife for a Hat* takes us into a strange world; but it is a human world, and we need to know about it.

A SCARY BOOK

THE SPIRIT CATCHES YOU AND YOU FALL DOWN
A Hmong Child, Her American Doctors, and the
Collision of Two Cultures
By Anne Fadiman

Anne Fadiman touched a few raw nerves in *The Spirit Catches You and You Fall Down: A Hmong Child, Her American Doctors, and the Collision of Two Cultures* (Farrar, Straus, and Giroux, 1997). I certainly found it to be an uncomfortable encounter, suffering flashbacks to times when a difficult patient would suddenly challenge my resources with an intense crisis, and then continue to dominate my existence for months at a time. This is the story of Lia, a four-year-old Hmong child with epilepsy who appears in a California emergency room with uncontrollable seizures and is transferred to a referral center where she is discovered to be in septic shock. There she receives heroic treatment but fails to improve. She fails to die as expected, but she suffers severe brain damage and survives for years, essentially brain dead.

Few worse scenarios can be imagined. Even a few of the circumstances in this case could lead to a memorable disaster.

The patient and family were from a much different culture. Even smaller cultural variations can make a significant difference: rural background or big city background; southern or northern or western; religious or secular; rich or poor; Native American or African American or Hispanic. Any of these gaps can be bridged by a conscientious physician, but the fewer the differences, the more likely the doctor is to understand what is going on. Walking along a street in Paris one day and seeing a brass plate with the physician's name on it, it occurred to me how difficult it would be to serve as a locum tenens for him, without a chance of knowing nearly as much about his patients as he did. It would be a bit like trying to write a novel in French, using a French-English dictionary as your only source of information about the French language.

In this case, the patient and family were Hmong. Much of the book is occupied with Anne Fadiman's exploration of the vast cultural differences between the Hmong, an Asian ethnic group, and modern American medicine, a curious culture in its own right. Lia's parents were convinced that her seizure disorder resulted from her soul leaving her body and becoming lost when an older sister slammed a door, and Lia had her first seizure. "They recognized the resulting symptoms as *quag dab peg*, which means 'the spirit catches you and you fall down.' The spirit referred to in this phrase is a soul-stealing *dab, peg* means to catch or hit; and *quag* means to fall over with one's roots still in the ground, as grain might be beaten down by wind or rain." And *quag dab peg* is generally understood as the Hmong word for epilepsy.

Not only did the Hmong speak a different language and require a translator, they brought their own concepts of medical treatment, a complex mix of tradition and superstition; and they didn't trust the American system. Their failure to use medications as prescribed posed such an impasse that their health care providers, when they became aware of the problem, became preoccupied with it (as did the author in her account). The Hmong showed no appreciation for the bona fide efforts of the American medical community, and they recognized no obligation to pay bills. These and other cultural issues resulted in a high level of stress among those who took care of them, such as the psychologist who sometimes had to throw up before going to work in the morning.

A second factor leading to disaster was the patient's reputation in the medical center. Everyone knew Lia, whose chart weighed

190

thirteen pounds eleven ounces and who had been admitted to Merced County Medical Center seventeen times. She had had more than a hundred outpatient visits. Everyone thought they knew her and her problems so well that, in the emergency that sealed her fate, her fever was overlooked – and the fever was the evidence of the septic shock that led to her severe brain damage.

Not only was there a false sense of certainty about understanding her condition, everyone dreaded her arrival. There are certain patients in every practice that none of the partners want to see when they are on call, and Lia was one of these. Under these circumstances, the caregivers' brains tend to go dead, revert to the algorithm, and get the job done as quickly as possible. One is less likely to think of it as an interesting challenge, less likely to keep an open mind for all diagnostic possibilities. Her primary physicians were Neil Ernst and Peggy Philp, married to each other and highly respected pediatricians in the medical community. They shared call with each other, and each prayed that the other would be on call the next time they had a call about Lia Lee.

The nursing staff dreaded her visits. She would create havoc as she ran through the corridors, banging on doors, entering other children's rooms, opening drawers in the nursing station and strewing the contents on the floor.

Among other things, Lia was fat, growing up in a culture that prized being overweight as a sign of good nutrition and good health. But especially in a pediatric patient in whom venous access is a challenge at best, excess fat can make it difficult to find veins for drawing blood samples and providing intravenous medications and fluids. In emergency situations, this is a significant risk factor, and it enhances the stress.

The family, on the other side of the cultural divide, was hardly supportive of the staff's efforts, leading the staff to exclude the parents even more. One physician likened this effect to a layer of Saran Wrap between the two sides of the divide.

"The big one" was Lia's arrival at the emergency room in status epilepticus, sometimes known as "status" in medical slang, a condition of uncontrollable seizure activity. This is one of those life-threatening situations where the caregivers feel, appropriately, that the patient's survival depends on how quickly and how well they perform certain tasks – assessing the situation, achieving and maintaining an airway for ventilation, obtaining venous access, delivering the appropriate medications. And besides all these efforts devoted to saving the patient's life, the attending physician knows that the family is outside the door and must be treated with kindness and consideration – a task that requires a slow and deliberate pace, at the same time that the pace at the bedside may be one of urgency and haste.

This happened on the evening before Thanksgiving; not necessarily a major disruption in the lives of Americans, but on this occasion, the night before Neil and Peggy were scheduled to leave town with their children. What doctor will tell you that this doesn't always happen? Schedule a trip, make arrangements for coverage, and just before you leave, an emergency rolls in. With coverage arranged, this should theoretically pose no problem. But it always does. In this case, after Lia's vital signs were stable, the sweat stains under Neil's arms ran down to his waist as he walked out into the hall. Through an interpreter, he explained to the parents that she needed to be transferred to a referral center for care that was not available in Merced. And the family seemed to understand when he told them that he and his wife were leaving town for a week.

What she understood, of course, was that her doctor was going on vacation to play, so they sent her away for someone else to take care of her.

It didn't turn out well. In retrospect, she had been in septic shock on arrival at the emergency room, due to a blood-stream infection from an unknown source and for an unknown reason. That this was unrecognized in Merced was an appropriate source of guilt for those in charge of her care there, though a reviewer said it was probably already too late even when she arrived at the Merced emergency room. The tragedy is that she wound up brain dead, and the family was still heroically caring for her at home years after the event.

The author searches for lessons and morals in this drama, and she receives three from Arthur Kleinman, chair of the department of social medicine at Harvard Medical School. The first is, "Get rid of the term 'compliance'." His point is that it "implies moral hegemony." There are other terms of the same sort that could be discarded in similar fashion, including: "good patient," "bad patient," "manipulative," "crocks." Once such terms are used, patients are put into categories and prejudged. Minds become closed. Nursing care and medical care are not enhanced.

Kleinman's second recommendation is to look for models of mediation, not of coercion. "Decide what's critical and be willing to compromise on everything else." And finally, he reminds us that as powerful an influence as the Hmong culture is, we should remember that biomedicine has its own culture, which is also powerful.

Perhaps the description of the two cultures is a major reason for the acclaim the book has received. It received the National Book Critics circle Award for Nonfiction, the *Los Angeles Times* Book Prize for Current Interest, and the *Boston Book Review* Rea Award for Nonfiction. It has been widely used in medical school curricula, and it is required reading for all first-year medical students at the University of Minnesota, the University of Virginia, and the University of California-Irvine.

Janelle S. Taylor has cited this rapid acceptance of the book into programs for enhancing cultural competence in health care providers in a lengthy and laudatory review, *The Story Catches You and You Fall Down: Tragedy, Ethnography, and 'Cultural Competence*,[10] which she offers as a tribute to the author. Here, she alludes to a feeling that she should bow down at the feet of Anne Fadiman in appreciation for her work. My own reaction was closer to terror than fascination.

---

[10] Medical Anthropology Quarterly 17 (2): 159-181, 2003

She discusses it as a tragedy in terms of the rigid personality of Dr. Neil Ernst, in a detailed review of Aristotle's definition of tragedy. And as a text for doctors and doctors-to-be, it can surely be read as a cautionary tale. At one level, it surely does deliver the lesson that bad results will occur if you don't work hard to communicate.

Reality is more complex, however, and rather late in the story, the author discloses that the horrible result may have been the result of chance rather than the errors in management which a perfectionist could cite from a review of the record. In its own way, this is a tough truth to learn. "Why has our son had three strep throats this winter?" my wife asked our pediatrician years ago.

The answer was simple but profound: "Bad luck."

What did the author think when she was told that Lia might have died no matter whether the parents were "compliant" or not, no matter whether the doctor missed a diagnosis in the emergency room or not? Her reaction may have been similar to that of a scientific investigator when his study yields, to his dismay, "negative results." "Oh, no, there goes my paper." If so, she was right in continuing with the book. Its acclaim validates its merits. We never really understand everything on the other side of the fence that divides one culture from another, and it takes flexibility, an open mind, and hard work to bridge the gap, even partially.

And the book is a tragedy. Perhaps, though, the real tragedy wasn't the individual story of Dr. Ernst, but the tragic result of a halfway recovery from the resuscitation efforts made possible by current technology, leaving Lia in such an unsatisfactory status for years and years.

For better or worse, the expectations that our society has for its medical care range from high to way too high. Its practitioners often respond to these expectations with a rather rigid set of standards. And a really rigid set of standards often results when the doctor's worst fears are realized and a malpractice suit is filed, which didn't figure in this story.

(High expectations and rigid standards lead to expensive medical care, but that is another story.)

Medical care is a rewarding calling, but all rewards carry their price; and part of this price is that it can be scary. This is a scary book.

WHY THE UNDERTAKER GETS UP AT 2 A.M.

THE UNDERTAKING:

Life Studies from the Dismal Trade

By Thomas Lynch

Sooner or later, everybody dies. Every patient dies. Somehow, I seem to have missed this lesson in medical school and in training. I don't think anybody even mentioned it. The more typical lesson was the one delivered one day by one of the professors at morning report, the daily ritual when the residents would give an account of their stewardship for the past twenty-four hours. After hearing a report of the death of a patient with severe diabetic acidosis, the professor said, "But you were wrong."

"But what did I do wrong?" the stricken resident asked.

Answer: "The patient died."

Perhaps there was an error in management. There almost always is. There's always something. And no one questions that young physicians should be trained to have high standards. Various postmortem conferences in training programs seek to teach by identifying errors in management. But perhaps as a result of this emphasis, many doctors in practice will go to almost any lengths to "save lives," without acknowledging that "saving a life" may only be prolonging it in an uncomfortable state until the inevitable finally happens.

My standard reaction to the death of a patient was to conduct an agonizing review of my own management in search of what I could have done better. And there were almost always things I wished I had done differently. I must confess that the constant threat of malpractice lawsuits made me fear that some lawyer might be searching my records for the same purpose. And so, with this fearful mindset, I was always determined to part with the bereaved family on the best terms I could achieve.

Ironically, the unintended consequence of such efforts was that some of my most faithful and loyal patients were widows, widowers, and children of my patients who had died.

In time, I began to think, on assuming the care of a patient with heart disease, that my job wasn't to save their life, but to manage the illness in such a way that when death occurred, the family would think their loved one had been cared for in the best way. And when death did come, my emphasis shifted entirely to the family.

And so it was that I discovered that some of my most deeply held principles corresponded to those of a conscientious undertaker.

When my daughter and her family lived in Milford, Michigan, one of my running routes led me by a neat, well-kept white frame building on 404 East Liberty Street, home of Lynch and Sons, Funeral Directors. It was only a few years later that *The Undertaking: Life Studies from the Dismal Trade* (W. W. Norton and Co., 1996), by Thomas Lynch, one of the Sons, became a finalist for the National Book Award.

The enduring image from *The Undertaking* is that of the undertaker receiving a call about a death in the middle of the night. When I received these calls as a physician, my duty was to get up, go in, and talk to the family. In later years, the nurse would sometimes ask, "Do you just want me to call the emergency room doctor to come up and pronounce her?" This was a temptation to be resisted. The family might have questions about the care, or about the diagnosis, and I felt better about it if the family appeared to be satisfied that we had done our job properly. Nowadays, I fear, this duty may devolve upon a hospital-employed doctor who may be in the hospital anyway, and who probably knows neither patient nor family. One never knows what the family's thoughts may be. I learned that I should never be too casual under these circumstances. One morning, I was called at the office about the death of a 108-year-old woman. Her home was near the clinic, and I drove over to find the family gathered so closely around the deathbed that I could hardly elbow my way to the bedside. I began asking the usual questions and making the usual comments when one of the young women in the circle asked, "Aren't you even going to examine her? Are you just going to take our word for it?" So of course, I produced my stethoscope and confirmed there was no heart beat.

We tend to forget that undertakers receive these same calls at all hours. When Thomas Lynch received a call from Mrs. Hornsby at 2 A.M. one winter night to report that her husband Milo had *expired*, his first impulse was to tell her to call him in the morning. But he didn't say that. He got up, shaved, put on his overcoat and Homburg hat, and headed the hearse out to the freeway, not for Milo, who had sent his laundry truck to Lynch's house twice a week for two months after Lynch's wife left him and his children, and refused to send a bill. He did it for the Widow Hornsby, "because she still can cry and care and pray and pay my bill."

I always counted it a privilege to have the opportunity to deal with people at one of the most important times in their lives: the immediate loss of a loved one. It is part of the job, but it is not written in the job description. Maybe it's taught in medical school now, but I missed it.

Of course there is more to the life of an undertaker. And Thomas Lynch is an original. He is a poet, and his prose shows evidence of care and appreciation for language. He uses short words and repetition, and his style is terse and more frank than expected from one who knows how to wear the "game face" at funerals. "Only the living care... The living have to live with it. You don't. Theirs is the grief or gladness your death brings... It's not your day to watch it, because the dead don't care."

This is his undertaker's creed, and it follows that he is no advocate of pre-planning of funerals. Funerals are for the survivors. Let them do it the way they want to. Don't try to control things from the grave (or the crematorium). As a customer rather than a professional, I agree with him that there is no substitute for a beautiful cemetery for a final farewell.

He was stung by Jessica Mitford's *The American Way of Death* (1963), a harsh critique of the funeral business. His response, that few could be paid enough to embalm a friend, particularly at Christmas, or talk to a recently bereaved leukemic mother who fears that her other children will soon be motherless, is his article of faith. His work, he concludes, is good for the species.

Milford, Michigan, is a beautiful little town with some large Victorian homes, spacious yards, snow in the winter and green, green trees in summer with lots of shade, and bunting on the houses to celebrate summer, all summer long. Thomas Lynch loved it. He likened it to a Currier and Ives in the snow; people on Main Street know each other and stop to talk. He continued this meditation, reminiscent of Thornton Wilder's *Our Town*, with other thoughts that pop into the mind of an undertaker: a brutal murder of two young girls, the rape and strangling of another by a serial killer.

And the undertaker's service, he reminds us, is to prepare the bodies so they can be viewed by the family as a fair recollection of how they were in life, not after the horrible disfigurement of their deaths.

My daughter used to tell me about the local celebrity who spent half the year working in Hollywood, where she played Miss Emily on "The Waltons," among other roles. She spent the other half of the year in Milford. This was Mary Jackson, and Lynch talks about her initiative in raising money to rebuild the bridge leading to the old town cemetery, along the route she wanted her body to be carried when her time came.

In his poem to commemorate the opening of the bridge, Lynch wrote,

> *A graveyard is an old agreement made*
> *between the living and the living who have died*
> *that says we keep their names and dates alive.*

The two hundred pages of *The Undertaking* constitute a long meditation on life and death by a poet who is a conscientious workman, true to his profession, always aware of the need to memorialize those who have just left us. He concluded with a few speculations about his own funeral, and his own request. February, preferably, and a cold day, but stay at the hole in the ground until it's all over.

I would hope for a nicer day in a warmer climate. But everyone to his own taste. And remember the undertaker's mantra: "The dead don't care."

WITH GUN AND CAMERA

THE PHOTOGRAPHER
Into War-torn Afghanistan
with Doctors Without Borders
By Emmanuel Guibert, Didier Lefèvre,
And Frédéric Lemercier
Translated by Alexis Siegel

Back in the good old days, Eric Newby, bored with his ten years in the fashion industry, wired a friend in the British Embassy in Rio de Janeiro: "CAN YOU TRAVEL NURISTAN JUNE?" When he received a three-word reply, "OF COURSE, HUGH," he chucked his job and began preparations, in 1952, to become the first European to visit this remote northeastern province of Afghanistan since 1891. The title of the book that resulted from this adventure, *A Short Walk in the Hindu Kush,* indicates the level of detachment with which the civilized world viewed Nuristan.

No more. The Taliban now control parts of Nuristan, having evicted Afghan police from one of the districts in May, 2010, and this remote province has demonstrated the difficulty of winning the war against terrorism that resulted from the attack on the Twin Towers in New York on September 11, 2001. It ain't funny anymore.

Somewhere in the transition phase in how the western world viewed Afghanistan is *The Photographer: Into War-torn Afghanistan with Doctors Without Borders* by Emmanuel Guibert, Didier Lefèvre, and Frédéric Lemercier, translated by Alexis

Siegel (First Second, 2008), a graphic book first published in France in 2003. The photographer was Didier Lefèvre, who accompanied a Doctors Without Borders mission into northern Afghanistan in 1986, during the war between the Soviet Union and the Afghan Mujahideen. He died of heart failure at age forty-nine in 2007. Guibert was the cartoonist, and Lemercier was the graphic designer.

The graphic format gives visual reinforcement to several aspects of a visit to Afghanistan that one may read about, but lose track of: the barren landscape, occasional black spells after dark in the absence of electricity, the universal eastern mode of dress, travel without cars or trucks.

A group of French physicians and journalists founded *Medécins Sans Frontières* in 1971 after having been frustrated by government interference in their attempts to provide humanitarian and medical aid during Nigeria's civil war in 1970. Its American branch, Doctors Without Borders, was founded in 1990. MSF was awarded the Nobel Peace Prize in 1999, and it now has offices in nineteen countries and provides aid in sixty countries.

Lefèvre was an ambitious young French photographer looking for adventure and some memorable images when he flew to Peshawar, northwest Pakistan, to meet the MSF team, who were preparing to set off for a three-month mission across the border. The reader is first introduced to Juliette Fournot, DDS, MPH, the leader of the team. Her father, an engineer, had settled in Afghanistan with his family in the 1960s. Shown in her photograph as a pensive, beautiful young woman, it was she who negotiated with various Afghan factions, planned the trips, and arranged the logistics. Her insights, faithfully recorded by Lefèvre, provide a primer in local mores.

John, the surgeon, spoke the local Afghan Persian language with an American accent, but Robert, the doctor, had the appearance and the air of a native. He had the look and the attitudes and was fluent in the language. He said he even knew their dirty jokes. Régis, the nurse anesthesiologist, explained himself: he had done the same mission two years earlier, and he was returning so he could practice surgery where there was no access to health care. This is so deeply fulfilling, he said, that he thought he would probably never return to the comforts of an anesthesiology practice in a well-equipped hospital in Bordeaux. His ambition was to learn how to make wine and buy a vineyard.

The mission of MSF is to provide medical care to civilians who are caught up in war and have no other medical care, with no consideration for which side they are on. MSF offered assistance to the Russians, who said, "Nyet." Yet when a physician required medical care, the Russians took care of him and returned him.

The photographer, in observing two of the surgeons at work, was impressed with their seriousness and concentration – though they could pass for a "hilarious stand-up comedy duet" the rest of the time. He learned that the MSF doctors sometimes undertook hopeless surgery because it was so important to the people there that their loved ones die treated. And on one occasion, they encountered a chief whose hand has been irretrievably injured. John tells Didier that although it was certain nothing could be done for the arm, they would take three hours to examine him to make it clear that he was the chief. Sometimes Afghan medical trainees watched the MSF surgeons, who provided a running commentary so they could perform the surgery when MSF was no longer present.

One striking photograph showed a young man who had the lower part of his face torn off by shrapnel. After surgery on site, he was sent to France through the efforts of an association started by two French doctors. Several more operations were done, but because of his initial repair in Afghanistan, no bone graft was required. He was sent back home, where he again saw Robert, his original doctor.

Didier expressed sympathy for school children hard at work reading their lessons, but Juliette told him they weren't overloaded with reading, and that the school wasn't open because of harvest time.

"They manage, Afghan style, to learn a thing or two, but on the whole they're really just little workers or little fighters. And the awful part is that, more and more, their only role models are teenagers who don't know anything other than fighting, and brag about it. Nothing else is available. There's no one to explain to them that knowing things is better than hacking each other to pieces."

This was 1986. In 2009, twenty-three years later, Juliette Fournot told an interviewer in New York[11] that she feared the years of war had shattered the concept of nationhood. Over seventy percent of the population had never known anything but war, and war was a normality for the children, who didn't go to school.

Juliette also explained to Didier that the all-covering *chadri* worn by the women was really an asset allowing the women more freedom of movement about town; women's real priorities, she explained, were access to health care, to education, to work, and to an adequate legal system; not clothes.

When the medical mission was complete, Didier had his own personal rebellion when Juliette announced that the route home would take a week longer than expected because she wanted to go through Keshem Valley to make a "quick assessment." He declared that he would go back to Peshawar alone, with hired guides. Big mistake. His guides deserted him. He gave himself up for dead when he lay down in the snow on a mountain pass, too weak to walk further; and he wrote a farewell letter to his girlfriend. Then a caravan came along and rescued him, but its leaders repeatedly extorted money. In a village familiar from the outward journey, he was embraced by the local chief, who recognized him, fed him, and allowed him to sleep for forty hours. But walking further alone, he was imprisoned by a corrupt local policeman who extorted money and demanded his camera and sleeping bag, which Didier refused to give. When his

---

[11] Published on Monday, May 11, 2009 by TruthDig.com. "Becoming What We Seek to Destroy," by Chris Hedges; reported in http://www.commondreams.org/print/41893

door was inexplicably left open, he escaped and caught a ride to Chitral in Pakistan, then caught a ride to Peshawar, where he arrived one day ahead of Juliette and the MSF team.

The account of these and other adventures is enhanced by the graphics. His crisis on the mountain pass is shown in five pages of gray and black cartoons, dramatizing the loneliness of the snowy mountain pass. And then there are twelve black panels when he wrote his letter and lay down to die, but was later almost trampled on by a passing caravan.

The epilogue told of what happened to the individuals we followed through this campaign. Didier lost fourteen teeth owing to the malnutrition and exhaustion on his arduous return. Of his four thousand photographs, he was only to get six published. But thirteen years later, Emmanuel Guibert suggested they make a book together, and he dug them out of storage. Régis, the anesthesiologist, eventually studied oenology and obtained a vineyard near Bergerac; Robert returned to a private practice in France for ten years, but then he too studied oenology and bought a vineyard next to the one owned by Régis. Juliette went to Minneapolis in 1988, and she and John started a family with a daughter. She was instrumental in founding Doctors Without Borders, the American arm of MSF, in 1989. She returned to France in 2003 to look after her parents. The members of the MSF team lost track of most of their Afghan friends after the 1980s.

MSF was forced to pull out of Afghanistan in 2004 after five of its aid workers were murdered. The Taliban took responsibility for the killings. MSF returned to Afghanistan five years later, but the conditions required for independent humanitarian aid were virtually nonexistent.[12]

The landscape and the people shown in Didier's photographs are strikingly similar to those shown only thirty years earlier in

---

[12] Afghanistan: A Return to Humanitarian Action by Michiel Hofman, Head of Mission for Médecins Sans Frontières (MSF) in Afghanistan, and Sophie Delaunay, Executive Director, MSF , www.doctorswithoutborders.org

A Short Walk in the Hindu Kush. But times had changed; things became serious, and they still are. Serious also, however, are caregivers such as these. One marvels at their altruism, their appetite for adventure, their resourcefulness under challenging conditions, their grace under fire. The images on these pages give the reader an understanding beyond that conveyed by the written word. These are stories that need to be shared.

HIGH STANDARDS

COMPLICATIONS: A Surgeon's Notes on an Imperfect Science

BETTER: A Surgeon's Notes on Performance

THE CHECKLIST MANIFESTO: How to Get Things Right

All by Atul Gawande

The list of physicians who are also excellent writers is not a lengthy one. Among them are Abraham Verghese, Oliver Sacks, and Sherwin Nuland in recent years. The late John Stone was a distinguished poet; and Lewis Thomas had a brief and brilliant career as a writer after a distinguished medical career. And the list must include Atul Gawande, who, like Sacks and Verghese, has published frequently in the *New Yorker*. His three books are based on these *New Yorker* essays.

Gawande wrote *Complications* (Metropolitan Books, 2002) as a surgical resident in his eighth and final year of surgical training. This is an impressionable period to say the least, and he has presented some vivid stories of his own experience. However, he ventured beyond the operating room and emergency room to review issues relevant to medicine at large. The *New Yorker* first published his account ("When Doctors Make Mistakes," 1999) of the achievements of anesthesiologists in reducing errors with techniques used by the airline industry to prevent pilot errors.

"Critical incident analysis" utilizes the insight that many errors are a result of faulty protocols and systems. Anesthesiologists have significantly reduced mishaps in the operating room by standardizing the dials on their machines so that they all turn in the same direction, using locks to prevent accidental administration of more than one gas; and by setting the dials so that oxygen delivery could not be reduced to zero.[13] He uses accounts of his own patients to tell the "war stories" that physicians use in sharing their work with one another; but he has gone further and followed up on his patients, going to their homes as long as one year after discharge, just to provide follow-up.

Some of the cases read like a thriller, so well has he handled the narrative. I think he left his best story for last, telling about a young woman, whom he calls Eleanor Bratton, who came to the emergency room with a swollen, red leg but no definite history of trauma. She had danced barefoot in the grass at a wedding. It looked like cellulitis, a rather common diffuse subcutaneous infection. Dr. Gawande had recently dealt with a case of apparent cellulitis that turned out to be due to necrotizing fasciitis, a horrible manifestation of streptococcal infection known as a disease of "flesh-eating bacteria." Out of around three million cases of cellulitis a year in the United States, only about a thousand are of this usually fatal type. I never saw a case of it. But Dr. Gawande set the wheels in motion to obtain a surgical biopsy to rule out necrotizing fasciitis. Here and at several points in this story, the author stepped back and discussed the general issues: medical decision-making, which is quite often arbitrary, as opposed to following a "decision tree" or an algorithm; or the extent to which patients make their own decisions. He gave an example of a woman whom he had seen

---

[13] From "Notes on Sources": "The history of anesthesia's success against error is described in Pierce, E. C., 'The 34th Rovenstine Lecture: 40 years behind the mask—safety revisited,' *Anesthesiology* 49 (1978), pp. 399-406."

who had refused a recommended operation and, when he called her a year later, was doing just fine. But we get back to the thread of the story, and it did indeed turn out to be necrotizing fasciitis; she had an emergency operation and a series of further surgical procedures; she didn't have an amputation, and when he went to see her at her parents' home a year later, she was doing well, beginning to jog. The author pointed out that it has been argued that doctors should have a "cook book" of solutions to every problem. But, he adds, a doctor finds peace in making decisions in the confidence that he or she is the one who can reason it out correctly and make the right decision. Even though we all have a history of errors of judgment, each of us can call on the recollection of some brilliant victory to reinforce our confidence in ourselves.

In a discussion of how some doctors have a record of bad results, leading to an intervention of some sort, he told the story of an orthopedist who made one horrible surgical error after another. Eventually, he was forced to seek help, and he visited a clinic dealing with such problems, where a psychiatrist and his team made a diagnosis of depression; after a long period of treatment and recovery, the surgeon returned to practice. Unfortunately, this clinic, quite busy and successful with similar cases, was forced to close because it was losing money. This story is a credible one; but the author's account of how doctors are slow to intervene to protect the public from doctors who perform poorly failed to put sufficient emphasis on the issue that, in my observations, is the major deterrent to the profession's dealing with its own problems: doctors know they risk serious retribution from other doctors whom they may call to account for errors. As much as doctors fear lawyers, who are often the agents of such retribution, they have more reason to fear colleagues they antagonize. Hell hath no fury like an offended colleague, who can sue directly, or can serve as a hostile witness in a malpractice suit. One of my classmates retired early because his clinic was destroyed in such a community quarrel among physicians. The power of the accused doctor to strike back seems to exceed the power to bring the accused to account, so that well-meaning efforts at "quality control" usually founder in committees because no one will stick his neck out.

Complications is one of the most credible, and best written, of the numerous revelations of what medical training is really like. I admit that I couldn't help wincing as I found someone spilling the beans about how doctors learn by doing on the vulnerable patient. My only consolation is that perhaps most of those who are "practiced on" won't have read it.

Somewhere along the path that included medical school and internship, I caught on to what I was supposed to be doing as a doctor. My professor in gross anatomy called me in for a conference one time and asked me why I always seemed to have such a placid countenance. How could I be doing well and not look like I was trying? I was taken aback, of course, and the only thing I could think to say was that in running the distance events in high school track, it didn't seem so agonizing if I tried to keep a calm look on my face. She seemed as puzzled by me as I was at the question, but that year my grades were good.

Three years later, I learned that the comments on my performance in my third year indicated that I was only going in "second gear." Apparently, my placid demeanor wasn't so well received on the wards where there was work to be done. I resolved to make a fresh start in my internship, and just as Benjamin Franklin learned as a young printer in Philadelphia to make his own deliveries so that he would be seen to be industrious, I learned to walk briskly down the hospital corridors. Subsequent performance reviews indicated I was doing better at keeping a "game face."

Dr. Gawande introduced *Better: A Surgeon's Notes on Performance* (Metropolitan Books, 2007) with a story from his own internship about how his resident asked him to keep an eye on a patient they had seen on morning rounds; she had not slept well and had had night sweats. However, her temperature, pulse, and blood pressure were unremarkable, and Dr. Gawande made a mental note that he would check on her at noon. The resident himself went from the second floor to the fourteenth floor to check on her twice that morning. Gawande's first-hand account conveyed the rookie's reaction to the subsequent events: "The second time, he found her blood pressure had dropped and the nurses had switched her oxygen to a face mask, and he transferred her to the intensive care unit. By the time I had a clue about what was going on, he already had her under treatment—with new antibiotics, intravenous fluids, medications to support her blood pressure—for what was developing into septic shock from a resistant, fulminant pneumonia. Because he checked on her, she survived. Indeed, because he did, her course was beautiful. She never needed to be put on a ventilator. The fevers stopped in twenty-four hours. She got home in three days."

How many of these stories are there? Every doctor can tell many of them. They are like war stories. In fact, they probably are war stories. Gawande is a good storyteller, and he placed this one well—right at the start of his book—to set the tone for his title and its implications. It is not enough to be smart; you have to go from the second floor to the fourteenth floor twice in the same morning. And you can learn to do it. (Oh, you can still look calm. But there is an appropriate "game face" for every situation. And "second gear" won't cut it.)

Better includes an account of efforts to improve care of cystic fibrosis. The hero of this story is Warren Warwick, pediatrician and head of the cystic fibrosis center at Fairview-University Children's Hospital in Minneapolis. Anyone who has ever heard a respiratory therapist encouraging a patient to breathe deeply, "Blow! Blow! Harder! Harder!" knows that patient care can include a good bit of cheerleading. Among other things, Warwick's patients wouldn't simply cough up sputum; they had to practice their cough in front of him, stretching the arms upward, pinching the nose, bending way down to let the pressure build up, and then rising up and blasting everything out. After describing his visit to Dr. Warwick's clinic and observing the details of care there, Gawande spelled it out: although we are accustomed to thinking that science and skill are what determine a doctor's ability, these are the easiest parts of it. Aggressiveness, diligence, and ingenuity can make a big difference.

Gawande not only recounted stories from his own experience; as in the trip to Minneapolis, he also went on the road to get his stories. He paid a visit to his ancestral home in India and also included three days in Karnataka, where he traveled with Pankaj Bhatnagatar, a pediatrician with the World Health Organization, to observe a regional mop-up operation in the worldwide campaign to eradicate polio. The target date has been progressively set back, but many observers think the campaign will be successful. It can still go either way. The contribution of Rotary International shows what an international civic organization can do. Rotary's campaign showed such early success that in 1988, the World Health Organization made a commitment to eradicate polio from the world. Rotary International pledged 250 million dollars that year, and has provided 350 million dollars more since then. It is a thrilling story, and Gawande gave the overview and history, and also the foot soldier's view as Dr. Bhatnagatar goes from village to village to review the work. Again, details, details, as he asked the local supervisor for his microplan, asked if he was sure the population estimate was correct, asked how the vaccine was distributed to distant vaccinators, how many vehicles he had, what kind of vehicles they were, and how the supervisor got out into the field. Pankaj learned finally that though ice packs were required to keep the vaccine cool and were kept in a freezer, the temperature in the freezer was above freezing because the electricity was out, and although there was a generator for this contingency, the generator wasn't working. Everything didn't have to be perfect; introducing the live vaccine into the community established a mild contagious infection that spread the immunity to others. The campaign may succeed. If it does, it surely will be one of the great victories for public health in the world.

In recent years, Gawande has become the leader of the World Health Organization's Safe Surgery Saves Lives program, and his experiences in this project have formed the backbone of his third book, *The Checklist Manifesto: How to Get Things Right* (Metropolitan Books, 2009). Its premise was validated by the first results from a pilot study in eight medical centers worldwide, showing a 36% decrease in major surgical complications and a 47% decrease in surgical deaths, by the use of a checklist to be followed at the time of surgery.

The value of the checklist concept has been demonstrated in other fields, and Gawande cited enough of these for the book to be shelved in the Business Self-Help section of the bookstore. Examples include the building of a skyscraper, flying a B-17 Flying Fortress, running a restaurant, managing investments, coping with Hurricane Katrina, and finally, the heroic landing on the Hudson River of an airplane that struck a flight of geese.

Especially in the field of aviation, the checklist concept has been widely accepted and is the norm. In medicine and surgery, despite the convincing results of early studies, one is less optimistic about a rapid change. Why are doctors so independent that they stubbornly resist changes in their routines, and prefer developing their own routine, or lack of routine, for procedures new and old? Gawande cites a seventeen-year lag before a new form of treatment was adopted in half the patients. It may be partly due to the pride that each doctor has in his own training, achieved with long hard work and sacrifice. "If it was good enough for my chief at University Hospital, it's good enough for me." New laboratory tests and medications serve to improve the efficiency of care, which is beneficial, but when the skin is cut and an operation is being done, it begins to get serious. Gawande demonstrates this with overall statistics and with specific examples. He told a nail-biting story of inadvertently cutting the inferior vena cava when attempting to remove an adrenal tumor, in which the patient immediately had circulatory collapse (in other words, he was about to die) from the massive sudden loss of blood. While Dr. Gawande quickly split the sternum and manually massaged the heart, a nurse was immediately able to produce blood for transfusion because the "surgery pre-flight checklist" included a question about having blood available in the unlikely event it might be needed. Nobody had told her to do it. She had just thought she ought to follow the protocol.

Gawande has gone public with his case for improvement of the results of surgical and medical care. One hopes that doctors these days are getting enough training in being flexible and open-minded to decrease the lag time in adoption of new ideas and routines. I paid lip service to the concept, but unless the younger doctors are more nimble than I ever was, we're still in trouble.

THE PLAGUE WE DIDN'T TALK ABOUT

THE GREAT INFLUENZA
The Epic History of the Greatest Plague in History
By John M. Barry

The Four Horsemen of the Apocalypse have ridden rampant over our world in the last hundred years. Of these, Death comes to us all; the United States has been spared the immediate visitation of War and Famine; but Pestilence didn't pass us by in the great influenza pandemic of 1918. Consider the experience of Philadelphia, the nation's hardest-hit city, where thousands of bodies arrived daily at a city morgue that had been built to hold thirty-six bodies. Burial of some corpses was delayed for more than a week with a backlog of as many as 500 bodies. During the worst week of the epidemic, in October, 1918, 4,597 Philadelphians died from influenza or pneumonia in a city with a normal average weekly death rate from all causes of 458. The details, as outlined by John M. Barry in *The Great Influenza: The Epic Story of the Deadliest Plague in History* (Viking Penguin, 2004), are horrifying. In families where everyone was ill, there was no one to feed them. The care of orphans became a problem. In plants employing thousands of workers, twenty to forty percent were absent. Medical and nursing personnel were overwhelmed. One organization received calls for 2,955 nurses; 2,758 of these calls weren't filled. Morbidity and mortality among the caregivers was high. Priests were enlisted to assist the police in removing bodies from homes. Bodies were collected in trucks and wagons. One observer reported that when his aunt's brother died, she saw the horse-drawn wagons pass by and then saw him placed on the wagon, wrapped in a sort of sackcloth as they all were, one on top of another, and taken away.

Whether or not the pandemic was entirely due to the crowding of soldiers and lack of sanitation in wartime, World War I certainly contributed to its severity. And the story of the Great War is well known, of course. Curiously, we know hardly anything of the pandemic. But it killed more people than any other outbreak of disease in history. World War I claimed fifteen million casualties; twice that many died of the influenza pandemic in six months. In the fourteenth century, the plague killed a greater proportion of Europe's population, about a fourth, but influenza killed more people in a year than the Black Death of the Middle Ages killed in a century. More than half of all the deaths from the influenza pandemic, which lasted over two years, were compressed into the three fall months of 1918. Roughly half of those who died were in their twenties and thirties.

Was the story of the pandemic suppressed? Yes, it was. Due to concern about the spread of negative publicity during wartime, the emphasis was on selling war bonds, not on reporting the deaths from influenza. *The Philadelphia Inquirer* counseled its readers to not even discuss influenza and to talk of cheerful things. "Worry is useless." And it relegated its coverage of the flu to the back pages. Virtually ignored in the press at the time, it has received so little mention in the history books that one might wonder if it really happened.

John Barry wrote *Rising Tide*, the story of the 1927 flood, and he went from that disaster to the public health disaster that occurred less than ten years before. He may have found more than he was looking for. He chose to frame his story in the history of American medicine, and the frame is too big; it distracts from the big picture. The first eighty-seven pages deal with the inadequacies of medical science in the nineteenth century, culminating in the formation of Johns Hopkins Hospital and Medical School. He wove into the story of the influenza pandemic the lives of several individuals who played a role in attempting to control it, including William Welch of Johns Hopkins, Oswald Avery of the Rockefeller Institute, William Park of New York City, and Paul Lewis of Philadelphia.

Barry mentions several possible origins of the influenza, but he presents evidence that the outbreak may have originated in Haskell County, Kansas, in January, 1918, traveled east across the state to an army camp, and from there to Europe, mostly on troop ships. One reads with horror the accounts of how the disease spread in army camps and on troop trains and ships. Consider the times of death of the soldiers on the troopship *Leviathan* as recorded in the ship's logbook: "two names at 2:00 A.M., another at 2:02 A.M., two more at 2:15 A.M.," continuing all through the night and morning hours: "7:56 A.M., at 8:10 A.M., another at 8:10 A.M., at 8:25 A.M."

Army Surgeon General William Gorgas urged that all movement of troops between infected and uninfected camps cease, but despite this recommendation, 3,108 troops boarded a train in Camp Grant in Illinois to Camp Hancock in Georgia. Hundreds of men were crowded into each car, with much less ventilation and much less space than in any barracks. On arrival, seven hundred of these men were taken directly to the hospital. In all, two thousand of these soldiers were hospitalized with influenza. The author speculates that troops poured out of the train at each stop, seeking any escape from the horrors on board. Men must have been coughing, sweating, collapsing, bleeding from the nose and ears, delirious, and panic-stricken.

How does a viral disease kill healthy young people within one, two, or three days of the onset of illness? The body responds to the infection with a massive immunologic response that becomes counterproductive, resulting in the Acute Respiratory Distress Syndrome, known as ARDS. This is seen in the intensive care units today as a result of various causes, often a viral infection of some sort. Other causes include toxic fumes and smoke inhalation. It can often be managed successfully with a ventilator, giving the lungs time to recover. But there were no ventilators in 1918. (And since most ventilators are in use nowadays, there would hardly be any to use for the overwhelming demand imposed by a pandemic today.)

There was little that doctors could do to modify what was later learned to be a viral infection. Nursing care was more important, and doctors and nurses were sought and recruited aggressively. One woman with nursing training went to the movies, where the lights were turned on in the middle of the show, and she was paged by name with a request to report to the lobby for service with the Red Cross. Although one physician fled from Philadelphia Hospital, certain she would die if she stayed, this was unusual. "Doctors died, and others kept working. Nurses died, and others kept working."

A surgeon, tired and disillusioned, had left his practice in Kansas City and moved to Texas as a farmer a few years before the epidemic; but the Hispanic farm workers learned that he had treated some workers for influenza.

> *A few days later his wife woke up to a disturbing and unrecognizable sound. She went outside and saw out there in the gloaming people, hundreds of people, on the horizon. They seemed to cover that horizon, and as they came closer, it was clear they were Mexicans, a few of them on mules, most on foot, women carrying babies, men carrying women, bedraggled, beaten down, a mass of humanity, a mass of horror and suffering. She yelled for her husband, and he came out and stood on the porch. "Oh my God!" he said.*

Dr. Ralph Marshall Ward and his wife used all their resources to feed and treat them; he later returned to his practice in Kansas City.

Doctors and nurses died in such great numbers so that the obituary pages of the *Journal of the American Medical Association* were expanded to page after page of tiny compressed type.

As with so many other epidemic diseases, life and death depended not so much on individual health care workers as on public health measures. Several towns in Colorado declared quarantine and isolation, but without success. One hundred twenty-five died in a single week in Silverton. But Gunnison isolated itself entirely, with lawmen blocking all roads through town and train conductors warning passengers that if they even left the train to stretch their legs at Gunnison, they would be put under arrest for five days and quarantined. Two travelers from Nebraska were put in jail when they tried to run the blockade to get to a town in the next county. Although six people died in the nearby town of Sargents in one day – out of a population of one hundred thirty -- there were no deaths in Gunnison.

Despite the satisfactory results in Gunnison, one wonders how the world survived such an onslaught. Barry attributed the end of the epidemic to two factors: the development of immunity, and mutation of the virus to a less virulent form, in accordance with the mathematical concept of "reversion to the mean," the probability that an extreme event is likely to be followed by a less extreme event. Losing streaks and winning streaks don't last forever. There is no evidence that medical progress had anything to contribute to the end of the epidemic.

Public health measures were also of limited value. The people of San Francisco utilized surgical masks and survived the first wave of the epidemic with fewer deaths than expected. But the epidemic came in waves. In most places, the subsequent waves were sequentially less severe, apparently due to development of immunity, but San Francisco had a second wave that was more severe, and although a third wave killed only half as many as the second wave, the final death rates for San Francisco were the worst on the West Coast.

Perhaps one individual case of influenza had an effect to rival that of the entire pandemic. President Woodrow Wilson is generally considered to have had a stroke late in his presidency, which left him virtually unable to govern. Barry, however, presents evidence for the hypothesis that Wilson caught the flu during the Peace Conference at Versailles, and that this happened at a crucial phase in the negotiations. French premier Georges Clemenceau was taking a hard line that Germany should pay in full for the damage of the war, and Wilson had opposed this approach. Then he fell ill, and as he recovered and returned to the negotiations, he yielded to Clemenceau in virtually every article he had previously opposed.

Did Wilson have a stroke, or the flu, or something else? Who knows? But if it was influenza, and if indeed the harsh terms imposed on Germany at Versailles led to the rise to power of Adolph Hitler and the resulting World War II, it is possible that the damage done by the influenza virus was far greater than the number of deaths from 1918 to 1920.

Clinical experience tells us that almost any virus can do almost anything, and that the mischief after the illness is supposedly over can include such disparate phenomena as peripheral neuropathy, central nervous system changes, and cardiomyopathy. I attributed some of the cases of "idiopathic cardiomyopathy" that I saw to a recognized previous viral illness. I have no difficulty in thinking it possible that a cascade of disastrous effects resulted from a viral illness striking the President of the United States.

One still hopes that basic research will lead to discoveries to diminish the impact of such a devastating pandemic; however, in the 1918 pandemic, the available weapons were in the field of public health.

The author added an afterword dealing with the probability of a new pandemic and its effect on our present world. We still have no "magic bullet" that would cure viral influenza. We can hardly expect a specific vaccine to be available in sufficient amounts in time to have any significant effect. Our health care system now works so close to full capacity that it would be overwhelmed by large numbers of cases. Perhaps our most effective measure would be one learned in 1918: "They knew so little. So little. They knew only that isolation worked." The quarantine measures at The New York State Training School for Girls even required people delivering supplies to leave them outside; it escaped with no cases of influenza.

One hopes that many of the mistakes of 1918 wouldn't be repeated. One wonders with apprehension whether knowledge of those mistakes will help us do any better the next time. We have learned that the Four Horsemen cannot be discounted. But we hope. In the words that William Butler Yeats used for his epitaph: "Horseman, pass by."

A FEW THINGS WE SHOULD ALL KNOW

THE STRONGEST BOY IN THE WORLD
How Genetic Information is Reshaping Our Lives
By Philip R. Reilly

Every New Year's Eve, a professor of surgery at Washington University sat by his fire, a glass of whiskey in one hand and a book in the other. It was one of his old medical school textbooks, and by custom he sat thus every year, purging each of those books of the pages that were no longer true, tearing them out one by one and casting them into the flames. Or so he loved to tell his classes. The point is, of course, that medical science changes pretty quickly. Doctors have to be nimble to keep up. Keeping up with one's particular field of medical interest is aided by daily exposure; but there are also rapid changes in the broad general field of medical science, and to a great extent these are things that you don't have to go to medical school to know. Genetics, microbiology, and molecular biology are covered by the weekly science section of *The New York Times,* the medical news segments on television, and other media sources. Do well-read, well-educated people pay as much attention to science news as they do to politics, business news, sports, and the arts? I doubt it. Some authorities urge that a good liberal arts education should include basic sciences as well as literature, art, history, and political science. And such basic education should be regularly supplemented with bits of new information.

The general reader has received a boost in this area by Phillip R. Reilly's *The Strongest Boy in the World: How Genetic Information is Reshaping our Lives* (Cold Spring Harbor

Laboratory Press, 2006). Philip R. Reilly is a professional scientist who received his M.D. from Yale in 1981 and subsequently received a doctor of laws degree. He was Executive Director of the Eunice Kennedy Shriver Center for Mental Retardation from 1990 to 2000 while also serving as an assistant professor at Harvard Medical School. Since then, he has served as Chief Executive Officer of Interleukin Genetics, Inc., in Waltham, Massachusetts.

Thus, he is qualified to review some of the recent advances in genetic research, a field that has advanced swiftly in the half-century since Watson and Crick's discovery of the structure of deoxyribonucleic acid (DNA), the nucleic acid that carries genetic information, particularly with the mapping of the human genome, which was completed in 2003.

Reilly could hardly have organized a table of contents more symmetrically: four sections, each with five chapters. This is a heroic effort, because new information and new techniques keep lots of people busy looking for ways to use these advances; since all living beings have genes, it is a pretty broad field. His four sections are entitled Humanity, Diseases, Animals and Plants, and Society. This takes the reader from the earliest origins of humans to the current techniques for preimplantation genetic manipulation, and from genetic diseases in humans to genetic analysis and breeding of corn and rice.

This material is quite accessible to the lay reader, and many health professionals will find significant help in these basic explanations of things they are supposed to know about. I certainly didn't understand preimplantation genetic diagnosis well enough to explain it to someone else, but with this account, I don't have any excuses.

There are a few broad themes, as indicated in the table of contents, but there are also many interesting little facts, with related observations. As a rice farmer's son, I was particularly interested in the chapter on rice, with its assertion that the most important advance in human health in history may well be the sequencing of the rice genome. This is because one third of the world's population depends on rice for survival, and the similarity of the rice genome to that of other grains and grasses will help improve our yields from other plants.

The public has great interest in the ethical and social implications of genetic research. Reilly acknowledges many of these concerns, but he generally then dismisses them with a refreshing reminder of what might be termed the "technological imperative." In other words, if people can do something, they will. For instance, he tells us that animal researchers will soon be able to find the human counterpart of the genes that govern a dog's behavior by merely doing a search on the Web. And he predicts that such a report will lead to impassioned arguments about such philosophical issues as determinism and free will, and subsequently to demands that the search for the genes that determine behavior in humans be forbidden. Not to worry, he says. This would be a tempest in a teapot. Our human brains and behavior are too sophisticated and complex. The dog genes wouldn't be applicable to this issue.

Reilly's survey of the controversy about genetically modified crops provides helpful historical perspective (a short history, of course—dating back to the late 1990s). Just as poor and poorly informed people sometimes refuse vaccination and proper medical treatment, so they sometimes refuse food. Zimbabwe, with three million people at risk of famine, would not accept genetically modified corn. "Unfortunately," the author allows himself to observe, "there are no genes to counter political posturing or overcome fear generated in Africa by well-meaning, but scientifically ill-informed, activist groups."

In discussing the issue of stem cell research, the author patiently cites several passages from the Bible that are used in arguments about when "humanhood" begins and finds that he could quote scripture to support the view that humanhood begins with implantation, when the embryo fuses biologically with the mother. According to Luke 2:21, "...his name was called JESUS, which was so named of the angel before he was conceived in the womb."

However, Reilly argues persuasively for the use of embryo tissue for research, posing a situation in which you find yourself in a building about to burn to the ground. A woman in a wheelchair is in the room to your left, and a tray of a hundred frozen human embryos is in a refrigerator in the room to your right. With only time to save the woman or the frozen embryos, which would you choose? "None of those to whom I have posed this dilemma, including many with strong fundamentalist views and deeply held pro-life stances, have said that they would save the frozen embryos."

This is an authoritative, persuasive, and entertaining survey of the field of genetics. But it was published five years ago. Is it time to review it on New Year's Eve?

POETRY AND DRAMA

The paradox of poetry in the literature of medicine is that although one might expect the interaction of physician and patient to yield great poetry, the result has been a surprisingly high volume of what one might call "medical poetry," but relatively little that is acclaimed as poetry of the first order. There have been some excellent physician poets. John Keats must be invoked as Exhibit A, but though he didn't live long beyond his medical training and didn't establish himself as a physician, he did establish himself in his short life as one of the great poets of the English language. Such poems as his sonnet, "When I Have Fears," touch on his reflections on his short life expectancy, due to tuberculosis, but in general his poems deal with matters of universal interest and appeal, and they have little to do with the practice of medicine. William Carlos Williams, a hard-working pediatrician and obstetrician, was perhaps the most notable of the twentieth century physician poets; he did write a few poems about the practice of medicine, but not very many. Rafael Campo's agenda included several social issues, and medicine is one of them; but it does not dominate his collection.

One of the better collections of poems dealing with medical

affairs is by Sharon Olds, not a physician, in her collection, *The Father*, which deals with the death of her father in great detail.

One is tempted to speculate that although physicians' encounters with their patients require concern and empathy, the job also demands that the intellectual problems of diagnosis and management must be addressed; and these problems require *aequanimitas*, the Oslerian detachment of the brain from the heart at the same time as there is recognition of emotional overlay that cannot be ignored. The doctor must be a doctor first and a poet second. Some can play both roles, but only a few.

There are more good physician-writers of prose than of poetry. Is this because more prose is written, or is there a qualitative difference somewhere?

The relatively few poets represented in this section are those whose works I would like to share; and as with other sections, this selection is not intended to be an exclusive list or a list of the best. To my mind, they can hold their own as portrayals of the issues doctors address; and they fulfill the role of poetry in stripping down layers of meaning to explore deeper meaning and even ambiguity.

One play is reviewed: *The Madness of George III.* There have been quite a few plays dealing with medicine in recent centuries, and if there should be a Volume II to follow this volume, it could very well include several of these. But how much fun can one have? Only one night at the theater on this tour, but this one is a good show.

MAKING ROUNDS IN NEW JERSEY

PICTURES FROM BRUEGHEL
And Other Poems
By William Carlos Williams

"And so it occurred to me that," the father begins, in a comic strip in today's newspaper, but he is interrupted by his son.

"Dad. People my age are used to quicker communication, okay? I'd appreciate it if you'd get to the bottom line a little quicker when you talk to me."

This must be what William Carlos Williams and other poets, sometimes known as "Imagists," were saying to Alfred, Lord Tennyson in the early twentieth century. Williams wrote *Pictures from Brueghel* in the 1950s, and by this time, he had adopted the triadic stanza of three lines as his basic form. John C. Thirlwall, in an afterword to the edition published by New Directions in 1962, quoted the poet as saying, "The key to modern poetry is *measure*, which must reflect the flux of modern life. You should find a variable measure for the fixed measure; for man and the poet must keep pace with this world."

And get to the bottom line a little quicker.

Here is an example of the kind of poetry that was *not* in pace with the modern world of the twentieth century:

"Angels of rain and lightning! there are spread
On the blue surface of thine airy surge,
Like the bright hair uplifted from the head

Of some fierce Mænad, even from the dim verge
Of the horizon to the zenith's height,
The locks of the approaching storm."

These lines are from the second stanza of "Ode to the West Wind," written by Percy Bysshe Shelley in 1819.[14]

Williams, on the other hand, describes the whisper of the wind with much greater economy:

> *"The whisper of the wind in*
> *That pine tree,*
> *goatherd,*
> *is sweet as the murmur of live water;*
> *likewise*
> *your flute notes. After Pan*
> *you shall bear away second prize."*

William Carlos Williams was the poet whose works I never read in my recent poetry course in my senior year in college. Oh, I scanned them, of course. The lines are so short that you can't help scanning them. But I didn't read them. Why not? Well, they are so spare. They look like hickory trees in winter, bare branches with no leaves. But one thing about Williams is this: he didn't care whether I read them or not. He was an experimentalist. And he made a little pact when he decided about his occupation: he would become a writer and a doctor. He would not be only a writer; he didn't want to have to write for money. He would make a living in medicine, and he would write what he wanted to, and how he wanted to.[15]

I should understand that. My own little pact was more modest. On deciding to pursue a pre-medical curriculum, my only reservation was that I would major in English because I enjoyed it. Literature would be a hobbyhorse, not a serious pursuit.

But Williams was quite serious. Like Anton Chekhov, he maintained that each of his two vocations made the other

---

[14] Edna Vincent Millay, a contemporary of William Carlos Williams, said that this stanza was "as fine a thing as ever was written in English."

[15] As it turned out, he practiced medicine much the same way. Many of his patients were in the poorer sections of Rutherford, New Jersey, where he grew up and later practiced; he didn't make a lot of money in his practice.

possible. As he wrote in his autobiography, "And my "medicine" was the thing that gained me entrance to... [the] secret gardens of the self. I was permitted by my medical badge to follow the poor, defeated body into those gulfs and grottoes."

He skipped undergraduate college altogether; but he had spent the years 1897-1899 in school in Switzerland and Paris, when his father, a businessman, had to spend time in Brazil and sent his family to Europe.

After graduating from high school in New York, he initially enrolled in dental school, but quickly switched to the University of Pennsylvania School of Medicine in Philadelphia. A mutual interest in poetry became the basis of a friendship with Ezra Pound, then a fifteen-year-old freshman at Penn. They remained life-long friends, even in the face of Pound's support of Mussolini in World War II, as shown in these excerpts from a letter from Williams to Pound:

"Dear Assen Poop: Don't speak of apes and Roosevelt to me -- you know as much of the IMPLEMENTATION of what you THINK you are proposing as one of the Wops I used to take care of on Guinea Hill... But you personally do write poems that are at best supremely beautiful."

When Williams died in 1963, Pound sent his widow a brief note from his home in Italy: "For you he bore with me sixty years. I shall never find another poet-friend like him."

After internship in New York and graduate study in pediatrics in Leipzig, Williams became a hard-working pediatrician and obstetrician in Rutherford, New Jersey, where he is said to have delivered more than three thousand babies between 1910 and 1952. His office was in his house and he made many house calls. He maintained that he could snatch five or ten minutes at work to write a few lines when words came to him. He wrote prolifically, novels, essays, plays, and an autobiography in addition to his poetry. He maintained friendships with several poets besides Pound, including Hilda Doolittle (also a college chum, daughter of a professor of astronomy at Penn, and engaged to Pound at one time), who published her poems as

"H.D;" Marianne Moore; and Denise Levterov. His friendship with the painters Charles Demuth and Marcel Duchamp helped him enjoy art; and paintings figure in several of his poems, as in *Pictures from Brueghel*. He often spent weekends in New York with literary friends, and in 1924 he took a sabbatical trip to Europe, where he visited with Pound and James Joyce.

Poets felt strongly about theories of poetry in those years, and Williams was an early advocate of Imagism, famously stating, "No ideas but in things." In contrast to such Victorian poets as Tennyson and Longfellow, who tended to be moralistic and discursive, the Imagists strove to be "curt, clear, and concise." An image was to be described precisely and in only a few well-chosen words. After a few years, Williams and Pound both began to stray a bit from Imagism, but Williams retained a fondness for brevity.

The poems in *Pictures from Brueghel* are among his last, and for this volume he was honored posthumously with a Pulitzer Prize. The title is taken from a group of poems describing ten paintings by the sixteenth century Netherlandish painter, whose earthy, vivid, and unsentimental style might have been expected to appeal to Williams. "Landscape with the Fall of Icarus" deals with the same painting described by W. H. Auden in "*Musée des Beaux Artes.*" Williams' poem, even shorter than Auden's, concludes his description of a farmer plowing his field with:

> *unsignificantly*
> *off the coast*
> *there was*
>
> *a splash quite unnoticed*
> *this was*
> *Icarus drowning*

Williams' place in the world of the twentieth century is emphasized in the similarity that has been noted between his poems and the paintings of Edward Hopper, a comparison that helps me to understand them both better. In "Exercise No. 2," for instance:

The metal smokestack
of my neighbor's chimney
greets me among the new leaves

One can see this metal smokestack portrayed by Hopper. They would be clearly delineated, and there might be two or three colors in simple rectangular shapes. Perhaps the old lady and the old man would be greeting each other, but the faces would show little interaction, certainly no sentiment.

This collection contains several references to flowers (Williams loved working in his flower garden) and birds, but hardly any to medicine per se. His house calls were a window onto the world for Dr. Williams, but his vision and concern were for all of life. He stayed on the liberal side of political issues, enough so that in the McCarthy era of the early 1950s, he lost a consultantship with the Library of Congress.

Some insight into his practice comes from his short stories, several of which have been compiled by Robert Coles in *Doctor Stories*. In his introduction to this collection, Dr. Coles recounts how he was encouraged to write to Dr. Williams in connection with his college thesis on *Paterson*, Williams' epic about the town where he practiced. This led to a friendship, and during Coles' senior year in medical school, he told his advisor about seeking his advice. "You're lucky to know him," the advisor replied.

And so are we.

AN INTERN IN A CITY HOSPITAL

WARD ROUNDS
Poems
By K. D. Beernink, M. D.

The hospital ward, an institution that seemed to be as immutable as schools, churches, and baseball, disappeared only a few years after I passed through the wards as a medical student and house officer. Wards persist now mostly as emergency wards and intensive care units in the United States, though more traditional inpatient wards are still to be found in other countries. The ward of St. Louis City Hospital in the 1960s, just like those designed by Florence Nightingale, had about twenty beds, ten on each side of the long room. The first two beds on either side were reserved for the sickest patients, perhaps a precursor of the intensive care unit. Barnes Hospital had a surgical ward, 1200, and a medical ward for white patients, 2400. In the basement was 0400, known as "O Fo'," which was the ward for African-American medical patients. These wards were for indigent patients; the private patients had private or semi-private rooms in Wohl Hospital, a different part of the Barnes complex.

The passage of Medicare in 1965 and the gradual decrease of segregation led to the disappearance of these wards. The concept of the big city charity hospital, such as Cook County Hospital in Chicago, Grady in Atlanta, and Charity in New Orleans, began to disappear. Indigent African-American patients in St. Louis were sent to Homer G. Phillips Hospital, which was closed in 1979;

City Hospital downtown, which was for whites, was closed in 1985. Its main building was spared from the demolition project and has been converted to a condominium complex.

The ward was a teaching institution, and the ward residents traditionally had a free hand in making decisions with relatively little input from the attending physicians. Since patients received care at little or no cost, there was a tacit understanding that they would serve as "teaching material" and might even be "experimented on." The ward service at Barnes was one of the nation's most prestigious internship appointments, whereas private service internships were less competitive. When my daughter-in-law was an internal medicine resident at Barnes a few years ago, 1200, 2400, and 0400 were distant memories. There were no more wards and there was no more ward service.

The experience of a sensitive intern on the wards at Yale University was memorialized in a slim volume of poems, *Ward Rounds,* by Kenneth Dale Beernink, first published privately in 1969, the year of his death from chronic myelocytic leukemia, and later in 1970 by Washington Square East. K. D. Beernink and I were both born in 1938; he grew up in Michigan and California and graduated from Stanford School of Medicine in 1965. He got married upon graduation, completed an internship at Yale, and learned that he had leukemia in May, 1966. He returned to Stanford as a research fellow, where, because of his own illness, he had the time to write his poems.

There are twenty-three poems, each representing a patient with a specific illness, except the last poem, which is more general. Each poem, he tells us, is about a single patient, but is based on several patients with the same condition. This is a subset of patients rarely seen in an office practice today. By definition, these are people who didn't have the option of outpatient care.

These are twenty-two more or less fictional patients with different diseases: rheumatic heart disease, delirium tremens, senility, exogenous obesity. Many of the problems are largely social in nature; teenage pregnancy is addressed in "Baby

238

Belinda Bulefsky: Failure to Thrive":

> *No one believed that your mother, just fifteen,*
> *Loved you like her record collection,*
> *Or that she had been trying to feed you*
> *Hamburger*
> *And beans.*

Cigarette poisoning has created a particular subset of patients and diseases that poses its own set of problems in a private practice with paying patients. These problems are ratcheted up in the indigent ward setting, as in the case of "Jackson Spander, Acute and Chronic Bronchitis," who lacked the wits to convince the doctors he was crazy enough to be committed, as his friend had done. But Mr. Spander was taken care of, spending the winter on a ward of the V.A. Hospital.

Several of the stories are tragic. "Child Tony Ribi: Septicemia":

> *Never saw my ward, contaminated*
> *With the wrecks of adult excess, drink*
> *Stained livers and smoke scored lungs.*

But when the intern found him in the E.R., his nares were moving no air.

Other patients included Bartholomew Stard, whose mother said he would soon be looking better and proudly enumerated the "gooks" he had killed before his brain injury left him with no intelligence. Then one morning, his corner was empty and his respirator was unplugged.

A grim humor surfaced in the story of "Jemimah Dill: Infectious Mononucleosis," whose missionary husband assumed her illness was fatal and began planning a mission in Africa without her. He didn't smile when he learned her disease wasn't fatal; kneeling by her bedside, he read a passage from Job about darkness coming while waiting for light, and the intern wondered whether he was disappointed with her prognosis.

A triumphant story is that of "Silas Gill: Osteoarthritic Cervical Spurring," who was found on the streets, unable to walk, but who limped off the ward three weeks later, twirling his cane, after successful neurosurgery.

The poems are powerful in their economy of words and ironic in tone, sometimes appearing to condemn a society or a world or a God who could allow such human tragedy, sometimes celebrating a rare victory over the forces that would destroy the body. The reader shares the coming of age of a young physician who gets a strong dose of the facts of life on the other side of the tracks, concentrated in this case by the knowledge that his own life, lived in privilege compared to his patients, would soon be forfeit to the same random forces of disease. Another irony is that if not for his illness, we would probably never have had the poems.

Every generation of physicians in training has its own challenges and rewards. The circumstances change with changes in our social consciousness and conventions; we no longer have a St. Louis City Hospital with a dormitory for interns. But the basic process surely remains the same: at some point, the young physician must learn through doing. This is what training is. One also learns from teachers, from peers, and from patients. Some learn more than others. Dr. Beernink learned a lot.

POETRY OF THE HEART

THE SMELL OF MATCHES
RENAMING THE STREETS
IN ALL THIS RAIN

By John Stone

I remember John Stone as a medical student. He was a year ahead of me, and we often ate supper at the same table in the Barnes Hospital cafeteria. We may have joined in the same table chatter, but I don't recall any conversations. He was a pleasant round-faced fellow, and I think I remembered his name because of its similarity to "Don Stone," the name of two of my college friends. I bought a copy of his first book of poetry, *The Smell of Matches* (Rutgers University Press, 1972) and I also bought copies of his subsequent collections when I happened to see them. I saw him again, this time as a senior bearded professor, when he discussed his poetry at one of the annual sessions of the American College of Physicians a few years ago, only a few years before his death in 2008, at the age of seventy-two.

His works have won awards from the Georgia Writers Association and the Mississippi Institute of Arts and Letters. He was a professor of medicine at Emory University, where he founded and directed the residency program in Emergency Medicine at Grady Memorial Hospital, and he later served as Associate Dean of Admissions.

Many of his poems have the stanzas of three short lines that

William Carlos Williams experimented with so often; but his poem about Williams, "Getting to Sleep in New Jersey," is composed of couplets in iambic tetrameter:

> *Not twenty miles from where I work,*
> *William Williams worked after dark.*

This tribute to the great poet-pediatrician-obstetrician concludes with an image of him walking in the snow along the banks of the Passaic River:

> *tracking his solitary way*
> *back to his office and the white day,*
>
> *a peculiar kind of bright-eyed bird,*
> *hungry for morning and the perfect word.*

The Stone poem that often occurred to me in the course of finishing up the day's duties at the hospital and going home, where I would exchange the role of the doctor who delivers information about life and death to a worried family, to the role of husband and father, was "Talking to the Family." Here, the doctor-poet puts on his white coat to visit with the worried family, realizing that

> *They will put it together*
> *and take it apart.*
> *Their voices will buzz.*
> *The cut ends of their nerves*
> *will curl.*
>
> *And after this,*
>
> *I will take off the coat,*
> *drive home,*
> *and replace the light bulb in the hall.*

The privilege of the poet is that he can deliver a pithy line to the reader and walk away, leaving the reader to digest it and "put it together and take it apart," not detracting from the power of his few words by having to explain them. But when the white

242

coat is worn and the family is hanging on every word, the doctor is then obliged to be sure he is understood as well as he can be. He must ask if there are any questions, if there is anything else they would like to tell him, and he must make eye contact with each member of his audience, including the silent sister in the corner who is staring straight ahead, because she is the one who can cause trouble after he leaves, and may do so anyway.

Oh, I know that some lordly physicians prefer to utter dogmatic revelations and leave the family to interpret them as best they can, but this style is becoming less prevalent, isn't it?

The title of a book of poems may be counted on to be the poet's selection of a phrase that he turned as well as he could. In *The Smell of Matches*, the phrase turns up in "To a Fourteen-Year-Old Girl in Labor and Delivery":

> *Your coming of age*
>
> *Is a time of first things: a slipping of latches;*
> *Of parallels like fire and the smell of matches.*
> *The salmon swims upstream. The egg hatches.*

Dr. Stone often spoke at the graduation ceremonies at Emory. Perhaps he read "Gaudeamus Igitur: A Valediction" on such an occasion, including such passages as this one, which merits being quoted simply because it delivers wisdom appropriate for one about to become known as a doctor:

> *For you will be invincible*
> *and vulnerable in the same breath*
> *which is the breath of your patients*

In our skeptical age, the traditional authoritarian role of the physician has been diminished; but it hasn't disappeared. Just as there are no atheists in foxholes, so the sick individual, threatened with unknown risks, tends to seek the authoritative voice of the doctor, perhaps even as he mocks its authority. And the doctor's job is to wear the mantle of authority appropriately, with humility and honesty, but also with evidence of concern that will meet most patients' criteria for authority. The assumption of this mantle of authority is the life change the young doctor must accept, and Stone, who had so many opportunities to observe this metamorphosis, amplified his explanation of it in further lines from the same poem, telling the students that the patient may live, and you will try to understand, or the patient may die, and you will try to understand.

The metaphor of the heart provides the physician-poet with a unique and powerful tool for coping with the mysteries of life, survival, and the failure to survive. Most of us who deal with heart disease simply stand and wonder, trying to make sense of it. We occasionally get some clues in the examination room when trying to help someone come to grips with their own personal mortality. "Ten Days in July" is a poem that is more like eloquent prose, describing a baby who died at ten days of age with a congenital heart defect that was incompatible with further survival: "The heart compensates for what it lacks by trying to pass for normal for as long as it can. That is never long enough. But it is still the heart's first lesson and its only language, however long it has."

One is constantly reminded that the physician's time is spent in moving from one time zone to another; from a critically ill patient to one who merely needs a checkup, or from the routine checkup to the emergency room. Somewhere, there is a code that says you cannot initiate withdrawal from one encounter to go to another simply because you have something more important to do. You can be summoned to an emergency, but you cannot declare one unilaterally as an excuse to leave an examination room. The seasoned veteran is the one who can compress an intense encounter into a relatively short time so that no one feels shortchanged. Stone addresses the issue of different time zones in the poem about "The Girl in the Hall," who has a Mickey Mouse watch and tells him the time. Having just come from seeing someone with a crushed leg, the physician-poet reflects that she has her clocks, and he has his.

According to one of his obituary notices, Dr. Stone once said that he believed his duty as a writer was to prepare for "a good death." *In All This Rain* (Louisiana State University Press, 1980) includes several poems addressing the finality of this event. Some of his most vivid imagery appears in "Death," in which it may "come on/ slowly as rust/ sand" or "suddenly as when/ someone leaving/ a room/ finds the doorknob/ come loose in his hand."

Dr. Stone was middle-aged when he wrote these poems about death, including a lighter touch in "How I'd Have It," concluding with his fanciful stage directions, with these lines for the mourners: "What/ A Pity A Pity/ And So Old, Too."

Unfortunately and ironically, he wasn't.

Dr. Stone is credited with having created one of the first medical school courses combining literature and medicine, teaching it at Emory and also in a summer studies program at Oxford. With Richard Reynolds, he edited *On Doctoring*, an anthology of selections from the "literature of medicine," which was given to every medical student by the Robert Wood Johnson Foundation. In their introduction, the editors provide a concise *apologia* for the literature of medicine, pointing out that while physicians have a unique window to human emotions, literature has the capacity of describing the reactions of both doctors and patients, defining the medical profession and its role in society, and conveying the legacies and traditions that are so important to understanding the function of medicine.

Poems about various aspects of medicine, usually written by physicians or patients, often appear in the *Journal of the American Medical Association* and the *Annals of Internal Medicine.* In style and content, many of these appear to be indebted to John Stone the poet, who, in turn, had his own debts, especially to William Carlos Williams. One cannot overlook John Stone as a significant figure in what we now think of as the literature of medicine.

WHEN YOUR FATHER DIES

THE FATHER
Poems
By Sharon Olds

Dealing with death on a regular basis is an occupational privilege, or perhaps an occupational hazard, of health care providers. It may even become commonplace. But Sharon Olds has brought us up short with her series of poems about her father's death, describing all too graphically the things an observant daughter sees, hears, smells, and feels during the time before, during, and after her father's death. Not surprisingly, there is a lot of baggage. He was alcoholic. He was married to the poet's stepmother for twenty years; we don't really get any information about her, or what happened to the poet's mother.

Doctors and nurses are trained to observe anything about a dying person that will help them to do their job; helping the patient get well, if possible, but providing comfort if not. Other details and emotional overlays are usually out of focus and not recalled. Some family members find it difficult to observe any of the details in emotional situations. Others, like the poet in this instance, notice everything, ruminate about everything, and incorporate everything.

Some of the details are particularly unpleasant. "The Glass" is a thirty-eight line poem about a glass of sputum always present at the bedside. Most observers turn their heads when someone spits; but this poet does not, even noting even how he scraped "the rim of his lower lip to get the last bit off his skin."

Providing mouth care was always an unpleasant duty for me. I did it. However, I never overcame my squeamishness when a patient in the clinic would fish a tissue out of a pocket or purse and carefully unfold it to show me just exactly what had been spat up, or blown out, earlier in the day, or perhaps the previous day. I could ask with interest and persistence about the nature of the sputum, or "phlegm". Was it thick or thin; clear or colored; red, brown, or black? Would there be enough in twenty-four hours to fill a cup, half a cup, a quarter of a cup, just cover the bottom of a cup? But I was always quite satisfied with the answers. Specimens weren't required. Other bodily fluids and products such as urine, feces, blood, sweat, and tears, I could address with equanimity; but I had a little thing about sputum.

In this direct and graphic style, Olds described other insights that the intimate caregiver acquires in the course of being a sensitive observer. In "The Stillness," she sees the quiet dignity with which he accepts the doctor's announcement that nothing further can be done to reverse the course of his fatal illness. She sees "The Struggle" her father makes to sit up when the doctor enters the room, not so much a gesture of respect as an effort to maintain his own dignity. She conveys the sense of awe that so characteristically accompanies "The Exact Moment of his Death," " when the "skin tightened" momentarily and "then it was not my father." And in "Death and Murder," she reflects on the futile measures made to prolong his life when we "cut him and/ piped him, tubed him, reamed him."

Delmore Schwartz's phrase, "The Withness of the Body," has stuck in my head for years as a reminder that for all our reflections and aspirations, we are only flesh and blood after all. The Withness of the Body gets its due in these poems, as well as the reflections of the spirit.

She had complex feelings about her father; she didn't have enough belief in a life after death to entertain any hope of seeing him again in heaven; but she continued to ruminate about him and their relationship. Grieving is complex, and its nature must surely vary with the circumstances. Her ruminations have their own specific features, but some of them must be typical: the transition from life to death, the contemplation of the corpse or of the ashes as the mortal remains, reflections of their relationship with each other throughout their life together, regrets and consolations, speculation about following in his footsteps. She spells out all these and more in these poems, with a candor that invites the reader to feel a sense of sharing. She is known as a confessional poet and this series is nothing if not confessional. It reflects the realities of dealing with death, specifically the death of a parent, which almost everyone must deal with at some time. It also reminds the reader, whether doctor or nurse, friend or other "caregiver", how profound this passage really is.

ALWAYS ON CALL

THE ENEMY
By Rafael Campo

We had just finished our fellowships, the last stage in our training. I was riding along the country road to Chapel Hill with my next-door neighbor, enjoying the June air in his MG. There had been no ceremony to tell the world we had graduated, but we had, and my feeling was one of accomplishment, of having completed a trial. But Bob, who was about to enter a pediatric practice, brought me up short when he said, "From now on, we're going to be on call all the time. We won't have any time off any more."

Of course, this wasn't literally true. I was determined to find a practice (after my two-year military obligation) where I could share call with others, so that I could have some time off. And I did. But Bob was right. Your patients are your patients, even though you may be out of town; and when you come back, they will be there unless they are dead (or unless they decide to see someone else; that is always the patient's prerogative). And, of course, there are always some patients whose needs may trump the doctor's night off. There are some phone calls that bring you into the emergency room immediately, in your Bermuda shorts, even though you may not be on call.

This is both the privilege and the responsibility of being someone's doctor. William Osler could divide his life into "day-tight compartments" and leave his patients behind when he went on to something else (this is my own impression of Sir William's personality, even though the death of his own son was something he couldn't overcome); but Rafael Campo, from the evidence in his poems in *The Enemy* (Duke University Press, 2007) couldn't dismiss the patients whom he had followed to their deaths, even when spending eighteen days in France, as in "Postcard Mailed from the Airport":

> *"They're here, you know, my patients,*
> *the ones who died on me too young – their passions,*
> *their laughter and first tastes of caviar,*
> *their spindly arms that reach out towards the sun*
> *amidst the plane trees and the monuments."*

Can one really get away from these memories and these responsibilities? One is reminded of the trend toward working vacations, where people in business take cell phones and laptops down to the beach. To be effective, a vacation must surely involve separation; Noël Coward praised "geographic distance." But there is always the knowledge that, for the doctor, the sick folks are waiting when they get back. Sometimes I would get away completely; sometimes I would attempt to soften the blow of returning to unsuspected disasters by making occasional calls to the office to ask what horrible things had happened. One of my partners routinely called me when he returned from a trip: "Do I still have a job?"

Campo is an associate professor of medicine at Harvard Medical School. He grew up in New Jersey with Cuban-American parents who had fled from Castro. His primary care practice is slanted toward care of Latinos, people with HIV infections, and homosexual people. Like Paul Farmer, also on the Harvard faculty, he reaches out to those who need an advocate. Medical care, at bottom, is personal, and it is the personal physician who is speaking in these poems.

Every field of medicine involves some bit of work that others would find tedious, distasteful, or too demanding in some other way. Plumbers and public sanitation workers must understand this. Surgeons may have to stand on their feet a long time, gastroenterologists may have to put up with gas and feces, and dermatologists may have to stare at some ugly rashes. There is a certain adaptation that permits one to take pride in dealing successfully with challenges that appear to be too much for ordinary people. And these poems are explicit in presentation of the details of caring for sick people: "her bony skin," "her bony arm," "diabetic feet and cataracts."

But the greatest burden is the psychological one, and Dr. Campo appears as one of the physicians who empathizes. He describes the man wearing a "stupid T-shirt" that belonged to a lost loved one, and "a hand I held, near death"; and he tells himself, "I'll diagnose a man with cancer, not know what to say."

He holds himself to high standards, asking himself why he didn't know enough to save them, remembering "blood poisoned by our bumbling acts." There is always the tension between knowing that death will come, inevitably – sometimes "speeding, inescapable" – but the physician still strives to postpone death and permit greater enjoyment of life. In an interview,[16] Campo distinguished between healing and curing, pointing out that even though a patient's cancer may not be cured, a sense of healing can be achieved that will not only sustain the patient through the course of the fatal disease, but may even persist in the memory of the survivors. Referring to "failure" of a course of chemotherapy may be an accurate descriptor of the course of management, but it adds little to the patient's ability to cope with the inevitable. I cringe when someone talks about "flunking" a treadmill test, as though it were an examination in school. At the risk of employing unrealistic optimism, there must be a way to accept the infirmities of the flesh without implying that disease and death represent failure.

Casual readers of poetry may be surprised to find that Campo is one of the current poets – A. E. Stallings and Marilyn Hacker are notable among the others – to celebrate the recent interest in "formalism" with intricate and complex poetic forms, some derived from medieval French troubadours. The sestina is a

---

[16] Birnbaum v. Rafael Campo by Robert Birnbaum - The Morning... http://www.themorningnews.org/archives/personalities/birnba

poem of six six-line verses, followed by a three-line concluding verse. The last word of each verse is repeated in one of the lines in the first six-line verse, in a fixed pattern: the first verse is ABCDEF; the second is FAEBDC; and each of the others is a prescribed pattern. The final three-line verse (the *envoi*), is ECA or ACE; but the remaining three end words, BDF, must appear in the final three lines.

"Sestina Dolorosa" follows this pattern of six six-line verses followed by an *envoi*; Campo does make the matching words similar, not identical: pursue, say, so, see, sea, she; and he takes a few similar liberties with the *envoi*. To the uninitiated, these may seem like word games for those who have already solved the end-of-the-week *New York Times* crossword. But a work of art is one that rewards the examiner with little lagniappes to be found for the searching. A whimsical variation on the theme of identity is the repetition of forms of catastrophe in "Catastrophic Sestina," in which the last word of the first line is repeated in its appointed place in succeeding verses as a different disaster: "blizzard," "volcanic eruptions," "flood," "earthquake," "tsunamis," "landslide," and finally in the *envoi*: "tornados."

And what of the title poem, "The Enemy"? It's a villanelle. A villanelle is a poem of nineteen lines, five three-line verses followed by a four-line verse. There's more: there are only two rhymes. The middle line of each three-line verse (tercet) rhymes; the other lines rhyme with one another; the last line of the first verse is repeated in the third, the fifth, and the sixth - the last line of the poem. The last line of the second verse is repeated in the last line of the fourth and the third line of the sixth. It is all very complicated, and none of it may be noticed by the casual reader. (One of my poetry professors used to say that students would complain to him that they couldn't understand poems as well as stories and novels. "I tell them that if they'd spend as much time reading a poem as they do reading a novel or short story, they'd begin to understand it.")

Campo employs a few variations on the classic villanelle form in "The Enemy," which stands as a meditation on the disaster of

9/11, concluding with three memorable lines, the last two of which are enhanced by repetition:

> *"We fear the enemy is all of us.*
> *The buildings' wounds are what I can't forget.*
> *I stared into their blackness, which was not."*

Such indulgences in poetic tradition may seem frivolous alongside the horror of terrorism in our largest city; the ravages of AIDS; the demands of erotic passion, love, and heartbreak; the rage against senseless war; and the various challenges of being a physician who is never really "off call." But Campo has shown both in his life and in his work that we are many-sided creatures. The doctor is always on call; patients get sick and die whether is the doctor is there or not. But things may turn out a little better when the doctor, when present, is one such as Rafael Campo who sees life steadily and sees it whole – and may even know something about poetry.

NOISES FROM THE ROYAL BATHROOM

THE MADNESS OF GEORGE III
Play by Alan Bennett

THE MADNESS OF KING GEORGE
Screenplay by Alan Bennett

I was on a predawn errand as an intern when I saw a figure approaching from the other end of the hall, in a hospital gown, holding on to an IV pole. Before me was the head of the department of internal medicine, whom I had rarely seen since my introductory interview, except for a few conferences, owing to his regional enteritis and angina pectoris, both of which caused him severe pain in the absence of today's pain-relieving measures. He wasn't among my patients at that time; we exchanged a few greetings in the otherwise deserted corridor and passed on. When I related this strange encounter to my father, he responded with a coon hunting saying I hadn't heard before: "The big coon don't walk till it's nearly day."

Dealing with the chief as a patient was a duty several of us experienced and in doing so, we began to learn some of the challenges involved. I had some vicarious training in another dimension of such situations when sitting at lunch with Dr. Willis Hurst when he was a guest of his old colleague and my chief of cardiology, Dr. Ernest Craige. Dr. Hurst had been cardiologist to President Eisenhower in the course of his myocardial infarction and thereafter, and though he was discreet, we were interested in hearing his comments. There was some mention of inappropriate disclosures to the press by others who had had such access, and Dr. Craige said, "I'm sure the Queen of England makes noises in the bathroom, but I don't think I want to hear them."

When such a patient appears in a doctor's practice, a new set of challenges appears. The "VIP" may be a colleague or member of a colleague's family. The celebrity may have some unusual demands, either spoken or unspoken. The treating physician may be hard-pressed to remember that his first responsibility is to deal with his patient's health problems. There is a temptation to use shortcuts in order to avoid inconvenience or embarrassment. There may be some temptation to give precedence to the patient's official responsibilities. If the patient should be a political leader, the issue of loyalty to the state or nation may arise. What information is the public entitled to know? Should the leader be a head of state, the doctor's position may be even more difficult.

These are among the issues that arise when we hear royal "noises from the bathroom" in Alan Bennett's play, *The Madness of George III*, a 1991 play that opened at the National Theater in London and was adapted for the screen in 1994 as *The Madness of King George*[17]. King George III may have had a brief episode of mental illness in 1765, but after losing the American colonies in the Revolutionary War, he had the first of several more prolonged bouts of apparent insanity in 1788, provoking a governmental crisis as to who should govern. His son, the Prince of Wales, claimed authority in family matters and had his father taken away for treatment. Just before the House of Lords was to vote on a Regency Bill to enable the Prince of Wales to act officially for his father, the King recovered. His triumphant return is the climax of the play.

Serving as the royal physician involved some difficulties. Sir

---

[17] The playwright tells us that the title was changed for the movie because of concern that the American movie audience might think that "George III" indicated that there had been two previous "George" movies: "George" and "George II." Some who had enjoyed *Henry V* said they were sorry to have missed the first four in the series.

George Baker, the king's first physician, voiced one of these when he asked Greville, a new equerry to the king, where the king's pain was located. Greville suggested it would be better to ask the king, but Baker replied that he couldn't address the king until the king addressed him.

Having thus described a formidable problem in obtaining a history of the king's illness, Baker goes on to give some insight into the role of the physical examination in his practice: "With any patient I undertake a physical examination only as a last resort; it is an intolerable intrusion on a gentleman's privacy. With His Majesty it is unthinkable. However, it's probably only a fever – a tax our constitutions must pay for this dreadful climate." Dr. Baker further demonstrates the limits of his concept of laboratory investigation when an equerry brings him a sample of the king's urine, telling him that it is blue, only to be told that whether a man's water is blue or not is insignificant.

The play was written shortly after several publications about the king's illness. Among them was *George III and the Mad Business,* by Richard Hunter and Ida Macalpine, credited by Bennett with having been the first to suggest that the king's illness was "physical not mental" and was porphyria. It was later reported[18] that hair obtained from George III contained high concentrations of arsenic, which is known to interfere with the metabolism of heme and could thereby have made porphyria worse. Review of the king's medical records showed that the most common medication he was given was James' Powder, often given for fever. It was made of antimony, which contained significant amounts of arsenic even when purified. So acute attacks of his illness could have been precipitated by his treatment.

His porphyria has been classified as variegate porphyria, which characteristically is associated with abdominal pain, headache, and psychiatric symptoms. Of course, this is a retrospective hypothesis and cannot be proven; but it does prove a satisfactory

---

[18] Cox, T. M., et al: King George III and porphyria: an elemental hypothesis and investigation. *The Lancet* 366: 332-335, 2005

hypothesis. Many would question the validity of continuing to separate "physical" from "mental" illness, which seems to imply there is a real cause for "physical illness," and that "mental" illness is left to the realm of original sin.

One of my psychiatry professors said all psychiatric diseases could be classified as either "C" or "Not C." "C" really stood for "crazy," but he said that a respectable psychiatrist couldn't use the term "crazy." According to this classification, there is general agreement that King George occasionally crossed the line to "C."

From the practical historian's standpoint, it really doesn't make much difference what the diagnosis was. The point is that the king sometimes became incapacitated, and the political powers called upon the medical profession to confirm what any observer knew: that the king was mad again.

Alan Bennett is a celebrated playwright who came to the theater from the academic life, having taught medieval history at Oxford; his account of King George's illness, though having taken a few dramatic liberties, may be taken as basically faithful to the known facts of George's life. He outlines these facts for us in his introductions to the stage play and the screenplay. Dr. Willis, the specialist in mental disorders who takes the king to his asylum in Lincolnshire, was historical, and his son undertook the king's care during a subsequent attack in 1802.

Dr. Willis comes across as the sensible physician, in contrast to the royal physicians who competed with one another to suggest remedies, including the infamous James' Powder. In their conference, they ask about the pulse, which varies but doesn't signify; the stool, which is "more eloquent than the pulse"; a gouty humour of the brain, for which James' Powder wasn't effective in sweating it out; emetics, which made him loose; laudanum, which made him constipated; and finally bleeding. "No expedient known to the most advanced medical opinion has been neglected."

Dr. Willis was summoned on the recommendation of Lady Pembroke, the Queen's beautiful and "statuesque" Mistress of the Robes, because he had cured her mother-in-law, who had lost her wits. An ordained clergyman as well, Willis appeared in simple clerical garb with an air of straightforward confidence and listed the problems: "Skin tender. Pains in the lower limbs. Talks continuously with varying degrees of sense." The prime minister, William Pitt the Younger, started to dismiss him when Willis acknowledged that he had never seen a case like this before, but he replied, "Oh, I can cure him. I'm just not sure what from."

And Dr. Willis proved himself up to the task of confronting the king. He is audacious enough to look the king in the eye, a liberty not permitted to subjects of the king. When the king responds to this steady gaze by rushing to attack him, Dr. Willis demonstrated his power by unveiling a restraining chair that looked much like a later-day electric chair, with bands and clamps. It was horrible to see the king being strapped down. When he howled, "I am the King of England," Dr. Willis responded, "No, sir. You are the patient."

There is more. We see the king being cupped against his will. Willing or unwilling, the dramatic portrayal of this treatment modality is unsettling to the uninitiated. (How will future generations view some of today's modalities, such as electroshock treatment?)

Treatment of a head of state characteristically touches in some way on the issue as to whom the doctor is responsible. In this case, the prime minister attempted to insert himself into the loop, asserting to Dr. Wills that he was *his* doctor. Dr. Willis understood, but he replied that he was the king's doctor.

Pitt replied, "It is the same thing," and the issue was left up in the air, as it often is.

As it turned out, the king started getting well spontaneously, without benefit of any more purges, bloodletting, cupping[19], laudanum, or James' Powder. His recovery became apparent when he, Dr. Willis, and Greville were passing the time at the asylum by doing a dramatic reading from *King Lear*. Thurlow, the Lord Chancellor, came along and was astonished that Dr. Willis

---

[19] A treatment in which evacuated glass cups are applied to intact or scarified skin in order to draw blood toward or through the surface

was allowing King George to read *King Lear*, fearing, no doubt, that the story of a king who goes mad would be disturbing to King George. He asked if it was wise, and Willis replied that he had no idea. King George read the lines:

> *I am a very foolish, fond old man.*
> *And, to deal plainly,*
> *I fear I am not in my perfect mind.*

He then added he was now himself again. And it was apparent that he had recovered.

The climactic scene is the approach to St. Paul's for a thanksgiving service for the king's recovery, in which the English people's love for their anointed sovereign is played to the swelling of a Handel anthem.

King George III had recurrences of his madness, and his last years from 1811 to his death in 1820 were spent in seclusion at Windsor Castle, while his son George served as Regent. He may have even walked the halls of Windsor Castle just before day.

FICTION

Imaginative literature, mainly in the form of the novel and short story, tells the truth in a way that is inaccessible to nonfiction. Writers have toyed with this opportunity in various ways, sometimes playfully providing alternative endings to novels, as John Fowles did in *The French Lieutenant's Woman*. Sebastian Barry provided contradictory accounts by different narrators in *The Secret Scripture*. Tim O'Brien dispatched the question of "What really happened?" when the narrator of *The Things They Carried* says he could honestly answer his daughter's question of whether he killed anybody as a soldier by saying that of course he didn't. But then he says he could tell her with equal honesty that he did.

Fiction explores the truth of the things that could really happen under certain circumstances, and in doing so it reveals certain truths about the human condition. In discussing William Faulkner's short story "A Rose for Emily" in a college classroom, we were told that the macabre events of the story, which stretched our sophomore imaginations in the 1950s, were later duplicated in a faraway town by someone who couldn't have been expected to be aware of Faulkner's story. Read the newspapers. Unbelievable things happen all the time.

Martin Winckler makes the point for fiction in *The Case of Dr. Sachs* when he tells us that "writing, for a doctor like for anyone else, is a way to take the measure of what we don't remember, what we don't retain." *Dr. Sachs* is a work of fiction, based on the author's experience as a rural physician in France, and the author has given us a picture of a medical practice that even those of us who have never lived in France can accept as credible, persuaded by details that ring true in any culture. He may be telling us that his progress notes may not tell the whole story; he may not remember all the details he was told. But writing in the fiction mode rather than in the clinical mode, he fills in the blanks.

The reviews of *The Great Influenza: The Epic Story of the Deadliest Plague in History* and *Pale Horse, Pale Rider* indicate how one can learn different things about the same event (in this case, the influenza pandemic that began in 1918) from a journalistic history and from fiction (which in this case was based on the author's own experience). Like Martin Winckler, Katherine Anne Porter surely filled in a few blanks. *The Great Influenza* conveys its powerful message with an overall summary; *Pale Horse*, on the other hand, has the advantage of being a detailed, skillfully written case history.

One of the fictional works that surely had some bearing on my early conception of the medical profession is one I read in high school: *Not As A Stranger* by Morton Thompson. Perhaps I will read it again some time. A high school friend told me that she read it because her mother forbade her to and hid it from her on the top shelf. I remember little of the book now, except my reaction at the time that it dealt with the trivia of medicine – not what I really wanted to know. *The Plague*, on the other hand, I read during my senior year in medical school, and its platitudes stuck with me.

Although I have always read a lot of fiction, it is surprising how little fiction I read in the literature of medicine during my years in practice: *Doctor Thorn*; the Ferroll Sams novels I was introduced to when I heard my wife Mary laughing in bed as she was reading *Run With the Horsemen* (though the Porter Osborne trilogy includes relatively little about Porter's exposure to the world of medicine); and in the later years of practice, *Middlemarch, The Magic Mountain, The Case of Doctor Sachs,* and *A Few Short Notes on Tropical Butterflies.* The last two of these would have served me well at a younger age, but the timing was off.

Some of the works reviewed here may be regarded as classics, particularly the works by Chekhov, Tolstoy, George Eliot, and Albert Camus. *Marion Fay* is probably the least familiar to most readers. Several are relatively recent, and it will be interesting to see how they settle out after a few generations. My enthusiasm for some of these is high and I hope they fare well in posterity. If I were teaching literature in medicine courses, they would all be eligible for my course syllabus.

CAKES AND PIES AND COOKIES

MIDDLEMARCH
By George Eliot

DR. THORNE
By Anthony Trollope

One of the highlights of the Christmas season for several years at our house was the arrival of a large cardboard box filled with two fruit cakes, about a dozen fried apricot pies, and several assortments of Christmas cookies; all the gift of a jolly lady whom I saw for management of high blood pressure and various minor illnesses. She was the mother of one of my college friends, and I made house calls from time to time, but I also saw her for unscheduled clinic visits occasionally, when she would usually bring something from her kitchen. So envied was I by my partners that one of them routinely demanded a portion from her as she proceeded past his office toward mine. She often had rather specific requests about her medication, usually about antibiotics, but we generally managed to find some mutually acceptable solution. On one occasion, however, when she called and told me she had a cold and wanted a shot of penicillin, I drew the line. Attempts to explain about viruses and antibiotics were fruitless; she was not pleased, and she may have subsequently gotten her shot elsewhere. In any event, there were no more cakes or pies or cookies, and I had to explain the loss to our children.

All doctors deal with similar issues, and my sad loss of cakes and pies and cookies may trivialize ethical issues such as those Tertius Lydgate raised when he started his rural practice in nineteenth century England in George Eliot's *Middlemarch* (1872), one of the highly acclaimed novels in our literature. A young man in his mid-twenties, Lydgate let it be known that he wouldn't prescribe any medications that had not clearly been shown to be effective – an early precursor of the "evidence-based medicine" of today. His "expectant theory" involved "watching the course of an interesting disease when left as much as possible to itself, so that the stages might be noted for future guidance." Furthermore, he would not follow the custom of compounding and selling his medications himself, so as to avoid the taint of self-interest in his prescriptions. And perhaps worst of all, "Especially it was to be expected, as the landlady of the Tankard had said, that he would recklessly cut up their dead bodies. For Lydgate having attended Mrs. Goby, who died apparently of a heart-disease not very clearly expressed in the symptoms, too daringly asked leave of her relatives to open the body."

Lydgate was an exotic specimen in the small medical community of Middlemarch. He had been trained not in a local apprenticeship, but in London, Edinburgh, and Paris. Travel from England to France had been re-opened in 1815, and Paris was at the cutting edge of European medicine in 1830-1832, the years of this story. Lydgate brought with him a stethoscope, which had been invented by René Laennec in 1816 as a hollow wooden tube, useful in listening to the heart when it was inconvenient to apply the ear to the chest.

The reader is introduced to Lydgate in the words of Lady Chettam, who described him as a "young surgeon... one of the Lydgates of Northumberland, really well connected. One does not expect it in a practitioner of that kind. For my own part, I like a medical man more on a footing with the servants; they are often all the cleverer." He was offered a part-time position as director (with no salary) of a new hospital to be built in Middlemarch, where he would have the opportunity to apply his theories.

He embraced this opportunity with enthusiasm. "There are few things better worth the pains in a provincial town like this," said Lydgate. "A fine fever hospital in addition to the old infirmary might be the nucleus of a medical school here, when once we get our medical reforms; and what would do more for medical education than the spread of such schools across the country?" His hero was Marie-Francois Bichat, "the father of histology," who, before his untimely death in 1802 after falling down a flight of stairs at age thirty-one, developed the concept of tissues, such as fibrous, glandular, or mucus tissue, which would react in a similar way no matter where they were located in the body. Lydgate aspired to go beyond Bichat by discovering some primitive tissue from which all tissue developed: "as your sarsnet, gauze, net, satin and velvet from the same cocoon."

Lydgate's idealistic ambitions were not achieved within the framework of Middlemarch. He laid the foundations of his failure early with an unfortunate matrimonial choice. The similarly idealistic and naïve Dorothea Brooke, ambitious, energetic, altruistic and philanthropic after the mold of Florence Nightingale, didn't interest him.

> *Plain women he regarded as he did the other severe facts of life, to be faced with philosophy and investigated by science. But Rosamond Vincy seemed to have the true melodic charm; and when a man has seen the woman whom he would have chosen if he had intended to marry speedily, his remaining a bachelor will usually depend on her resolution rather than on his.*

And of course, her resolution soon terminated his bachelorhood. But the fair Rosamond didn't share her new husband's idealistic approach to medicine, a fact that never dawned on Lydgate until after he had been made the happiest of men. Why should she be denied the good things appropriate to their station in life just because he had some scruples about dispensing medicines that the patients expected? He was obliged to give up his hopes in Middlemarch, and we learn his fate in the last chapter: "He had gained an excellent practice, alternating, according to the season, between London and a Continental bathing-place; having written a treatise on Gout, a disease which has a good deal of wealth on its side. His skill was relied on by many paying patients, but he always regarded himself as a failure: he had not done what he had once meant to do."

Anthony Trollope's *Dr. Thorne* (1858) appeared in English fiction about a generation after the time of Mr. Lydgate. Lydgate's training had apparently been that of a "surgeon," so he was known as "Mister." Dr. Thorne, in contrast, was a "graduated physician," entitled to be addressed as "Doctor." There was a third class of medical practitioners in England, also descended from the medieval guilds, known as "apothecaries." They compounded and sold medications, the practice Lydgate had avoided. Here again, Dr. Thorne differed from Lydgate: "As was then the wont with many country practitioners, and as should be the wont with them all if they consulted their own dignity a little less and the comforts of their customers somewhat more, he added the business of a dispensing apothecary to that of physician. In doing so, he was of course much reviled." Lydgate had suffered the scorn of his Middlemarch colleagues because he would not dispense medications; Dr. Thorne was "reviled" in the nearby towns of Barchester, "where there was a regular depôt of medical skill," and Silverbridge, "where a properly established physician had been in residence for forty years," because he did dispense medications.

In this arcane classification of health care providers, so strange to us today, the "general practitioner" apparently played a role similar to that of the "nurse practitioner" in today's rural practice. "Dr. Thorne's predecessor at Greshamsbury had been a humble-minded general practitioner, gifted with a due respect for the physicians of the county; and he, though he had been allowed to physic the servants, and sometimes the children of Greshamsbury, had never had the presumption to put himself on a par with his betters."

At the time of his story, Dr. Thorne had been in practice in the small town of Greshamsbury for over twenty years. He was described as a proud man with a sharp tongue, but his outlook was so similar to that of the author that Trollope has been said to have poured those characteristics which he most admired into the character of Dr. Thorne: the ideal of the conservative English country gentleman. His integrity obliged him to be open about his fees; he had a fixed schedule of how much was to be charged for each visit, with allowance for the distance he had to travel. His colleagues considered this to be unprofessional. "A physician should take his fee without letting his left hand know what his right hand was doing; it should be taken without a thought, without a look, without a move of the facial muscles; the true physician should hardly be aware that the last friendly grasp of the hand had been made more precious by the touch of gold."

Would Dr. Thorne, a seasoned veteran in his rural practice, have alienated a good cook who provided Christmas treats? I'm not sure. "To trifling ailments he was too often brusque. Seeing that he accepted money for the cure of such, he should, we may say, have cured them without an offensive manner. So far he is without defence. But to real suffering no one found him brusque; no patient lying painfully on a bed of sickness ever thought him rough."

We see relatively little of Dr. Thorne in his role as physician. There was one visit to his childhood friend who had become Sir Roger Scatcherd, the wealthiest man in the county. Sir Roger refused to accept a recommendation of abstinence from alcohol and rest from work, and he threatened to call another of the town doctors, Dr. Fillgrave. Dr. Thorne called his bluff: "Well, send for Fillgrave, only do it at once. Believe me at any rate in this, that whatever you do, you should do it at once. Oblige me in this; let Lady Scatcherd take away that brandy bottle till Dr. Fillgrave comes."

Of course, a consultation with a childhood friend can hardly be considered a representative sample of Dr. Thorne's bedside manner. But it can be assumed that he made himself sufficiently acceptable to make a living in his country practice. We are told he was occasionally summoned to neighboring towns to consult with colleagues on difficult cases.

The great crisis in Dr. Thorne's practice had to do with Lady Arabella Gresham, who viewed with alarm the growing friendship between her son Frank and Dr. Thorne's niece Mary. In one of the dramatic "serious interviews" that Trollope loved to describe,

Dr. Thorne refused to forbid his daughter to see her son. She angrily transferred her case to the infamous Dr. Fillgrave, but she still did not thrive, and as she became worse, the desperate family sent to London for the great Sir Omicron Pie, who came and assessed her condition. "You should have Thorne back here, Mr. Gresham," said Sir Omicron, almost in a whisper, when they were quite alone. "Dr. Fillgrave is a very good man, and so is Dr. Century; very good, I am sure. But Thorne has known her ladyship so long." And so Dr. Thorne was recalled to the care of Lady Arabella.

He was more fortunate than Lydgate in his personal affairs. After being disappointed in an early love affair, he remained a bachelor until the last chapter of the next novel in the Barsetshire series, *Framley Parsonage*. Miss Martha Dunstable, a wealthy young heiress, had distinguished herself by refusing the proposals of several inappropriate suitors and by subsequently inviting Dr. Thorne, whom she had always admired, to London to advise her on some financial affairs. They were soon married.

Dr. Thorne was also fortunate in that his niece, in the fairy tale love story of *Dr. Thorne*, inherited the Scatcherd fortune as niece to Sir Roger, and married Frank Gresham, heir to the impoverished Gresham estate. So his author saw to it that he lived happily ever after, in contrast to Lydgate, who died at age fifty, unhappy in a prosperous practice.

Lydgate sacrificed his idealistic principles and was forced to accept what was an unhappy fate for him. Dr. Thorne's major ethical standard was his integrity. He found a way to serve his patients and meet their needs. I don't think Mr. Lydgate received many parcels of sweets. I'm sure Dr. Thorne was more successful in this regard; I only wish that Sir Omicron Pie could have been consulted by the nice little lady who made my cakes and pies and cookies.

THE CURSE OF CONSUMPTION

MARION FAY

By Anthony Trollope

I was six years old when I met Tommy Wallace. He spent a good bit of time with his Aunt Rushie, who lived two doors down from us, while his mother spent a year at the Booneville Sanatorium with tuberculosis. We still see an occasional patient with tuberculosis nowadays, but the sanatoriums, including the Wildcat Mountain Sanatorium which was on the site of the present Methodist Nursing Home, are all closed or used for other purposes. However, it still causes 1.5 million deaths worldwide each year, trailing only respiratory diseases, AIDS, and diarrheal diseases as the leading infectious killers.

Tuberculosis, known back then as consumption, was widespread in the nineteenth century, causing one out of four deaths in England in 1815. It only began to subside between 1850 and 1950, when deaths due to tuberculosis decreased tenfold, from 500 per 100,000 population in 1850 to 50 per 100,000 population in 1950. Improvements in public health reduced the incidence of tuberculosis even before the advent of antibiotics in 1946 with the introduction of streptomycin. Poor living conditions and the development of resistance to antibiotics have contributed to its resurgence and worldwide threat.

Before the discovery of the tubercle bacillus in 1882, the common understanding of consumption was that it was a constitutional disorder with a strong hereditary element, giving a pale, even "haunted" look to the sufferer. As such, it played a prominent role in literature and the other arts. John Keats, Frederic Chopin, and Franz Kafka died of consumption, as did Edgar Allen Poe's wife, Virginia. Among the familiar victims in our collective consciousness are Mimi in Puccini's *La Boheme*, Violetta in Verdi's *La Traviata*, and Camille, played by Greta

TAYLOR PREWITT

Garbo in the MGM film of 1936. Doc Holliday died of tuberculosis in 1887, and his bloody cough figured prominently in the 1993 film *Tombstone*. Consumption claimed a number of characters in Dickens' novels: Little Nell in *The Old Curiosity Shop*, Nell's friend Kit, Nicholas Nickleby's faithful companion Smike, and both Richard Carstone and the boy Jo in *Bleak House*. Thomas Mann's *The Magic Mountain* portrays a sanatorium in the Swiss Alps. Other victims include Ralph Touchett in Henry James' *A Portrait of a Lady*; Edmund Tyrone in Eugene O'Neill's *Long Day's Journey into Night*; Fantin in Hugo's *Les Miserables*; Katerina Ivanovna in Dostoevsky's *Crime and Punishment*; Kirillov in *The Possessed*; and Jane Eyre's best friend in Charlotte Bronte's novel.

Anthony Trollope's two sisters and two of his three brothers died at a young age with consumption, an "established sorrow" described in his autobiography as the horrid word, Consumption. With this experience, it is no surprise that Trollope should write a novel, *Marion Fay*, about a young woman with consumption. The wonder is that it took him so long to write it; it was more than thirty years after his first novel that he wrote *Marion Fay*, which was finished in 1879.

Marion Fay's story is a sad one. A Quaker's daughter and the eldest son of a marquis meet and fall in love with each other. She refuses to marry Lord Hampstead, however, pleading first that it would be an unequal match for him, but finally admitting she has a strong family history of early death and does not expect to have a long life. Hampstead's emotional reactions are described in great detail, and much of their story is told from his point of view. She is determined from the first that she will not marry, and there is little more to think or say about it. She gradually becomes more open with him as her illness progresses, writing frequent letters from her seaside location. Most of the agonies belong to him, while she appears relatively tranquil, though she does indulge in a Trollopian flop onto the sofa to bury her tearful face in a cushion.

The reader is shielded from some of the details. For one thing, the descriptions emphasize the mental processes. There are no bloody scenes. The color would sometimes rise to Marion's cheeks, and those in the room would hear only a preparation for a cough, not the cough itself. This preparatory sound, the author tells us, is the one so familiar to those obliged to follow the downward course of someone dear to them. And that's it. Marion's illness is said to be a description of the course of Trollope's sister Emily, and she is said to have had a quiet and peaceful course and death. Apparently, if she had a hacking cough or brought up bright red blood, Anthony missed it. In any event, the reader is spared.

As Marion becomes more ill, a frustrated Hampstead, who has fallen under the Victorian illusion that a woman is obliged to obey the man she loves, fails to understand how he cannot control the situation. He has difficulty accepting the inevitable fate she has predicted. A woman has no right to accept such a fate. Such things must be left to "Providence, or Chance, or Fate, as you may call it."

On the other hand, George's mother and Marion's friend, Mrs. Roden, confirms her understanding and acceptance, and she marvels that she can soar above weakness and temptation. This angelic portrayal is surely influenced by Trollope's recollection of his sister Emily.

Two chapters of comic relief follow the end of Marion's tragedy, and the author's ironic touch is shown in his summation of the Civil Service, which had figured in the novel's subplots and was personified by Lord Persiflage: "Everybody knew that Lord Persiflage understood the Civil Service of his country perfectly. He was a man who never worked very hard himself or expected those under him to do so; but he liked common sense, and hated scruples, and he considered it to be a man's duty to take care of himself, -- of himself first of all, and then, perhaps, afterwards, of the Service."

Interestingly, the word "consumption" is never mentioned. Trollope had written about Henry and Emily's illness in his autobiography, saying that though she was doomed and he knew it, the word was never spoken.

The edition published by the University of Michigan Press in 1982 features the original illustrations of William Small, in which we see the Marquis of Kingsbury (father of Lord Hampstead) looking remarkably like the author, who was used as the model for the Marquis.

No one can begrudge Trollope his novel about consumption. His brothers and sisters died from it, and he used his observations of his sisters to create Marion Fay. The tragedy of the fatal familial curse is presented, and, though it is quite sentimental, it is not badly done. The artist in Trollope knew that he had to leave 'em laughing, and he backed away from the central sadness of the story to return to his objects of fun. Good. He was better at comedy than he was at tragedy.

DEATH COMETH TO EVERY MAN

THE DEATH OF IVAN ILYCH
By Leo Tolstoy

EVERYMAN
By Philip Roth

Death is a downer, by and large. And what may be even worse to those who stand at many bedsides is its ordinariness. There may be an occasional utterance of dramatic last words, but the more usual course is simply the cessation of vital signs.

Life goes on, we say. The Earth shrugs. That's the way it goes. Death is part of life. The funeral director gives a warm smile. But despite all this evidence from direct observation, the grieving survivors continue to cry, "But that's not all! There's more to it."

Two writers have addressed this issue with fairly clinical descriptions of an ordinary death of an ordinary man, raising questions in each case, and perhaps implying answers, but leaving the real answers to the reader.

The imminent approach of death assumes such ominous and final importance that there is often a tendency to change the subject and allow the intrusion of less relevant issues, such as wondering what the diagnosis might be. Modern medicine, of course, has postponed death in many instances by identifying a specific diagnosis and bringing some form of treatment into play, often referred to as life-saving. Perhaps so, but the funeral director merely smiles. Pay me now or pay me later. And if you don't pay me, pay my son when he succeeds me in the business.

With this in mind, it is interesting that Ivan Ilych died without benefit of diagnosis. By today's standards, both medical and literary, this is highly irregular, and I must confess that I began trying to formulate a differential diagnosis as soon as he bumped his side and began to complain of pain. A convenient list can be readily generated. His progressive painful course would be consistent with malignant disease, perhaps carcinoma of the pancreas or kidney. One must keep an open mind, and poisoning by his wife, perhaps with arsenic, has been suggested.

Who knows what the master had in mind? In the absence of specific revelation in the text, a more prudent reading would be to take Leo Tolstoy's story, *The Death of Ivan Ilych* (published 1886), at face value, and to accept that the author was more concerned with the process of coping with one's imminent death and its attendant angst and discomfort than with any particular disease process.

We are told at the beginning that Ivan Ilych is dead and that nobody misses him. The ritual phrases are uttered and the ritual acts are performed. But the concerns are merely for how his place will be filled, and for how affairs will be arranged for his wife and family, not for the poor late and unlamented Ivan Ilych himself.

And as we become acquainted with Ivan Ilych, we learn that he is Everyman, just like "Everyman" in Philip Roth's novel (Vintage Books, 2006) of the same name. Ivan Ilych is a lawyer, a civil servant, and finally a Public Prosecutor, though not a particularly distinguished or heroic one. He is scrupulous in separating his public role from his private life, and he plays his public role by the book, accepting and following the letter of the law. As a young man, his youthful indiscretions are carried out "with clean hands, in clean linen, with French phrases, and above all among people of the best society with the approval of people of rank." He marries as a matter of course rather than in the course of deep love and understanding; when his wife becomes more irritable, he transfers the "center of gravity of his life" to his work.

And then, after seventeen years of marriage, he slips on a ladder and hits his side against the knob of a window frame. He begins to notice some pain in his left side, though the injury was only a slight bruise. And he begins to notice a queer taste in his mouth. As these symptoms progress, he consults a doctor. He discovers in his medical visits that the doctors regard him with the same indifference that he maintained for those who were brought before him as a magistrate.

He becomes disillusioned with the society of the best people, whom he has attempted to cultivate throughout his life. The only interest they have in him is whether he will soon vacate his place. His only friend in his despair is the butler's young assistant, Gerasim, the only one who will acknowledge the situation and address it. Everyone else appears to accept the falsehood that Ivan Ilych is merely ill, not a dying man, and this is a source of torment for him. Gerasim alone doesn't lie. "We shall all of us die, so why should I grudge a little trouble?"

Alas, none of his physicians are frank with him. As he undergoes the ritual of interview and physical examination, Ivan Ilych sees through their nonsense and deception.

At some point along the sad course of Ivan Ilych's terminal illness, it becomes more difficult to forget that Ivan Ilych is a creature of the author of two of the world's greatest novels, *War and Peace* and *Anna Karenina*. Leo Tolstoy renounced these works as not being true to life, and *Ivan Ilych* was written after his conversion to an unorthodox form of Christianity, which embraced the teachings of the Sermon on the Mount, endorsed ascetic rejection of the comforts of the world, and rejected the dogmas of the Russian Orthodox Church, which excommunicated him. "Live seeking God and then you will not live without God," he concluded. Tolstoy himself died at the age of eighty-two, just after renouncing his ancestral estate and all his worldly goods and taking off by himself in the middle of winter to live the life of a Russian peasant. He made it as far as the Astapovo train station, where he caught pneumonia and died in the stationmaster's home.

The Death of Ivan Ilych speaks for itself; but as it does so, the reader begins to realize that Everyman is becoming more and more an individual unique in details as he faces the fate awaiting us all. Is he a mouthpiece for Tolstoy's own philosophy? Yes, to a certain extent, he is. But in this work, the artist won out over the preacher. The reader begins to root for poor Ivan.

"What do you want?" he asks himself. "To live and not to suffer."

His illness is long enough to allow him to pursue his ideas and change some of them. He initially rejects any feeling of remorse for how he has lived his life. "And whenever the thought occurred to him, as it often did, that it all resulted from his not having lived as he ought to have done, he at once recalled the correctness of his whole life and dismissed so strange an idea."

But then, in seeing the falsity of his footman, his wife, his daughter, and his doctors, he also sees himself as one great deception, concealing both life and death. As death approaches, he is given a large dose of opium, but the subsequent three days of continual screaming, using variations of the vowel "O," indicate that his end of life care might have been handled more skillfully. And then, two hours before his death, he finds himself being thrust into a black hole, but not able to get right into it because of his conviction that his life wasn't a good one. Then at the last moment, feeling a sudden blow to his chest and side, he "fell through the hole and there at the bottom was a light." He realized that though his life had not been what it should have been, he could still take action. And he attempted to say words of understanding to his wife and son, "Sorry for you," and ask for forgiveness. "He whose understanding mattered would understand."

He sought his former fear of death, but instead of the fear there was light. These final words form his coda: "Death is finished. It is no more."

At some point, the author has changed from the acute imaginative observer into the mystic who sees light instead of death. But who can deny the vision to the mystic? One of my cousins told me of a near-death experience after a nearly fatal car wreck, with a detailed account of seeing his deceased family members and even his childhood dogs. The reporter can relate these experiences even if he cannot explain them.

Having followed the thoughts of Ivan Ilych in his terminal illness, it is apparent that Tolstoy had no concerns about the clinical diagnosis of the cause of death. The persistent diagnostician might call for some details about the urinalysis, the results of which would alter the physician's directions. But then there was some contraindication between the findings of the urinalysis and the patient's symptoms. If there was an abnormality in the appearance of the urine, the progressive pain in his side may have been related to carcinoma of the kidney. And tumors can sometimes be associated with a disorder of the sense of taste. Surely his wife wasn't slipping him arsenic, was she?

That is a question for Agatha Christie, not Leo Tolstoy, who showed us the doors of the shadow of death. The end is always the same, but the details are always different. "Why these sufferings?" Ivan asked. "For no reason – they just are so," his voice answered him. But Ivan Ilych persisted, and his search for meaning in death has become a classic. Tolstoy couldn't have rejected this story, even in his right mind.

Philip Roth takes a more moderate, or perhaps a more devious, approach in describing Everyman. Whereas Ivan Ilych is led by his painful suffering to explore the meaning of suffering in life and seems to see the light in some way in the end, poor Everyman is caught blindsided by death. Some deaths, often those from cancer, follow a course so relentlessly downhill that one can almost predict at what point the downward slope will intersect the baseline and death will occur. This was Ivan Ilych's course. Other deaths, often those from heart disease, follow not a progressive downhill slope, but a more horizontal line interrupted by sudden events. You know what is going to happen, but you don't know when. This was the fate of Everyman, who had the misfortune to be an "arteriopath."

Every cardiology practice has its share of "arteriopaths," people who are afflicted by "hardening of the arteries," not just those to the brain, as is sometimes implied in popular use of this term, but those throughout the body – the pipes that go to the legs, the heart, the brain, everywhere. Often appearing at a young age in smokers and diabetics, who are particularly prone to this affliction, it may subject the victim to a long series of operations and other procedures in an effort to restore circulation and stave off the symptoms of angina pectoris and myocardial infarction, strokes and transient ischemic attacks ("TIAs"), and intermittent claudication (pain in the leg on walking) and gangrene.

Everyman was such an arteriopath. We are not told whether he was a smoker and no mention is made of diabetes mellitus, but we are told that his older brother was healthy with no such problems.

He died of a cardiac arrest at seventy-three, at the time of a carotid endarterectomy, his seventh vascular procedure in seven years. He had a five-vessel coronary artery bypass at fifty-six in 1989, and nine years later he had the first of seven annual vascular procedures. He had a renal artery stent in 1998, and then in following years a left carotid endarterectomy, a stent in the left anterior descending coronary artery, a stent in one of his grafts, three coronary stents, and then a defibrillator.

The death of this most ordinary of men was bereft of any drama; his demise was due to a cardiac arrest while he was under a general anesthetic for surgery. None of his family or friends even knew he was in the hospital.

Almost an elaborate case history, the book validates the dictum, "Every patient has a story." And in this story, we see the world through Everyman's eyes. He is Jewish and this is pertinent mainly in that he denies any religious faith; he certainly has no expectation of life after death. He sees his daughter Nancy as his major success in life, who still wanted to praise him even after all he had put her through by betraying her mother, Phoebe. She was "a pure and sensible girl, besmirched only by her unstinting generosity, harmlessly hiding from unhappiness by blotting out the faults of everyone dear to her and by overloving love."

Roth's ear for the question-and-answer rhythm of Everyman's speech gives the reader a feeling of knowing this kind of man.

Here, he calls the widow of an old advertising colleague who died recently:

> *"Was it a stroke or was it a heart attack?" he asked her.*
> *"It was a myocardial infarct."*
> *"Had he been feeling ill?"*
> *"Well, his blood pressure had been—well, he had a lot of trouble with his blood pressure. And then this past weekend he wasn't feeling so great. His blood pressure had gone up again."*
> *"They couldn't control that with drugs?"*

In the course of a relatively routine operation that carries a mortality rate on the order of five percent, Everyman became one of the five percent and failed to wake up. On the day of his funeral, "Up and down the state that day, there'd been five hundred funerals like his." His brother Howie told a few details from his childhood, but otherwise it was an ordinary funeral for an ordinary man who had an ordinary death. "But then it's the commonness that's most wrenching, the registering once more of the fact of death that overwhelms everything."

Everyman's struggle with his mortality was accelerated by a condition, atherosclerosis, that shortened his life; but because "hardening of the arteries" is not cancer or a raging infection, it seems less like a terminal illness and more like a process of aging. There was so little drama in his last days that he didn't bother to tell his daughter Nancy he would be having another surgery. He went to the hospital alone, recalling a similar trip to the hospital with his mother when he had an inguinal hernia repair at the age of twelve.

Roth leaves the reader feeling that Everyman had had a life; a tawdry one, perhaps, with three wives and three divorces, but a life all his own and then a rather commonplace death, with not even a whimper. In *Everyman*, we see the tension between the ordinary and the extraordinary. We are all alike, and we are all different. And we all die.

"Any man's death diminishes me," John Donne wrote. And

what would the great poet have said about the death of Philip Roth's Everyman? "Well, yes, of course. A little, perhaps. But not too much."

Life goes on. Death is part of life. I hope the funeral director had a warm smile for the survivors of Everyman.

THE RUSSIAN MASTER OF
LITERATURE AND MEDICINE

CHEKHOV'S DOCTORS
A Collection of Chekhov's Medical Tales
Edited by Jack Coulehan

"He (or she) is our Chekhov," has become a cliché in recent years, used in praise of a more recent writer, such as Peter Taylor, Alice Munro, or Tennessee Williams. "Our Chekhov" implies that "their Chekhov" must have been different; and he was indeed of a different time and place: Czarist Russia in the nineteenth century. But Chekhov's fiction may have been stranger to his contemporary Russian readers than it is to us. We have become accustomed to the kind of trivia that he emphasized, showing the world as it is rather than how it should be. The resolution of the story's problems is left to the reader's imagination; nobody spells out all the consequences. We have learned this from "our three Chekhovs" listed above, and also from Raymond Carver (who referred to Chekhov as the greatest short story writer who ever lived), Ernest Hemingway, Katherine Mansfield, and others who have acknowledged their indebtedness to him.

He has been recognized as a giant in the world of literature, yet he was also a physician who continued to practice medicine until his own tuberculosis forced him to give it up, a few years before it caused his death at the age of forty-four. There have been quite a few physician-authors, but few if any of his literary stature. In his introduction to *Chekhov's Doctors: A Collection of Chekhov's Medical Tales* (The Kent State University Press, 2003), Jack Coulehan quotes the twenty-eight-year-old Chekhov in a letter to his editor, "Medicine is my lawful wedded wife and literature my mistress. When one gets on my nerves, I spend the night with the other."

His life and work as a physician have been well described by Richard Carter, M.D. in "Anton P. Chekhov, MD (1860-1904): Dual Medical and Literary Careers"[20]. The physician who treated Chekhov for peritonitis at seventeen encouraged him to go to medical school, though Chekhov wrote years later that he didn't remember why he chose medicine, but he didn't regret it. He began coughing up blood in the year he graduated from medical school, indicating the presence of tuberculosis then. In spite of his chronic illness, he had great energy, working to support his bankrupt father and the rest of his family while attending medical school, earning money by private tutoring, catching and selling goldfinches, and by writing short humorous sketches for newspapers and magazines.

After working in a small town hospital, he started practice in Moscow at the age of twenty-four. A year later, he wrote in a letter that he stayed busy with his medical practice, had many friends and acquaintances, and therefore had quite a few patients. Half his patients had to be treated gratis, and the others paid three to five rubles a visit. He didn't expect to make a fortune any time soon.

He made a heroic trip across Siberia to the penal colony at Sakhalin Island, off the east coast of Russia, where he spent three months studying conditions there, subsequently reporting his findings in a paper he submitted as a Ph.D. thesis. Though he didn't succeed in receiving his degree, his report, *The Island of Sakhalin*, was regarded as the definitive account of Russian penology. Millions of people had been made to rot in prison in a barbaric manner, he concluded.

He worked both as a physician and as a medical administrator during the devastating famine of 1891-1892. Exhausted by this effort, he bought a run-down estate in the village of Melikhovo, about fifty miles south of Moscow, where he devoted himself to

---

[20] *Annals of Thoracic Surgery*, volume 61, pages 1557-1563, 1996

improving the farm, raising money for the village schools, and entertaining his many visitors. He no longer accepted fees for his medical services, but he treated the peasants who came from miles away to seek his care, without charge.

Dr. Coulehan, who is a retired professor of preventive medicine at The State University of New York in Stony Brook, New York, selected stories where physicians play a major role. (Chekhov's overall work could be used as a sociological source of everyday life in Russia.) Some of his stories are pretty short, probably because he started out writing short little pot-boilers for the popular press and then developed them into an art form. To the present-day reader, Czarist Russia was a strange and varied place; and Chekhov's medical practice brought him into contact with all levels of society. There must have been little concern about patients' privacy in those days; there is no report of any concern about identifying any of his characters with patients he saw, or their families.

Life is hard, doctors are sometimes put upon, and one doesn't have to spend much time in the doctor's lounge to hear complaints from doctors suffering from the "working too hard syndrome," where there's a mismatch between the demands of the job and the doctor's physical and emotional resources to deal with them. Reading the story "Enemies" brought to mind the prediction made by one of my new partners after I had just started in practice. At an introductory supper at his house, he told me, "Some day you will have been up all night, and the clinic will be busy, and you'll have a hospital full of sick patients, and when you finally get through you'll be so tired that you can't wait to go home and go to bed, and that's when the phone will ring, and Joe Roberts in Booneville will be calling to tell you that he's just sent an ambulance with a comatose patient in heart failure to be admitted to you."

"Enemies" describes an even worse situation: the doctor's six-year-old son has just died of diphtheria, his wife is distraught, and a man at his door demands that the doctor come with him immediately to see his wife, who is dangerously ill. The doctor complains bitterly but finds that the path of least resistance is to accompany the man to see his wife. As it turns out, however, she was only pretending illness and has run away with another man. When this sinks in, the doctor explodes: "I am a doctor; you look upon doctors and people generally who work and don't stink of perfume and prostitution as your menials and *mauvais ton*; well, you may look upon them so, but no one has given you the right to treat a man who is suffering as a stage property!"

This story can be taken as a parable, and it is amenable to a number of interpretations. Should the doctor's responsibility to his bereaved wife have outweighed his responsibility to respond to the distraught husband's demands? Should the doctor have preserved his professional dignity? Although Chekhov rarely pointed morals, he did conclude this story with a look inside the doctor's mind, which may resonate with the thoughts of some of today's physicians as they drive to the hospital in the middle of a cold night, beset with ungenerous thoughts. Dr. Kirilov condemned the man and his wife and the other man and everyone who was comfortable at that moment. "Time will pass and Kirilov's sorrow will pass," the story concludes, "but that conviction, unjust and unworthy of the human heart, will not pass, but will remain in the doctor's mind to the grave."

Chekhov worked hard at his practice; he worked hard on his writing; and he considered himself apolitical, but he did have his own views on a number of social issues. This concern for the victims of institutionalization appears in "Ward No. 6," one of his best-known stories, which describes a lodge that has all the signs of a neglected institution: "a stench of sour cabbage, of smoldering wicks, of bugs, and of ammonia."

This is only the setting. The story concerns Dr. Andrey Yefimitch Ragin, the medical director, who realized when he took the job that the institution was in terrible condition. At first, he thought it should simply be closed, but he later reflects that if such impurities should be expunged from this place, they would only appear in another. He was attentive and clever in his diagnoses at first, but in time the monotony and uselessness of his situation have sapped his energy. What was to be gained by adding five or ten years to a shopkeeper's life? Why should one attempt to alleviate suffering anyway? Was it not suffering that led man to perfection? And if medications should relieve suffering, would not man then abandon religion and philosophy, which not only brought him protection but also happiness?

Hard to believe? Perhaps so, but the son of one of my patients told the doctor at the bedside of his dying mother that he shouldn't use medicine for pain because it would only make his mother spend more time suffering in purgatory.

Ragin eventually became interested in one of the paranoid "lunatics" and spent long hours in conversation with him. This was so irregular that he was relieved of his position and he eventually found himself to be a patient in Ward No. 6, where he soon had a stroke and died. "The hospital porters came, took him by his arms and his legs, and carried him away to the chapel."

Chekhov, it has been said, could not accept the views on nonviolence and radical Christianity then being propounded by Leo Tolstoy, and he wrote "Ward No. 6" to express his disagreement with the born-again master. He also inserted his own opinions about social issues into "A Doctor's Visit," a story about a young physician called to see a factory owner's daughter with spells of fast heart beat. Just as his patients' chronic complaints were incomprehensible and incurable, so too were factories also baffling. The doctor began to look at all possible improvements in the lives of the factory workers as achievements to be compared to the treatment of incurable diseases.

The prevailing impression of these stories is one of detached irony. The writer appeared to have feelings about what he described, but he preferred description to preaching. A physician struck an orderly and expected to be sued and dismissed in "An Awkward Business". The magistrate, however, merely scolded the orderly and said there was no need for a trial. "How stupid," the doctor thought, that after all his worries, the end should be so absurd and vulgar.

A princess wept after being scolded by a doctor for her lack of sympathy and humanity in "The Princess", but on the next day she congratulated herself for bringing warmth, light and joy everywhere she went, smiling graciously even on her enemies.

A law student became obsessed with the idea of trying to rescue prostitutes and was taken to a mental specialist, marveling that his scholarly achievements were highly praised, but that he was now considered mad because he was more concerned about fallen women than he was about the furniture in the room. And immediately after being examined, he felt immediately cured.

An obviously guilty murderer was found not guilty in court in "The Head Gardener's Story," because the jury couldn't believe anyone would have murdered the good doctor.

A physician's approach to his job is opposite to that of the novelist, in many ways. The physician listens to his patients' stories; their drama, their sadness, their humor are not lost on him; it his duty is to be sympathetic. But the physician's job is to minimize the drama and cut through the complex to arrive at the simple in an effort to help alleviate distress and solve problems. The novelist, on the other hand, loves complexity and ambiguity; he loves taking a simple story and developing all its ramifications. The practicing physician, though, is not at the bedside merely to be entertained by a fascinating life story, or even by an "interesting" diagnostic problem. The important thing is that the patient gets better. I sometimes told patients that I would rather have a cure than a diagnosis.

It is of interest that Chekhov, the physician-artist, wrote plays and short stories, and some of the stories were very short indeed. He never wrote a novel. He described with precision and he sometimes seemed to concentrate on small things. He left the big picture and the long novels for his friend Tolstoy. Richard Ford has written in his introduction to a selection of Tolstoy's stories, "Chekhov is *not* famously aphoristic, and seems mostly to prefer stressing the way life struggles unheroically toward normalcy rather than serving up moments in which it is exceptional or by canny observation caused to seem so... His stories rarely resolve in highly dramatic, epiphanic endings. And by largely eschewing this strategy they seem to refer us back to their own often unsensational, interior details."

And in this way we can see how Chekhov maintained that his writing benefitted from his medical career. Whether he said so in so many words or not, he had one of his characters put it the other way around by protesting that medical studies that provide no general culture lead to a profession that is half-educated and underdeveloped.

Chekhov married relatively late in his short life and died only a few years later. On his deathbed he was brought a glass of champagne to stimulate his failing heart; he observed that it had been a long time since he had had a glass of champagne. He emptied his glass, began to ramble in his speech, turned on his side, and stopped breathing.

Irony to the last.

NOT SUCH A MAGNIFICENT OBSESSION

OF HUMAN BONDAGE
By Somerset Maugham

Unread books on the shelf hardly qualify as old friends one knows well, but their familiarity may grant them the status of old friends one might like to know better. Or, in the case of Somerset Maugham, whose face I knew from the dust jacket of *Mr. Maugham Himself*, a Book-of–the-Month Club selection standing unread on the living room shelf when I was a boy, they may continue to exist as old family acquaintances. So when I happened to notice on Abraham Verghese's web site that reading *Of Human Bondage* by Somerset Maugham was the experience that prompted him to become a doctor, I thought to myself, "Oh, yes. Mr. Maugham. It's time I read that."

Maugham declares in the foreword that though *Of Human Bondage* is not an autobiography, it is an autobiographical novel, and that as the memories of his past life became an obsession, he found the only way to free himself of them was "to write them all down on paper." Such an avowed purpose could hardly lead to a light-hearted novel. This one is serious.

Like his protagonist, Philip Crain, Maugham attended medical school. However, although Maugham became so successful with his writing that he never practiced, the book ends as his hero resolves to enter a private practice in a small coastal town, becoming a junior partner to a crusty senior physician who practices mainly among the poor. Philip's path wasn't a smooth one, though. He had an unhappy childhood in his uncle's vicarage after his mother's death; an unhappy time at a boarding school; a brief respite at Heidelberg where he studied German and French, another unhappy time; a rather frustrating and unsuccessful effort to become a painter in Paris, when Manet's *Olympia* was causing a sensation; and finally a fairly satisfactory time in medical school in London, marred by the "bondage" of an obsession with a plain, unimaginative waitress, and also by the later necessity of interrupting medical school to work in a department store to keep from starving.

It is generally assumed that Maugham exorcised a number of demons in the writing of this novel. Philip had a clubfoot; it has been speculated that this might have been a surrogate for Maugham's homosexuality, or perhaps his stammer. Like Philip, however, the author had also lost his mother at an early age; had been raised in a vicarage; had an unhappy time in The King's School in Canterbury; pursued a course of study in Heidelberg; spent a short time in an accountant's office; and finally attended medical school in London. Growing pains are an occupational hazard of youth, as Philip learned in his loneliness and sexual frustration in Heidelberg: "It is an illusion that youth is happy, an illusion of those who have lost it; but the young know they are wretched, for they are full of the truthless ideals which have been instilled into them, and each time they come in contact with the real they are bruised and wounded."

Both Maugham and Philip Crain certainly had their share of these growing pains, and the *bildungsroman,* a coming-of-age novel, can be an effective vehicle for seeing the world with the fresh eyes of a young person viewing it for the first time. England at the end of the nineteenth century had not changed very much from the England of Charles Dickens, and Philip's adventures bring David Copperfield and Oliver Twist to mind. After his mother's death, Philip was sent to live with his uncle, a vicar would say grace when it was time for his afternoon tea, cut the top off his egg, and offer it to Philip as he ate the rest of it himself.

Philip encountered the English concept of the "gentleman" at Tercanbury (Canterbury) School, which he attended at the age of thirteen. Some of his classmates had made up their minds to be ordained, but others observed that the church wasn't what it used to be. Some of the curates were sons of tradesmen, that is, anyone so unfortunate as not to be a landowner or a member of one of the four professions that marked one as a gentleman: medicine, law, the clergy, and service as a military officer. It would be better to go to the Colonies than to serve under some fellow who wasn't a gentleman.

Like Dickens, Maugham kept his story going with a host of vividly portrayed minor characters coming in and out of Phillip's life, including Miss Wilkinson, a family friend, thirty-something but close to forty, who initiated him into the facts of life; Hayward, a dilettante a few years senior to Phillip who told him that "accuracy is for clerks," and who gave him Newman's *Apologia* to read "for its style, not for its matter"; Cronshaw, the drunken poet he met in the back corner of a bar in Paris, who told him that sobriety disturbed conversation, and that if he looked at Persian carpets long enough, he would learn the meaning of life; and Miss Price, the homely little painter who befriended him in Paris, was reluctant to acknowledge that her work was mediocre, and hanged herself.

Larger parts were played by his uncle, the vicar of the topped egg, who finally died leaving Phillip with enough money to finish medical school; and by Thorpe Athelny, a short man given to wearing blue linen trousers and a very old brown velvet coat, who invited Philip to Sundays with his large family, saving him from starvation. Thorpe told him of his travels to Spain, and he may or may not have come from an old and honored family and a Winchester education.

Then of course, there was Mildred the waitress. Who knows what Mildred represented in the author's life? It must have been something significant to warrant the title and so much space in the book. Mildred was presented as a boring young woman, "tall and thin, with narrow hips and the chest of a boy," anemic with delicate skin "of a faint green colour," a waitress who "went about her duties with a bored look." The more indifferent she remained to him, and the more attention she paid to other men, the more he was infatuated with her. She concluded the first phase of his courtship by telling him she was to be married, and for a time Philip found consolation in a comfortable relationship with Norah, a married but separated woman with a "pleasant, ugly face," who wrote penny novelettes and gave Philip a solid and durable happiness. But Philip wasn't governed by reason in choosing his path, and he accepted Mildred when she returned to him after her preferred lover couldn't free himself of his wife and family. "He was a little horrified by her feeling that her body was a commodity which she could deliver indifferently as an acknowledgement for services rendered." He saw her off to a nursing home to have her former lover's baby, and after her confinement, he lost her to his best friend. Disgusted with himself and feeling that he was a bit mad, Philip happened to see Norah, who introduced him to her fiancé. There was nothing left so he devoted himself to his medical studies.

How had Philip decided to be a doctor? After abandoning his apprenticeship in accounting, he had been obliged to face his uncle's questioning, declaring himself now ready to settle down after having had his fling. And what was he to settle down to? He hadn't made up his mind; there were any of a dozen possibilities. Therefore, his uncle told him, the best thing for him to do would be to follow his father's profession and become a doctor.

"Oddly enough, that is precisely what I intend."

Philip's migration from accounting and art to medicine is surely not unique. I still don't know whether my own call to medicine was due more to its appeal or to a negative perception of myself in the business world. But Philip wasn't so flippant as his conversation with his uncle implied. His serious reflections run throughout the book, as shown in this rather tedious train of thought:

> The thing then was to discover what one was and one's system of philosophy would devise itself. It seemed to Philip that there were three things to find out: man's relation to the world he lives in, man's relation with the men among whom he lives, and finally man's relation to himself. He made an elaborate plan of study.

One would hope the plan would be elaborate. Such issues

hardly lend themselves to casual thought.

The author tells us that medical school was no longer as it was in the day of Dickens' Bob Sawyer. But his account of gross anatomy suggests that some things don't change much. His anatomy professor told the students they would be required to learn many tedious things that they would forget as soon as their examinations were over. But "it is better to have learned and lost than never to have learned at all."

Philip found life in the raw in the outpatient clinics, where alcoholism was the most common diagnosis among the men, and malnutrition most frequent in the women. We are reminded that a hospital was a charitable institution in the pre-National Health Service days in England. Most patients, however, thought of the hospital as a state institution paid for by their taxes and provided for them as one of their rights as a citizen. The physician who gave his time to care for them, they assumed, was handsomely paid.

Two particularly vivid experiences stand out in his medical school years. The first was his own episode of near starvation, resulting from the loss of his patrimony in an unfortunate venture into the stock market. His state of homelessness and exhaustion was relieved by his friend Thorpe Athelny, who took him in, saw that he was fed, and helped him find employment in a department store until his uncle died, finally leaving him enough money to resume his medical studies. Here, incidentally, is a revealing look at the life of department store employees, who received only subsistence wages and slept and ate in a communal existence in a dormitory sponsored by the store. The other experience was his duty in midwifery, in which he visited crowded, filthy houses where babies were unwelcome as one more mouth to feed. There was often a wish that the child might be born dead or else die quickly.

Here he found that the greatest tragedy in these people's lives was the loss of work, greater even than separation or death.

He wasn't quite through with Mildred, whom he found walking the streets as a prostitute. He took her in as his domestic help, but he declined to sleep with her, and eventually the scorned woman left after trashing his apartment.

Philip wasn't left without a mate, however. He spent a fortnight in the hop fields of Kent with the Athelny family, an agricultural sabbatical reminiscent of the mowing scene in *Anna Karenina* when Levin cut the field with a scythe. Here his attention was drawn to Sally, Athelny's oldest daughter, whose easy and assured gait attracted his notice; she seemed to walk the earth with decision.

Philip was no match for the commonsense of the seventeen-year-old girl, and for her he forsook his dream of going to sea as a ship's doctor.

Philip came a long way in his first thirty years. A likeable young man who enjoyed other people, he finally released himself from the "human bondage" that was painful for him and almost exhausting for the reader. The overall impact of *Of Human Bondage* is that it shows much of life and shows it well. So much of life is trial and error. And so much of it is error. But it is good to be reminded that beauty can arise from ashes, to paraphrase Maugham's first projected title. One can understand that a sensitive, intelligent young person could find the inspiration to become a physician in this story.

A SABBATICAL FROM LIFE

THE MAGIC MOUNTAIN
By Thomas Mann

My internship year, 1963, included two months at the Gravely Sanatorium in Chapel Hill, North Carolina (which we referred to as "The Grave", of course), a quiet respite from the fast pace of the internal medicine service. On walking across the street from North Carolina Memorial Hospital, one entered a different world in time. No one was in a hurry. Patients' lengths of stay were reckoned in months, not days and weeks. We made rounds on each patient every day, but new developments were unusual. Even the cultures for *Mycobacterium tuberculosis* took six weeks to grow, not twenty-four hours. Oh, there was the occasional emergency. Sometimes a patient would be transferred with a "hemorrhage," coughing up large amounts of blood, but I don't recall such a thing happening during my rotation. Interns were still required to be on call every other night, but we could usually count on a good night's sleep in the interns' quarters. It was a different world.

The sanatorium era didn't last much longer; it's surprising that it lasted as long as it did, after the discovery, in 1944, that streptomycin, and later other antibiotics, could usually cure the disease. My next experience with tuberculosis was in the Sebastian County Health Department in 1975, filling in for the pulmonary disease specialist who was away for a year. The Arkansas Tuberculosis Sanatorium at Booneville had closed in 1973, and tuberculosis was treated on an outpatient basis. Even here, the pace was much slower than in my office practice. Patients were ushered in and out of the director's office, the nurse placed chest x-rays on the viewing box, and the physician thumbed through the chart and followed a set routine of management, without being required to stir from his chair.

On the belief that rest, good nutrition, and fresh air would help the body's immune system wall off pockets of tuberculosis infection in the lungs, sanatoria began to appear in Europe and subsequently in North America in the late nineteenth century. Mortality from tuberculosis in Arkansas decreased from eighty percent to fifty percent with treatment at the state sanatorium in Booneville. The discovery of streptomycin in 1943 offered the first successful drug treatment for tuberculosis, and treatment gradually shifted from sanatoria to general hospitals, and then to outpatient clinics.

Thomas Mann tells us in an essay introducing *The Magic Mountain* (first published in Germany in 1924) that his wife entered a sanatorium high in the Alps at Davos, Switzerland, in 1912. She stayed there for six months for treatment for a "lung complaint," while he stayed at home with their children. He visited her for three weeks, and out of this experience he wrote *The Magic Mountain,* ostensibly an account of coping with the natural history of tuberculosis in the isolated and rarefied atmosphere of the snowy Alps, but also a leisurely exploration of another pathological process, the development of the mentality that led to the devastation of World War I in civilized Europe.

The author tells us that he developed a "bronchial cold" during his three-week visit. He accompanied his wife to see the doctor for her regular examination, and he consulted the doctor, who told him he had a "moist spot" in his lung and advised a six-month stay. Mann declined, and when he returned home he began writing *The Magic Mountain.* But then World War I began, the writing was interrupted, and when it was finally resumed in the early 1920s, the author's views about Germany and the war had changed a bit. So did the scope of the novel.

The reader's first impression of *The Magic Mountain* is that it is a long book and moves rather slowly. My most vivid recollection from an earlier reading is the fresh, clean, cold, clear mountain air high in the Swiss Alps. "Hans Castorp took in a deep, experimental breath of the strange air. It was fresh, and that was all. It had no perfume, no content, no humidity; it breathed in

300

easily, and held for him no associations."

If the air is free of any associations, so too is Hans Castorp's brain an empty vessel to be filled. And there is all the time in the world, it seems, high above the civilization of Europe. The leisurely pace is part of the treatment program, as Hans Castorp learns; once the reader adjusts to the pace, however, one begins to appreciate the change that tuberculosis and its treatment imposed upon its victims at that time. And on another level, one enters into the world that took Europe into The Great War of 1914-1918.

The Magic Mountain will not yield its secrets to a quick-in-and-out reader, too accustomed to the blistering pace of today's movies. The trick is to pretend that time is no more urgent in the reading of the book than it was in the rarefied atmosphere of the sanatorium. Hans' cousin Joachim tells him on his arrival, "They make pretty free with a human being's idea of time, up here. You wouldn't believe it. Three weeks are just like a day to them. You'll learn all about it... One's ideas get changed."

And indeed this is a novel of ideas, framed in the sanatorium setting and delivered by mouthpieces conveying the author's reflections after Germany, his own country, had been devastated by the war. One of the mouthpieces, Lodovico Settembrini, is an Italian gadfly who, in attempting to dissect the complex German spirit, concedes that he admires German Protestantism as the "historical opponent of the enslavement of knowledge," explaining that the two major contributions to humanity made by central Europe are the printing press and the Reformation. But then he warns that the German heritage of Lutheran Protestantism also contains elements of quiescent beatitude and abstract abstraction, which are foreign to its laws and customs. Beware. There madness lies. And this was written before the advent of Adolf Hitler.

The foil to Settembrini is a Jewish Jesuit, Leo Naphta, to whom nothing is complex. It is all too black and too white with no gray areas. Neither torture nor capital punishment pose any moral problem for Naphta, as long as it's carried out trying to save souls and advance the cause of the true religion (his own brand of the Catholic religion).

There is a third character, who appears relatively late: Mynheer Peeperkorn, a giant of a man who is presented as a Dutchman from the colonies in Java, a retired coffee-planter with alcoholism and an intermittent, malignant tropical fever. He dominates every group he finds himself in, more by force of his personality than by any eloquence, for he has great difficulty in completing sentences. Hans Castorp, our "empty vessel," follows him devotedly. The reader finds little of substance behind the great personality of Mynheer Peeperkorn, but if Hans Castorp is in any way the personification of the gullible German public, we see that the people could be easily swayed by the influence of a forceful personality. Again, this was written before Hitler appeared.

The cure always requires months, often years. "But after the first six months the young person has not a single idea left save flirtation and the thermometer under his tongue." Hans becomes infatuated with an exotic woman from somewhere across the Caucasus Mountains, but poor Hans is a bit out of his depth, and their most intimate relationship is a flirtatious conversation in French.

Even by the standards of mid-twentieth century sanatorium care, the pace of disease management in this mountain retreat was leisurely. The physical examination was an elaborate ritual, with the head physician's terse observations faithfully recorded by the doctor who was his assistant. Diagnostic x-rays were used much more sparingly than in subsequent decades. The specialty of the house was the therapeutic pneumothorax, developed in the late nineteenth century after it was observed that tuberculosis patients sometimes had a paradoxically beneficial course after spontaneous rupture of a cavity into the pleural space. The Hofrat (the head physician) was said to be quite skillful with this procedure, and it is described from the patient's point of view in great detail. "It is as though you were being tickled – horribly, disgustingly tickled – that is just what the infernal torment of the pleura-shock is like, and may God keep you from it!"

Just as one may judge a chef by his skill with something so simple as an omelet, so one might measure a writer by his ability to describe something so commonplace as snow. Hans' foolhardy venture into the teeth of a snowstorm conveys the mismatch between foolish man and the impersonal force of a monstrous and immeasurable snowstorm: "Day in, day out, and all through the night." In contrast to the power of the storm, which is described over several pages, we see Hans as a confused soul, torn between the arguments of Settembrini and Naphta, standing with his head bent and his stick burrowed in the snow, "pondering the vasty confusion of it all."

Hans has a surprisingly easy return to supper after becoming lost in the storm, but only after having a vision of dancing girls in paradise, then of Macbeth-like witches dismembering a child, leaving him to wonder how such a vision can bring both bliss and terror at the same time. Death and destruction are on the other side of the sabbatical from life that the sanatorium at Davos offers. Joachim is one of the patients who don't survive. Hans is eager to learn about death, but the Hofrat gives a matter-of-fact account of it, saying that it is not so unpleasant in most cases. The doctors do their duty with such measures as injections of camphor. Sleep is more frequent, the dreams are pleasant ones, and the crossing is a short one. Death is overrated.

I learned and observed many times that death is rarely as dramatic as it is in the movies. When my childhood friends and I mimicked the deaths that we saw in the Saturday afternoon westerns, we would stagger, grimace, fall, and have time for some profound last words before the sudden drop of the jaw and twist of the head. The Hofrat's description was more accurate in most cases I attended.

We don't know about Hans Castorp's death. We aren't even told for sure that he died in The Great War, but the odds weren't in his favor. A complex mixture of feelings and events led to a horrible war. And when it came, Hans "stormed with them." We last see him straggling up from the mud, untouched by a "huge explosive shell" that killed two of his companions. But "thy prospects are poor."

The Magic Mountain is no more. A magic cure for tuberculosis closed it. But now resistant strains are appearing, showing the potential ability to emerge triumphant after shaking off the potency of the antibiotics. And The Great War and its successor, World War II, came and went. But war has not gone away, and we have seen examples of how it can reach and destroy any of us. Thomas Mann analyzed and described, in retrospect, how its seeds can take roots in what we assume to be a civilized society. The Kingdom of God and the brotherhood of man are now known to be farther away from us than we thought they were a hundred years ago.

THE FLU IN 1918, CLOSE UP

PALE HORSE, PALE RIDER
A Short Novel
By Katherine Anne Porter

Katherine Anne Porter had a severe case of influenza during the pandemic of 1918 and almost died from it. Her fiancé did die from it. Their story is the basis of the short novel, *Pale Horse, Pale Rider* (1939), which is one of the few first-person reports of the disease that swept the world in 1918 and 1919. The big picture of this pandemic has been outlined in several books, including *The Great Influenza: The Epic Story of the Deadliest Plague in History*, by John M. Barry. In contrast, Katherine Anne Porter's story is short, not long; fiction (though based on fact), not history; and describes only one case. But case reports convey an immediacy lacking in statistical summaries. Her story excels because of its simplicity. The narrator, a twenty-four-year-old woman named Miranda, tells what happened to her, and what she dreamed and thought about. She tosses off little details about the flu and the war that bring us up short. "Was it really like that?" It probably was. She presents herself as a reliable witness.

Influenza made its appearance in army barracks and spread to the civilian population during World War I. Every effort was made to rally the citizenry to support the war effort; people were encouraged to buy war bonds to finance the war, but they weren't told about the influenza epidemic. In a time when stories that might be disturbing or inflammatory were suppressed, the public wasn't told the extent of the civilian casualties due to influenza; what the public was told was to buy war bonds.

Two men came to Miranda's desk at the newspaper office to ask her why she was the only one in the office not buying a Liberty bond. "Miranda, startled by the tone, met his eye; his stare was really stony, really viciously cold, the kind of thing you might expect to meet behind a pistol on a deserted corner." It sounds like an old movie just after the talkies came out. People must have really talked and acted like that. "At the head of the stairs her inquisitors had stopped in their fussy pride and vainglory, lighting cigars and wedging their hats more firmly over their eyes."

She shook them off, but later when taking a bath, Miranda was aware of a headache.

She had a headache that might have started with the war, but it had not been like this. And we start to follow with apprehension the course of her headache, her dizziness, her weakness.

She reflected on her visits to one of the soldiers' wards, as one of the young women "who were wallowing in good works." Most of the men had picturesque bandages over some part of their body. The girls had been warned not to ask questions if there was no bandage; if one of them forgot and asked anyway, the answer was always "rheumatism." We know from John Barry's book that the flu wasn't to be mentioned. Wartime morale required that everyone be positive. Newspapers ignored it. (What a difference a century makes.) Failure to acknowledge the extent of the pandemic and address issues of public hygiene undoubtedly added to the toll of the pandemic.

She met her new boyfriend Adam and they took a walk. It was a fine fall day with blue sky and bright leaves, but at the first corner they were obliged to stop and wait for a funeral to pass by. They saw several others on their walks. Miranda asked Adam how he got his leave. No reason, he replied. There was this funny new disease. Men were dying like flies.

> "It seems to be a plague," said Miranda, "something out of the Middle Ages. Did you ever see so many funerals, ever?"
> "Never did. Well, let's be strong minded and not have any of it."

Both Adam and Miranda smoke quite a bit. He alluded to what it did to the lungs, but he didn't really expect to return alive from the war. The risks of combat could be mentioned, but the greater risk of mortality from the influenza was not so acknowledged. Miranda's early symptoms progressed. Feeling lightheaded, she held onto his arm for support. We fear that this was due to more than love.

Fearing that Adam wouldn't survive the war, they were reluctant to admit their love for each other. "A deep tremor set up on Miranda, and she set about resisting herself methodically as if she were closing windows and doors and fastening down curtains against a rising storm."

Miranda's severe illness is told in only the last few pages of the story. Adam found poor Miranda sick and alone in her room, sleeping. Her landlady insisted she be taken to the hospital immediately. No ambulances, Adam told her, and no beds. No doctors or nurses, either. All busy.

Adam went further. Theaters, shops and restaurants were closed. Funerals all day. Ambulances all night. "But not for me," Miranda said.

She and Adam sang an old spiritual they both remembered: "Pale horse, pale rider, done taken my lover away..." The rider has taken pappy, mammy, brother, sister, the whole family. "But not the singer, not yet," said Miranda. "Death always leaves one singer to mourn."

She was taken to the hospital the next morning, carried out in an "interne's" arms. (Before the days of Emergency Medical Technicians, "internes" like Dr. Hildesheim apparently rode the ambulances and brought in the patients.) In her delirium, she "lay like a stone at the farthest bottom of life." After a month that she couldn't remember, she recovered to learn that Armistice had been signed. Among the letters was one telling her that Adam had died of influenza in a camp hospital. She left the hospital, where there was "No more war, no more plague, only the dazed silence that follows the ceasing of the heavy guns; noiseless houses with the shades drawn, empty streets, the dead cold light of tomorrow."

It's not too surprising that there aren't many stories of the great influenza epidemic of 1918 that are this well written. What is surprising is that there aren't very many stories at all.

REFUSING TO BOW DOWN TO PESTILENCES

THE PLAGUE
By Albert Camus

At times when hustling from the emergency room to the intensive care unit in the middle of the night, I would ask myself, "Why am I doing this?" I wasn't always quite up to answering that question under those conditions, but sometimes, passages from Albert Camus' *The Plague*, which I first read and underlined as a senior medical student, would come to mind; not word for word, like verses from some holy scripture, but close enough to serve the purpose. For instance, "On this earth there are pestilences and there are victims, and it's up to us, so far as possible, not to join forces with the pestilences."

Camus, who won the 1957 Nobel Prize for Literature, was born in 1913 and grew up in French Algeria, where he was a goalkeeper for his university soccer team until tuberculosis forced him to give up sports in 1930. (When once asked whether he preferred football or the theater, he quickly replied, "Football.") He studied philosophy, formed a short-lived theater group, wrote for a socialist newspaper, and after witnessing the German takeover of Paris, he fled to Bordeaux and became editor of the underground newspaper published by the French Resistance.

He wrote *The Plague* in 1947, ostensibly a novel about an outbreak of bubonic plague, perhaps based on a cholera outbreak in the Algerian city of Oran, in 1849. The novel, however, is set in the 1940s, and it is difficult to read it without thinking in terms of the Nazi occupation of France in World War II. It's a pretty preachy book, the sort of novel one might expect from a philosopher. The reader will search in vain for a touch of irony or humor to relieve the seriousness of the situation. And there is little in the way of beauty. Oran is described as "ugly," with only the sky to identify the season, flowers only in the marketplaces in the spring, dust in the summer, mud in the autumn. The only pleasant season is winter.

Not exactly Camelot, but not an inappropriate setting for presenting a series of philosophical issues. Indeed, the story seems to be but a delivery system for a philosophical discussion. Camus rejected the label of existentialism, but the term is sufficiently broad that some of his ideas continue to adhere to the sticky surface of the word.

An invasion of rats came to an ordinary north African city in April in the 1940s, to be followed soon by a series of cases of a disease marked by swollen glands, fever, black patches on the skin, delirium, and death. Dr. Rieux, a young physician, recognized these cases as the beginning of an epidemic of bubonic plague. The people of the town, being humanists, had difficulty believing this. It couldn't happen here. These things don't happen anymore. (The wars in Europe come to mind. This was the twentieth century. People don't do this anymore.)

And if it was indeed plague, and if it didn't soon end, then at least we would know what it was and what to do about it. But pestilence is not made to the measure of man. And slowly, slowly, the people and the magistrates began to accept the enormity of the plague. The prefect sent an official telegram: "*Proclaim a state of plague stop close the town.*"

The people reacted in various ways. Several attempted to flee. Father Paneloux explained to his parishioners, in a rather orthodox statement from his pulpit, that God had sent the plague to punish the people for their sins. But a visitor to the town, Tarrou, told Dr. Rieux that Paneloux was a man of learning who hadn't come into contact with death. The priests in the country would think as Tarrou did and try to relieve human suffering before trying to point out its excellence.

Dr. Rieux discounted the philosophical questions. There would be a time for such thoughts and conversations later. For now, there were sick people and they needed help. Sick folks came first. When Tarrou reminded Dr. Rieux that his victories would never last, he replied he knew that, but it was no reason to give up the struggle.

If this all sounds like the script from a B movie, it is because this is the kind of novel you get when a philosopher writes it. Nobel Prizes in Literature have been known to be awarded on the basis of ideas. But however presented, there is some importance to the ideas.

Through the narrator, the author goes on to explain that evil comes from ignorance, and that the good intentions of ignorant people may do as much harm as the evil intentions of smarter people. The worst vice, he adds, is when ignorance thinks it knows everything and claims for itself the right to kill.

This "incorrigible vice" brings to mind the ideas of another thinker who pondered the disaster of the Second World War. Reinhold Niebuhr attributed this "ignorance that fancies it knows everything" to original sin: the sin of pride.

Many of the people of the town volunteered to do what they could to fight the plague, working to maintain public sanitation in the face of dangerous and disagreeable conditions. This was the obvious thing to do. But again and again, men have been killed for doing the right thing and speaking the truth. (Again remember the author's experience in working with the French Resistance during the war.)

Another bit of B movie dialogue appears as Dr. Rieux mused with Rambert and Tarrou about people's motives, saying that it wasn't a question of heroism; it was a matter of common decency. And what is common decency? "In doing my job," Rieux replied.

Tarrou later made a long to speech to Rieux, reminding us of original sin as he declared that he had no innocence. No one on Earth is free from the plague, and we have to be always careful not to breathe on someone else and pass it on. Here, he described the world as consisting of pestilences and victims, saying he had decided to take the victims' side. But there is a third category: that of the true healers. They are the ones who can find peace. And how does one attain peace? Only by way of the path of sympathy, he said, adding that his major interest was learning how to become a saint.

Tarrou was among the last to succumb to the plague, and the narrator reflects that Tarrou had lived without illusions and without hope. He had searched for peace in the service of others; perhaps this accounted for his aspiration toward saintliness.

The plague ran its course, the gates of the town were opened, and the citizens who happened to be out of town when the city gates were closed could now return. Amid the celebration, Dr. Rieux walked alone in an uproar of bells. His wife, who had been away in a tuberculosis sanatorium, had died there. The sick have no holidays, so neither did he, and he had not been able to take time off to visit her.

Dr. Rieux revealed himself at the end to have been the narrator, so that he could bear witness to the outrage and injustice done to these plague-stricken people, "and to state quite simply what we learn in time of pestilence: that there are more things to admire in men than to despise."

He concluded that there was no final victory. It could be only the record of what had had to be done by "all who, while unable to be saints but refusing to bow down to pestilences, strive their utmost to be healers."

Concluding, the narrator backed off from the details of the scene in the memorable passage that reminds us that the plague bacillus never disappears for good, that it can lie dormant for years, and that the day might come when, "for the bane and enlightening of men, it would rouse up its rats again and send them forth to die in a happy city."

This is the paragraph for the anthologies.

Perhaps some of the difficulty in coming to grips with *The Plague* is in the problem of considering it as a novel. Yes, it is a novel; it is a fictional prose narrative of considerable length. But if we think of it as one of a subset of the novel, perhaps an allegorical novel in the group that includes *Lord of the Flies* and *Moby Dick,* we are closer to the mark. Perhaps this is what the Nobel Prize committee had in mind.

Truly, the physician, and indeed anyone who has not had to cope with a pandemic – bubonic plague, influenza, or other pestilence – has led a sheltered life. But trials do come upon us all; even the daily grind can be a trial at times. For such stresses, a little collection of proverbs such as those recited by the narrator of *The Plague* can lend a bit of perspective.

.

SOLDIER'S HEART, SOLDIER'S NERVES

REGENERATION
By Pat Barker

A physician doing research on nerve regeneration in 1903 had the superior ramus of his own left radial nerve cut so that he and a colleague could study the problem properly. The subject of this experiment was Dr. Henry Head, and his associate was Dr. W. M. R. Rivers. Their studies, done over a five-year period on weekends in Head's rooms at St. John's College in Cambridge University, documented the process of nerve regeneration and became a landmark in the field.[21] Dr. Rivers, a versatile fellow who also had careers in ethnology and psychology, went on from the study of regeneration of the sensory nerves to the study of regeneration of mental health in soldiers suffering shell shock in World War I.

Hence Pat Barker's *Regeneration* (Plume, 1993), a historical novel centered on the work of Dr. Rivers with a famous patient, the poet Siegfried Sassoon. Sassoon was one of the "war poets," the group of gifted English soldiers who left behind them a body of verse that may be unmatched in the literature of war. Few of them survived World War I; the world lost Rupert Brooke, Wilfred Owen, and John McCrae, among others.

But Siegfried Sassoon survived. He was a hero; he had single-handedly captured a German trench in the Hindenburg line, and he became known as "Mad Jack." While back in England recuperating from a shoulder wound, he became convinced that the war should be concluded with a truce to stop the killing. He declined to return to duty and published "Finished with the War: A Soldier's Declaration," beginning, "I am making this statement as an act of willful defiance of military authority, because I

---

[21] Pearce, J. M. S.: William Halse Rivers Rivers (1864–1922) and the Sensory Nervous System *European Neurology 60*: 208–211, 2008

believe the war is being deliberately prolonged by those who have the power to end it." The English army, confronted with the problem of what to do with this soldier-celebrity, hospitalized him for "shell shock."

"Shell shock" is a term I first knew as a name for a condition afflicting some who suffered severe mental disturbance as a result of combat experience. Terms change and it is now known as Post Traumatic Stress Disorder, or PTSD, defined by the National Institute of Mental Health as "an anxiety disorder that can develop after exposure to a terrifying event or ordeal in which grave physical harm occurred or was threatened. Traumatic events that may trigger PTSD include violent personal assaults, natural or human-caused disasters, accidents, or military combat." The literature of war rarely fails to include it in one form or another.

At Craiglockhart Hospital, Sassoon met Dr. Rivers, whose theory of treatment of shell shock was that the soldier's repressed memories of the horrors of combat should be recalled and told, perhaps in the same way that a boil should be lanced to let the pus out. But, of course, Sassoon held little back in his graphic poems, as in "Counter-attack":

> *The place was rotten with dead; green clumsy legs*
> *High-booted, sprawled and groveled along the saps*
> *And trunks, face downward, in the sucking mud.*

Sassoon's treatment consisted mostly of lengthy conversations with Dr. Rivers, who knew that Sassoon had had some nightmares and scary hallucinations, dreams that didn't quit when he woke up. But Dr. Rivers knew from the first that Sassoon wasn't "sick." "No, of course you're not mad... As a matter of fact I don't even think you've got a war neurosis." But then Rivers recalled his duty: "I can't pretend to be neutral." In essence, though, Rivers was faced with having to decide whether agreeing to go to war and kill people is normal, while not wanting to kill people is abnormal. And how was he to decide when a man would be fit to return to combat duty?

Some of his colleagues believed that the victims of shell shock were degenerates who would have eventually showed evidence of psychiatric disease in civilian life, but Rivers saw no evidence for this view. Hardly any of his patients had any history of mental disease. The problem with his assessment was that if a soldier's breakdown was due to war itself, not to his own pre-existing condition, then war became the issue.

Rivers and Sassoon both wrestled with their own reactions to the stress imposed by the war. Rivers initially survived the stress of his job by repressing his questions about the war. But then Sassoon came along and made the war a matter of debate. What to do about Sassoon? Rivers' initial strategy was to make Sassoon feel guilty about sitting out the war in a relatively comfortable situation, "playing golf in the loony bin," while his comrades were fighting and dying on the front.

But when Dr. Rivers woke up in the night with a fast pulse, breathlessness, a cold sweat, and chest pain, his commanding officer put him on medical leave. After a visit home, he returned in time to sit in on the Board's review of Sassoon's case, to determine his fitness to return to duty. Sassoon's celebrity status was limiting the Board's options. Such a high-profile figure could never be court-martialed now; the English people were already absorbing such a terrible casualty list that the government wanted nothing that would stir up public debate about continuing the war. It would have been easy for the Board to assign him to a desk job in England, far away from harm's way; but now Sassoon was requesting a return to combat duty so he could rejoin his comrades in arms.

"And, indeed, he was discharged to duty."

A historical novel leaves the reader wondering, "Did he really think that? Did she really say that? Did they really do that?" The author in this case preempts the question in her "Author's Note": "Fact and fiction are so interwoven in this book that it may help the reader to know what is historical and what is not." Then she lists the basic historical facts that are the framework of the story. In general, it appears that the situation was historical and that the details are the author's. This is almost always the case. A few historical facts are all that are needed to construct a story or even a myth. As a general rule, a good story is true, whether strictly factual or not.

We hear many war stories in these pages. We meet several other soldiers undergoing treatment. Two of them were historical friends of Siegfried Sassoon: the war poets Wilfred Owen and Robert Graves. The stories of men who have been so strongly affected by their war experiences help remind us of the horrible waste of human lives that occurred in World War I. One of the consistent features of war stories is that most of them are never told. Many soldiers die in the war without telling their stories; many of them find the experiences too painful to tell and relive. Some of them are indeed so horrible that the participant thinks nobody could understand them without having been there to experience it all first-hand. Dr. Rivers, believing that victims of "shell shock" could best overcome their problems by forcing themselves to remember and talk about them, dragged out a number of these stories. Siegfried Sassoon, after his Declaration and his stay at Craiglockhart, returned to combat just before the end of the war and was very soon shot in the head by friendly fire, ending his combat experience. He subsequently wrote *Memoirs of a Fox-Hunting Man,* the first volume of a fictionalized three-volume autobiography, and later a genuine three-volume autobiography. He died in 1967, just before turning eighty-one, of carcinoma of the stomach. He was one of the sixteen poets of the Great War included on a memorial in Poets' Corner, Westminster Abbey, which was unveiled in 1985 on the 67th anniversary of the Armistice. Six of these sixteen died in the war.

Pat Barker wrote two subsequent novels about Dr. Rivers in the war: *The Eye in the Door,* which won the 1993 Guardian fiction prize, and completing the trilogy, *The Ghost Road,* which won the 1995 Booker Prize. Dr. Rivers himself died of a strangulated hernia in 1922. Since then, almost a century of wars has produced generation after generation of participants in these wars, who have died and suffered physical and

318

psychological trauma, providing all too much material for novelists and poets exploring the results of all this trauma. *Regeneration* helps us to put this aspect of the horrors of our wars into historical perspective.

THE GREATEST SHOW ON EARTH

MARTIN WINKLER
The Case of Dr. Sachs

The practice of medicine is the greatest show on Earth. But the tickets aren't cheap. For the good seats, the tickets are among the most expensive. One of the problems is that you can't talk about the show very much with your friends. Oh, of course, doctors do share some of their stories in the name of consultation and collegiality. But sometimes, some of the best stories just cannot be divulged. There is an element of the confession booth in the examining room. Some of my colleagues told me they never took notes while with a patient; and a more retentive listener than I may not have to do so. But I did take notes while patients told me their stories. This was primarily because I was afraid I would forget something important. Details are important. It also implied to the patient that we were "on the record," even though the record was to be a confidential one. Sometimes a patient would say, "Don't write this down," and then I would put away my pen and paper. And if the story veered into sensitive areas, I would sometimes, rather obviously, put the pen in my pocket. Immediately after the patient visit, I would go to my dictation machine and rattle into it as many details as possible for my clinical notes. And there were so many of these stories. Sometimes while driving home, I would recall several riveting stories from just that one day. But this was the raw material of a medical practice, and it was to be used for the benefit of the patients who told the stories, not for a book for the entertainment of the reading public.

Martin Winckler has written that book: *The Case of Dr. Sachs*, published in 1998 and translated from French into English by

Linda Asher (Seven Stories Press, 2000). Martin Winckler is the pen name of Marc Zaffran, a French physician who was born in Algiers in 1955, and who practiced in a small town in southern France from 1983 to 1993, when he became a full-time writer. His Facebook page indicates that he now works for a magazine under his real name, Marc Zaffran. He is a part-time doctor at Le Mans public hospital. Dr. Sachs is the fictional physician in a rural general practice who is the subject, and sometimes the narrator, of the book.

This is a personal, meticulously detailed account of a medical practice, told in second person by multiple narrators. I found myself sitting in the examination room as a little fly on the wall, listening to the direct words of each patient, transcribed as though into a dictation machine. The result is that the reader gets a powerful sense of sharing the doctor's experience; the mere act of reading these accounts leads to the same sense of fatigue from having done a good day's work that a busy doctor would feel after seeing a full schedule of patients. (Pity any poor actor who would take on the job of reading this one for an audio book presentation and would feel obliged to find a different voice for each patient.) Here is one example: The reader is introduced to Dr. Sachs' story and his practice by following a generic patient into the office for a visit. The patient is asked to undress for examination: "I put my clothes (my polo shirt or my blouse, my trunks or my skirt) on the chair in front of the window, between the cot and the shelf-unit. You rinse your hands and you wipe them with paper towels that you discard in a small metal trash can with a pedal opener."

The next two chapters are generic chapters describing visits for health permits and for prescription renewals, described in detail, with interruptions for telephone calls – including the woman who repeatedly dials the wrong number and asks for Edmund, always answered patiently and politely.

Twelve itemized blanks to be filled in on the prescription pad are documented word for word, and the details of a conscientious physical examination are recorded: "The 'cold doohickey' on the chest, the flashlight in the throat, nose, and mouth, the palpation of neck and axillae for lymph nodes."

These are the humdrum details of humdrum routines in a busy office practice. But the next chapters deal with individual patients and with the supporting cast: the clerk at the abortion clinic, Dr. Sachs' appointment clerk Madame Leblanc, and his next-door neighbor. Some of the patients begin stories that are followed in subsequent chapters, some to a conclusion, others not.

The reader sees Dr. Sachs as a single, thirty-four-year-old family practitioner, one who excelled in his one-year internship, who forgets where he put his keys and his papers, who patiently bears with those sometimes called "crocks" in this country – such as Madame Renard, who has come by "just in case" some three or four times since he started his practice. (Such patients often get in on the ground floor by switching to a new doctor as soon as he starts, because he will be more willing to put up with them; the duration of this relationship may depend on the patience of the physician, and on the length of time before another new physician comes to town.)

From what I've heard nurses say, I'd estimate that perhaps one physician in ten is courteous to someone who awakens them in the middle of the night. The woman who answers Dr. Sachs' telephone at night reports that she enjoys working with him because he tells funny stories and doesn't treat her "like shit." She thinks her own reflexes aren't good enough for the job of handling night time phone calls, and his demeanor calms her down.

The difficult thing for sleepy doctors to remember on the front end of a night-time summons is that they will understand it better on the back end. On the way to a call, the doctor vows that the patient will have to pay for this. Extra charges will be added. But when the doctor gets back home the mood is changed because of having seen such heartbreak, misery, hatred, and misunderstanding.

The pharmacist tells the doctor that he is the only one who

comes by regularly for morphine. And the people tell him that Doctor Sachs was so kind to them – he gave a father a shot that really helped his terrible pain, or someone would have never made it through the night if Doctor Sachs had not given her a sedative. The mothers call him Doctor Aspirin; the seniors call him Doctor Relief. (In my first couple of years in practice, I found myself making frequent house calls to an elderly woman who was a patient of the senior surgeon in our group. I asked Dr. Hawkins if it was wise to continue giving her the shots of intramuscular Vistaril that she requested. He smiled and said just to do it. As our health care delivery system has changed, I don't think such issues arise very much anymore. Who even makes house calls anymore?)

The pharmacist didn't really understand all this very well, but then one Sunday, a woman called him to see her mother, who had slipped on some gravel and broken her hip. A neighbor called Dr. Sachs, who came quickly and gave some subcutaneous morphine without hesitating, and also some new pill under the tongue that wasn't in the pharmacies yet, but which he had gotten at the hospital. In five minutes, the woman could bear to be lifted and taken into the house. And Doctor Sachs stayed with her, holding her hand and telling her she would have an operation that would help her to walk better than before.

All too often, the most conscientious doctors are those who eventually leave their practice because their self-imposed standards exceed their own physical and psychological resources. And this is the case of Dr. Sachs: he pushes himself to the point of breakdown in his efforts to render personal care to his patients. Perhaps this was partially due to a feeling of guilt for not having read a paper given to him by his dying father about his terminal illness, so he could have relieved some of his father's discomfort. He turns to writing and finds a means of identifying and relieving some of his frustration in this activity. In a tenderly told love story, he falls in love with a young woman he met when he performed an abortion on her. She is an editor;

she returns his love, and she provides the support he requires.

Gray pages identify the notebook entries of Dr. Sachs himself, as he experiments with different ways to express himself. The reader is almost overwhelmed by the mass of detail he catalogs; just as the doctor himself is almost overwhelmed by the baggage each patient brings. In these gray pages Dr. Sachs delves into his childhood thoughts and fears, and he ventilates his frustrations about his profession: "Doctors conceal from everyone – especially from themselves – that they have no idea what nine-tenths of their patients are saying, and that they're wrong about what the rest are saying."

Dr. Sachs works through his own "case": his office assistant notices he becomes less tense as his romantic relationship with Pauline Kassel develops; the reader can follow the evolution of his writing style through the gray pages of his journal; he obtains the assistance of another physician and offers him a job in his practice; and his book is published and celebrated. He reflects that his writing "is a way to take the measure of what we don't remember, what we don't retain."

The Case of Dr. Sachs is framed as a case presentation, with Dr. Sachs' "case" divided into the sequential components of a patient encounter: Presentation, History, Clinical Investigations, Diagnosis, Treatment, and Prognosis. The many details are intimate individually and powerful collectively. Someone sits in his waiting room reading his book, waiting while others are called back to see the doctor, and while the doctor himself is called away on emergencies. In a playful twist, this unidentified reader finally achieves an interview with Dr. Sachs, in which the question is asked: "I know there's a different name on the shingle, but you are Martin Winckler, aren't you? You *are* the person who wrote *The Case of Dr. Sachs*?"

The Case of Dr. Sachs is one of the most significant books I have read. Its account of the challenges and rewards of a medical practice meshes closely with my own concept of them. Dr. Sachs' idea of his job description includes the little extras: the menial hands-on services beneath the dignity of most physicians, which are the most appreciated by the patients and the most rewarding to the physician. One of my partners often made it a point to wheel his patients on a gurney himself, saying he had learned to do it when he was an orderly. I discovered early in my practice that when looking at an X-ray with a patient and seeing evidence of a previously unknown tumor, one of the best things I could do was to take the X-ray immediately to a radiologist or other specialist for an opinion before returning to the patient with the confirmation of a suspected cancer. This is the sort of thing Dr. Sachs would have done. After all, he helped prepare the body of a patient he had been called to pronounce dead, cleaning and dressing the body; he wrote his prescriptions so clearly and explained the effects of the medication so thoroughly that the pharmacist complained he had encroached on his professional prerogatives. Needless to say, most of his patients were fiercely loyal; but nothing is a hundred percent. One man says that Doctor Sachs is a good guy but that some of his questions are too personal. What does his private life have to do with his health anyway?

The only one of Martin Winckler's books to be translated into English, *The Case of Dr. Sachs* was a bestseller in France and was awarded the *Prix du Livre Inter*. The details of a rural practice may differ in some ways from those in the United States, but the essentials are the same; the truths presented are universal. It is said to be required reading in some medical school courses; and well it should be. Ushers should hand out this program to all who enter the theater of the greatest show on Earth.

MEDICINE WITHOUT BORDERS

A FEW SHORT NOTES ON TROPICAL BUTTERFLIES

Stories

By John Murray

More than twenty percent of graduating medical students in 2003 reported having had an international health care experience. Twenty years earlier, it was six percent. Fifty years ago, when I was a medical student, it was almost unheard of. "Global medicine" is now a regular source of reports in standard medical journals and news publications. Some United States training programs regularly send residents to serve in certain programs abroad. A few years ago, most doctors serving abroad went to the "mission field" under church auspices, as Albert Schweitzer did. Nowadays, they are more likely to be secular in outlook and sponsorship, and a role model is more likely to be someone like Paul Farmer, one of the founders of Partners in Health. There is, however, often a strong sense of mission.

My own personal experience is meager: I spent a few days in Belize surveying rural health care (there wasn't much), and I spent a week with a Methodist mission group conducting clinics in rural Guatemala. Both trips showed the immense needs, the scanty resources, and what I considered to be the heroism of those who served. (But I was dealing with short-term volunteers, probably a different kettle of fish from the full-timers.)

Is this heroism? This is just one of the issues addressed in a collection of eight stories by John Murray, *A Few Short Notes on Tropical Butterflies* (Harper-Collins Publishers, 2003). Murray is an Australian physician who received a master's degree in public health from Johns Hopkins and subsequently served with the Epidemiology Intelligence Service of the US Public Health Service. As a medical epidemiologist, he investigated outbreaks of cholera and later participated in child health care programs, spending time in Ethiopia, Tajikstan, Gaza, Eritrea, Ghana, and Uganda. He became a full-time writer in 1999, entering the Iowa Writers' Workshop in Iowa City, where he has continued to live and write, while still making occasional medical trips to Africa.

His collection of stories covers a lot of territory, including a cholera clinic in Bombay; a mission hospital in the mountains of Africa; a village in New Guinea; a solo practitioner's clinic in the slums of Bombay; the operating room of a Catholic mission hospital near the Democratic Republic of Congo; a cottage in Gippsland on the coast of Australia; a mountain peak in the Himalayas; and the riverside home of a surgeon born in New Delhi and practicing in Iowa. Some of the stories also take place in New York and Florida; all, peripherally if not primarily, concern the practice of medicine. These are not stories where nothing happens; an Indian woman born in the USA visits Bombay and, becoming immersed in its teeming throngs, decides to marry and stay there; mission medical facilities are attacked by soldiers; a young man climbs a mountain under impossible conditions; lives are changed by a neighborhood love affair. People move around all over the world, coping with extreme challenges. Issues often filter through two or three generations.

The attraction of such a collection of stories is that it implies a wide view. What takes these people around the world? Personal reasons, many times; sometimes leaving India for the USA; sometimes, leaving "civilization" to go to the jungle. In "Watson and the Shark," the narrator meets five Russian military men in a solitary hotel somewhere in Africa. "There were green lizards on the ceilings." The Russian helicopter crew was hired by the local USAID office, and one of them says how good it is to get out of Russia. "You don't come out of the goodness of your heart," he adds. He wouldn't be here if he were happy at home.

Storytellers run some risk of being preachy, even in putting heavy speeches in the mouths of certain characters. The art lies in showing the reader what a strange world is like, and what its inhabitants are like. Murray does this. The reader learns exactly what a surgery theater in the jungle is like. But why is the surgeon there, when similar labor could be expended in other, more comfortable parts of the world for a significant income?

The narrator in "Watson and the Shark" thinks he sounds naïve when he says he came because he thought he could make a difference. Stefan, a Frenchman who has been a surgeon with the International Committee of the Red Cross for ten years, replies that nothing they do can make a difference. And it is a waste of time to look for common sense in their situation. But he adds that every life saved is a triumph and that that is what keeps us human.

People come and go. In "Acts of Memory, Wisdom of Man," we see an Indian surgeon emigrate to Iowa, where he drills his young sons on human anatomy. "Without discipline, we are nothing... All is lost." In "White Flour," a North Carolina medical student goes to India and marries a young Indian girl who returns to the States with him, where she pursues a career in paleontology; he returns alone to India and establishes a clinic for the poor.

The title story, "A Few Short Notes on Tropical Butterflies," is a showcase for the features of Murray's stories: it ranges from New York City to Pondicherry in southern India; it covers three generations, going back to the narrator's grandfather, who chased butterflies among the cannibals of New Guinea; it tells the story of two health professionals: the narrator, who is a plastic surgeon, and his wife, twenty years younger, who is a neurosurgeon. The story deals with an unusual disease, *kuru*, common among New Guinea cannibals and transmitted by direct contact with human brains. It also deals with a more common disorder, alcoholism, which the narrator begins to recognize in himself. The story skips nimbly along with a touch as light as that of Maya, the neurosurgeon: "Her touch is as light as that of a butterfly on a leaf." When the narrator describes his trip with his father to the New Jersey coast to count the monarch butterflies, he contrasts their silent, clean, and airborne migration to the noisy, dusty, and terrestrial movement of the wildebeest in the Rift Valley of Africa: "You could live right under a monarch butterfly migration and never know that it was happening."

The narrator assesses himself with a bit of revelation that comes to him when in bed with his wife in India, where they go to visit her family. After saying to her there must be something liberating about being away from one's family, he reflects that he could never really escape from his family; he carries them with him all the time. Maya, who at thirty-eight has been trying to persuade her husband they should have a baby before she becomes too old, has a miscarriage in India. Back in New York, she observes that his previously youthful energy has completely disappeared. (And it doesn't occur to him that it might have something to do with his alcoholism.) One night, she comes into his study, shouts that the butterflies he keeps from his grandfather's collection are a curse, and while he watches, unable to speak, she destroys them with a hammer.

Feeling relieved but needing some air, he drives to the coast to look for the migrating monarchs, and as he thinks of his own past beginning to drift out of his reach, it occurs to him that an adult monarch butterfly has a life-span of four weeks, during which time it is a short burst of color that dazzles and blinds, and must then reproduce before its fleeting moment is gone forever.

Butterflies fly from New Jersey to Mexico. The world is shrinking. Corporations are multinational, and the world is flat. Diseases are spread from continent to continent in the time it takes an airplane to cross the ocean. People move around from India to New York, from Florida to Australia. Some go to save the world, some go for a place to work; and when they go, they take problems with them, and they find new ones. It is little wonder that "global medicine" is a discipline increasing in importance and in its appeal to medical students. Adventure, altruism, intellectual curiosity, a sense of mission, maybe just something to do; all these must be part of the draw. John Murray has written one of the textbooks for the course.

JUST ANOTHER DAY IN THE LIFE OF A NEUROSURGEON

SATURDAY
By Ian McEwan

Henry Perowne, the fictional neurosurgeon in Ian McEwan's *Saturday* (Nan A. Talese, Doubleday, 2005), selects Angela Hewitt's performance of Bach's "Goldberg" Variations when he operates on the depressed skull fracture of the young crime boss who had threatened Perowne's family that day. At the end of the operation, as his assistant is closing, he gets the nurse to play Barber's "Adagio for Strings," its "languorous, meditative music" suggestive of a long labor finally coming to an end. But after he leaves the theatre (that's the operating room in England) to speak to two policemen and returns, the atmosphere has changed. The anesthesiologist's country and western music has replaced Bach and Barber. Emmylou Harris is singing "Boulder to Birmingham," and the nurses are gossiping.

We don't know whether Dr. Neil Kitchen, neurosurgeon at the National Hospital for Neurology and Neurosurgery in London, whom McEwan observed in the theatre over a period of two years, preferred Bach while working; but all the surgical details in the novel indicate that McEwan must have learned a lot more than I did when I was observing surgery as a medical student. My brother-in-law, a thoracic surgeon, considers this the most realistic operating scene he has read. I can believe this. It's written with a sure sense of detail, describing a major blood vessel, the superior sagittal sinus, running right below the depressed fracture, "vulnerable to the sharp edges of displaced bone tilted like tectonic plates," but its economy of words conveys the operating room atmosphere where actions are more important than words. The surgeon doesn't have to ask for the scalpel; Emily puts it right in his hand. This also avoids the melodrama built into so many popular accounts of surgery.

McEwan uses the convention of describing one eventful day in order to portray the life of this neurosurgeon. We see his two gifted children beginning to excel, one as a poet and the other as a guitarist, certainly not near the field of medicine or even science. His wife has a career as a lawyer. Her father is a famous poet; Henry visits his mother, who has Alzheimer's disease, in her nursing home.

The Saturday of the book's title happens to be the Saturday of the big march to protest the war in Iraq, and we follow Henry's ambivalent feelings about the war, due largely to his having seen an Iraqi professor as a patient, a victim of Saddam's terror. He disagrees with each of his children, who have no reservations about protesting against the war.

The central event of the day for Henry is the experience of encountering a trio of young toughs who demand satisfaction after Henry's Mercedes knocks off their rear-view mirror in a traffic scrape. Henry escapes a beating by making a brilliant diagnosis of Huntington's chorea in the leader of the gang. His arrival at the diagnosis is facilitated by some acute observations at a distracting time; the chain of reasoning is brilliant. It is the sort of performance that a professor might pull off in the more leisurely setting of a clinico-pathological conference.

To the extent that one wants to see inside the brain of a brain surgeon, here we do so. Perowne is nearing fifty, still vigorous, experienced, fit and skillful in the operating room, still playing competitive squash and running an occasional half-marathon, anticipating a drop-off in these activities in just a few years. We see him potter about the kitchen and ponder all aspects of the terrorist threat, apparently an unassertive Englishman at home. But it's impossible for a neurosurgeon to be unassertive.

There are many sides to Henry Perowne. He has begun to read more widely after being challenged by his daughter, Daisy, who has provided him with a Darwin biography and a Conrad novel. His medical training and practice had not left much time for non-medical reading, a deficiency she has set about remedying.

He thinks this has been offset by the extensive experience he has had with death, fear, courage, and suffering, but his willingness to take on her reading list has provided a means of staying in touch with her, on her own in Paris.

Common issues of the time and of his own station in life are shown in their impact on his thinking. He is sandwiched between his children and the older generation. The son and daughter are advancing to independence even as they retain their connection, playing strange music but desiring their parents' approval. When he visits his now demented mother in a nursing home with Alzheimer's, he recalls her as a strong swimmer and as his teacher. (In an appearance at the public library in Tulsa, Oklahoma, McEwan said he wrote down, word for word, comments by his own mother, who had vascular dementia, and used them for this passage.) His father-in-law is a gifted figure whose various gifts pose numerous problems in the family interactions.

Just another day in the life of a neurosurgeon. How does the day end? Finally, having dissected the minute aspects of Perowne's life, the author closes with a receding shot showing him looking out over the city square, as the camera moves farther and farther away: "A hundred years ago, a middle-aged doctor standing at this window in his silk dressing gown, less than two hours before a winter's dawn, might have pondered the new century's future. February 1903. You might envy this Edwardian gent all he didn't know."

McEwan is a gifted novelist, having won a Booker Award for *Amsterdam*. *Atonement* was a bestseller and also became a successful movie. He did his homework for this one, showing us Henry Perowne as a skillful and heroic surgeon who is also qualified to cope with the other stresses of this life, which we all know so well.

SWEEPING AND ROLLICKING

CUTTING FOR STONE
A Novel
By Abraham Verghese

"When I decided to go into pre-med," one of my fellow interns
once told me, "I went to see my home town doctor. He took care
of our family for years. He made house calls. We could always get
hold of him when we needed him. That was the kind of doctor I
wanted to be. I knew he'd be proud of me, so when I got back
home for the holidays, I went straight over to his office and told
him I was going to go to medical school. And do you know what
he said? I couldn't believe it. He looked at me for a minute, and
then he said, 'You've got to be crazy.'"

Maybe so. "I've told my kids never to be a doctor," I've heard
too many of my colleagues say. Medicine is not like it used to be.
You'd make more money as a plumber. The government has
ruined it. The paper work will drive you crazy. The young doctors
don't want to work. Night call is much worse now.

Maybe so. There is some truth in all these assertions, but not
everybody believes them. Marion Stone didn't believe them.
Marion is the narrator in Abraham Verghese's novel, *Cutting for
Stone*. His father was a surgeon, his mother was a nurse, and his
adopted parents were physicians. He went to medical school as a
matter of course and became, perhaps excessively, devoted to his
calling as a matter of vocation.

Abraham Verghese is Professor and Senior Associate Chair for
the Theory and Practice of Medicine at Stanford University
School of Medicine. His parents were Indian teachers in Ethiopia,
where he grew up and began his medical training until Emperor
Haile Selassie was deposed. He finished his medical training at
Madras Medical College and then came to the United States for

residency training. All these facts are pertinent to *Cutting for Stone*, his first novel (Alfred A. Knopf, 2009). He had previously published two acclaimed memoirs, *My Own Country: A Doctor's Story*, one of five chosen by *Time* magazine as *Best Book of the Year*, an account of his efforts to treat AIDS as a private physician in Johnson City, Tennessee; and *The Tennis Partner: A Story of Friendship and Loss*, a *New York Times* Notable Book, an intensely personal account of his reaction to the breakup of his marriage and also of the drug addiction of one of his medical students, who had become a close friend on the tennis court.

The story qualifies as a sweeping novel covering seven years before and fifty years after the birth of Marion Stone, born in Addis Ababa to Thomas Stone, surgeon at Missing Hospital (which received its name in the misspelling of "Mission Hospital" from a phonetic spelling of the name in local dialect), and Sister Mary Joseph Praise, a nun sent on a mission from Madras, India. It also qualifies as a rollicking novel, describing the coming-of-age adventures of Marion and his identical twin, Shiva, during times of political change and revolution in Ethiopia. They trick a marauding soldier into crashing his stolen motorcycle, and after the villain dies in a gunshot accident, they bury the body in quicksand and keep his death a secret.

There are even bits of magical realism in Marion's uncanny ability to identify his friend Genet's presence with his dog-like sense of smell, and the diagnostic powers of the sense of smell in some circumstances.

We have to remember that though the medical and surgical details identify the author as a physician, he and the reader are not limited by the laws of probability and credibility that we ordinarily expect in a rigorously trained medical scientist. The author is a good storyteller, and the entrance of the obstetrician, Dr. Kalpana Hemlatha (Hema), into the operating theater as the twins are being born, is nothing if not dramatic.

> *The doors to the operating theater burst open. The probationer shrieked. Matron clutched her chest at the*

> sight of the sari-clad woman standing there, hands on
> her hips, bosom heaving, nostrils flaring.
>   They froze. How were they to know if this was their
> very own Hema, or an apparition? It seemed taller and
> fuller than Hema, and it had the bloodshot eyes of a
> dragon. Only when it opened its mouth and said, "What
> bloody nonsense is Gebrew talking? In God's name,
> what is going on?" did their doubts vanish.

In this case, a lot was going on. The hospital personnel had all just been stunned to learn only at the time of delivery that Sister Mary Joseph Praise, now in shock from blood loss, had been pregnant; everyone correctly assumed that the father was Thomas Stone, the hospital surgeon; but he had no experience in obstetrics, and Hema, the obstetrician was on a return flight from India when labor began. The addled Dr. Stone had been about to crush the skull of the fetus in an effort to save the mother. It turned out that the source of bleeding was a uterine rupture, and there were twins, joined at the head and lacking fetal heart tones.

This extraordinary birth is the mainspring of the story; the mother dies, the father departs immediately and leaves no forwarding address. Hema and her colleague Ghosh raise the twins as mother and father, and Shiva grows up as a strangely different identical twin: brilliant, but lacking in some of the sensitivity and scruples of his brother. The humanistic values of medical service are nicely brought out in the story of Shiva's career. He doesn't bother with medical school; he works with Hema in the obstetrics and gynecology clinic, devoting himself to the problem of women with vesico-vaginal fistulas. Besides suffering the inconvenience of having a communication between the bladder and the vagina, these women are shunned by all because of their bad smell emanating from the incontinent flow of urine and sometimes blood. In time, his picture appears in the *New York Times* as the world's expert and leading advocate for women with vaginal fistula. Hema explains that fistula surgery, which requires constant attentiveness, suited a single-minded person like Shiva, who would spend hours preparing for each case, anticipating every possible complication.

This story seems too good to be fiction. Is there a fistula clinic somewhere? A quick internet search leads to the web site of the Addis Ababa Fistula Hospital, founded by Reginald and Catherine Hamlin, Australian obstetricians who were "called upon" to come to Addis Ababa, where they first saw a case of obstetric fistula and learned that, though it had almost disappeared with the surgical techniques of the developed world, it was still an unsolved problem in Ethiopia. They worked ten years to open the Addis Ababa Fistula Hospital in 1974; it is the only medical center in the world dedicated exclusively to fistula repair. Reginald Hamlin died in 1993, and Catherine Hamlin has been nominated for the Nobel Peace Prize. This is too good a story not to appear, in slightly amended form, in a story about medical care in Ethiopia.

The plot works itself out in the natural history of the transmission of tuberculosis and hepatitis B, the effects of isoniazid and alcohol on the liver, progression to fulminant hepatitis, and another dramatic operating room scene toward the end of the story, where medical and surgical history are made. These events are echoed in similar events described in the recent medical literature, so that, as in the story of the fistula clinic, the medical events are on the cutting edge.

Doctors from abroad form an integral part of the health care work force in America. After finishing medical school in Addis Ababa, Marion was forced to flee from Ethiopia's political unrest, and his arrival in the United States provides an opportunity to describe the challenges facing foreign medical graduates. Marion finds himself hijacked at La Guardia Airport by a driver from Our Lady of Perpetual Succour, and Marion naïvely thinks he is fortunate to find work there and that he might have been working at Massachusetts General Hospital if he had only applied there. The other residents explain the facts of life to him: there are "Mayflower hospitals," flagship hospitals that are teaching hospitals for big medical schools, staffed by descendants of those who came on the Mayflower. And there are

"Ellis Island hospitals," where all the house staff and most of the attending physicians come from the other side of the world. They are Indians, Pakistanis, Filipinos, Arabs and Africans; somehow they get the word, somehow they make it.

And when they finish their training, where do they go to practice? They go anywhere, perhaps to the small towns American doctors don't want to go to because those places have no symphony, no professional team of any kind, no culture. (Remember that Abraham Verghese began his career as a doctor in the United States in Johnson City, Tennessee.)

Marion's American experience constitutes only a part of his story, which begins and ends in Missing Hospital in Addis Ababa. Missing is run by Matron, a pragmatic administrator who shares the approach to health care so often found in those who serve in third world countries. But Matron also has a responsibility to Missing to encourage donations from churches in the developed world. In these situations, there is almost always a difference in perception of how these funds can best be used. It so happens that the Ethiopian church is an ancient one that claims its origins at the time of the Acts of the Apostles when Philip baptized an Ethiopian eunuch. The Ethiopian church did not accept the "two-natured" doctrine of Christ decreed in a church council in 451 A.D, continuing to hold to a single unified Nature of Christ. This ancient doctrinal difference rears its head in the story of a representative from a generous Texas church who complains that the watchman at Missing adheres to a Monophysite doctrine that Jesus had only a divine nature, not a human one.

Matron's reply to this complaint is a bit strongly worded, but it is reminiscent of the way Jesus responded to the Sadducees and Pharisees who tried to trip him up with questions about the Jewish law. She asks if the Monophysitic nonsense makes any difference to shivering barefoot children or to starving lepers, and then she answers her question herself by saying that God will judge us by what we did to relieve the suffering of our fellow human beings.

TAYLOR PREWITT

Hema and Ghosh, who become parents for the twins, work at the hospital in obstetrics and surgery. Ghosh is basically an internist, and he is pressed into service as a surgeon after Thomas Stone's abrupt departure. Matron, Hema, and Ghosh are all presented as heroic figures. But to those of us who live sheltered lives in a developed country, anyone who works in Missing or one of its counterparts has elements of the heroic. The Missing community is shown as an earthy one, dealing with life as it happens.

Marion finds direction in Sir William Osler's aphorism, "The master-word is work," as a guide to his own life, and he finds that his biological father, Thomas Stone, has retreated to his work and little else. Many physicians do this, and such single-mindedness can lead to much good being done. Paradoxically, however, pursuit of this particular master-word may also lead to legend or scandal. The resulting stories can keep communities entertained for months or years. In this coming-of-age novel, we follow Marion as he matures into a physician of such dedication to his work that he rivals any priest in poverty and chastity. One hopes that as he enters his second fifty years, he will take a little time to stop and smell the roses.

Abraham Verghese has skillfully knitted together a collection of legendary and sometimes scandalous stories into one "sweeping, rollicking" novel with enough authenticity to prompt the reader to reflect about our world that is still a work in progress, with much work to be done. But it is sweeping and rollicking and entertaining. And to the prospective medical student: this is one to read before you go talk to your dad or your dear old family physician.

ACKNOWLEDGEMENTS

I've been rather shameless in soliciting help with this project. The first filtration process has always begun with my wife Mary; we often made significant changes before I punched the "Send" button.

The next filtering process has been through the children. Sally has provided encouragement and comments on particular books. Kendrick, now Head of the English Department at University of West Alabama, let me know whenever some word or passage would be shot down immediately by academic guns. But if a book is usually the joint effort of writer and editor, this one can be attributed to Ellen, who has been encouraging this effort for years and did the heavy lifting with the editorial pen. Children tend to set high standards for their parents, and she never relaxed her efforts, having clearly picked up several things in her college English courses that I must not have bothered with. Perhaps the number one lesson was, "Read it over to yourself. If it doesn't sound right, you probably need to change it."

Besides our own children, two children of my clinic partners have stepped up. Todd Stewart, now an internist and author, has been helping to ease me from paper and pencil to the digital age for some ten years now, bringing me along to the world of publishing on demand. Chip Paris raised his hand when his dad and I were discussing the need for a graphic designer for the dust jacket. Chip utilized his personal skills and the resources of Williams-Crawford and Associates so well that his father conceded he may have gotten the right DNA. Charles, his dad, took on the job of photographing me for the dust jacket.

Todd introduced me to Mark and Angela Hooper of Angel Editing, who were patient, thorough and workmanlike in polishing the text into something that I felt a lot better about. (Every time I start to write "which" or "that" I think about them and think again.)

J. P. Bell and I spent a pleasant afternoon in the St. Edward Intensive Care Unit, starting from scratch on the cover photograph with the assistance of Autumn Moore, head nurse and an old friend from my ICU years.

My first collection of book reviews was a birthday present for my sister Mary Wheeler Brown. Her husband Spencer, a retired cardiac surgeon, pitched in on all the reviews, providing background information and a helpful perspective.

Jack Coulehan, who edited *Chekhov's Doctors* reviewed in this collection, answered a cold call from an unknown Arkansas cardiologist on a snowy day in Stony Brook, New York, and offered encouragement and advice; he also published a version of the review of *Cutting for Stone* in *Pharos,* where he is book review editor. Clif Cleaveland, a retired internist in Chattanooga and author of *Sacred Space: Stories from a Life in Medicine*, reviewed my early efforts and also provided counsel and a sympathetic ear.

Anita Paddock is an old friend who uses her position as a branch library manager to promote creative writing in the community. Her daughter Jennifer, a long-time friend of my daughter Sally, is also now the author of two novels, *Point Clear* and *A Secret Word,*with a third one forthcoming. Both mother and daughter have helped me to understand the world of books and have shown me how to do a better job with my own.

The late Virginia Cowart, wife of an old college friend and a successful writer on medical affairs, expressed enthusiasm for my project and agreed to edit my manuscript for me just before she learned about her own cancer, which swiftly carried her away.

I also shared parts of the manuscript with George and Peggy Ackerman, old family friends who have worked with me on the Reading Retreat, which bears his name, of the Arkansas Chapter of the American College of Physicians. George is a retired

342

professor of medicine at the University of Arkansas Medical School and also an expert on the writings of Chekhov.

Not the least of the sons of encouragement was my late friend and neighbor, Dr. Leon Woods, whose wife Ann requested new reviews to read to her husband in his terminal illness so faithfully that I felt like Scheherazade trying to keep the king entertained.

Dr. Sandra Johnson, a dermatologist with a background in research at UAMS, helped me bring Lewis Thomas' musings about warts up to date with a report of her immunologic work on curing warts.

A number of friends have been complimentary about previous collections of book reviews and have shared them with others. To all of you, thanks for your encouragement and for your tolerance of my eccentricities.

Taylor Prewitt

Taylor Prewitt grew up in McGehee, Arkansas and received his BA in English from the University of Arkansas and his MD from Washington University. His training in internal medicine and cardiology was at North Carolina Memorial Hospital in Chapel Hill and he practiced Cardiology at Cooper Clinic in Fort Smith, Arkansas, from 1969 to 2003, interrupted only by spending the year 1974 as a Senior Fellow in Cardiology at the Brompton Hospital in London. He has been named a Master of the American College of Physicians. He has published six previous collections of book reviews.

Cover Design by Amanda Osterman

Author Photograph by Charles Paris

foxboro press

www.ingramcontent.com/pod-product-compliance
Lightning Source LLC
Chambersburg PA
CBHW070201260626
47160CB00002B/414